GoldenPhi Press, LLC

Minnesota

Copyright © 2018
All rights reserved.

ISBN: 978-0-9863928-4-9

This book is dedicated to...

To those who have decided to protect themselves
and their loved one in an ever changing world.

To those who took the time to teach me
the ways of carrying concealed
and the thousands of rounds of ammo
we shared together on the range to success.

Copyright © 2018 by Grandpa "G"

All right reserved under International Copyright Laws. No part of this publication may be reproduced, distributed, or transmitted in any form or by any means, including photocopying, recording, or other electronic or mechanical methods, without the prior written permission of the publisher, except in the case of brief quotations embodied in critical reviews and certain other noncommercial uses permitted by copyright law. For permission requests, write to the publisher, addressed "Attention: Permissions Coordinator," found at either the website below or the email provided.

GoldenPhi Press, LLC – Minnesota
www.GoldenPhiPress.com

Way of the Concealed Carrier
The Concealed Carry Lifestyle
for Our Modern Day American Samurai
by Grandpa "G"

ISBN: 978-0-9863928-4-9

Cover Design by GoldenPhi Press, LLC
Edited by Grandpa "G"
Images from DepositPhotos
Photos by Grandpa "G"
First Edition

Published & Printed in the United States of America
First Edition: January 2018
♄○♋■ ♪⌂○ ☺✳□&

If you find any errors in this book, please email the editor at:
WayOfTheConcealedCarrier@GoldenPhiPress.com

The books focus is on providing quality and reliable information in the topics covered. The information provided herein is stated to be straightforward and consistent, and under no circumstances will any legal responsibility or blame be held against the publisher or the author for any reparation, monetary loss, personal injury, or damages due to the information herein, either directly or indirectly.

Although the author and publisher have made every effort to ensure that the information in this book was correct at press time, the author and publisher do not assume and hereby disclaim any liability to any party for any loss, damage, or disruption caused by errors or omissions, whether such errors or omissions result from negligence, accident, or any other cause. The material herein is offered for <u>informational purposes only</u>.

Recording of this publication is strictly prohibited and any storage of this document is not allowed unless with written permission from the publisher. <u>The views and opinions expressed in this book are those of the authors and do not necessarily reflect the official opinions expressed by GoldenPhi Press, LLC.</u>

As a gun owner, always follows the universal safety gun rules when handling a firearm. This is your responsibility while using any technique throughout this book. Any firearms used to perform any exercises in this book must not have any live ammo. We <u>never</u> recommend using live ammo during our training exercises. If you perform an accidental discharge, this is not the responsibility of the author or GoldenPhi Press, LLC., this responsibility lies with you.

Contents

PREFACE 13

ABOUT THIS BOOK 16

NOTE TO CRIMINALS 20

THE AMERICAN SAMURAI 23

GRANDPA "G's" CONCEALED CARRY CREED© 26

CHAPTER ONE - *The Basics* 27

PREPARE BEFORE YOUR FIRST CLASS 28

ALWAYS THINK T.A.N.K. SAFETY© 29

BE AN AMBASSADOR FOR THE REST OF US 34

BEFORE YOU CARRY 36

KEEP YOUR CONCEALED CARRY SECRET AND PRIVATE ... 37

NEVER TRUST YOUR MEMORY 40

GRANDPA G'S FIVE RECOMMENDATIONS FOR KEEPING SHARP AND BEING SMART WHILE CARRYING CONCEALED 42

WHERE TO CARRY YOUR SIDEARM 42

GUNS SCARE ME 44

GIVING IT THE FINGER 45

NOMENCLATURE OF A SIDEARM 47

PICKING OUT YOUR SIDEARM 49

STOP TOUCHING YOURSELF 52

CHAPTER TWO - *Holsters* 54

   HOW TO FIND THE RIGHT HOLSTER 55

   GRANDPA "G's" GUIDE TO FINDING THE PERFECT QUALITY HOLSTER 57

   IS THAT A HOLSTER IN YOUR PANTS OR ARE YOU GLAD TO SEE ME? 61

   HOLSTER DRAWING & THE CLOTHES YOU WEAR 62

   HIP VS. APPENDIX CARRY 64

CHAPTER THREE - *Heading Outdoors for the First Time* 66

   GOING OUT FOR THE FIRST TIME 67

   FIRST TIME CARRYING 69

   PACKING ON THE WEIGHT 70

   SPARE MAGAZINES (MAGS) 71

   KEEP YOUR GUN HAND FREE AT ALL TIMES 72

   WALKING THE DOG 73

CHAPTER FOUR - *Lifestyle Changes* 75

   BEING THE GRAY GHOST IN A DIGITAL AGE 76

   GETTING INTO THE HABIT 78

   A CHANGE IN LIFESTYLE 79

   CHANGING THE WAY YOU DRIVE 81

   TYPE OF SHIRTS/TOPS TO AVOID 82

   DON'T TALK GUN SMACK 83

   ADVERTISING T-SHIRTS 84

LIVING A RESPONSIBLE CONCEALED CARRY LIFESTYLE 85

GUNS AND CAMELS JUST DON'T MIX 87

CARRYING CONCEALED IN YOUR DREAMS 88

I AM TOO OLD FOR THIS SHIT!! 90

PREGNANT AND ARMED 91

CHAPTER FIVE - *Samurai Self Training* 96

BEING THE STUDENT ARE YOUR FIRST STEPS IN BECOMING A MASTER 97

DRY FIRE PRACTICE 99

HOLSTER DRAWING 105

DON'T STOP READING OR WATCHING VIDEOS 107

PRACTICING IN THE DARK 110

REPETITION & RETENTION 111

GRANDPA G's WARRIOR WORKOUT 111

OUT FOR A WALK 114

HOW'S YOUR SIX? 115

MEDITATION FOR THE ARMED WARRIOR 116

"NO MIND" SHOOTING 122

GUNFIGHTING & SPIRITUALITY 124

KNOW THY SIDEARM 128

HOLLYWOOD IS NOT YOUR TRAINING INSTRUCTOR 129

SAMPLE SCENARIOS 130

THAT ITCHY TRIGGER FINGER 141

FIRST TIME AT THE RANGE 142

CHAPTER SIX - *Inside Establishments* 148

WORKING OUT IN THE GYM 149

SHOPPING WITH YOUR SIDEARM 150

AT A RESTAURANT 151

SIDEARMS AND FURNITURE 152

RUNNING OUT OF HAIRCUTS 153

ACTIVE SHOOTER TRAINING IN THE WORKPLACE 154

CHAPTER SEVEN - *Involvement With Law Enforcement* 163

WHAT NOT TO CARRY FOR A DEFENSIVE SIDEARM 164

YOU DON'T NEED NO STINK'N BADGES 165

GETTING PULLED OVER BY THE POLICE 167

YOU ARE NOT THE LAW 173

IT'S A PAIN IN THE ASS, BUT IT'S THE LAW 174

CONCEALED CARRY CARD HOLDER FOR PERMIT 177

CHAPTER EIGHT - *Have Gun Will Travel* 179

TENTS, NATURE, & FIREARMS 180

AIRLINE TRAVELING & DECLARING A FIREARM 185

BOATING & CARRYING 190

CHAPTER NINE - *At Home* 192

IN THE BATHROOM 193

IN THE SHOWER 197

ALARMS AND SECURED DOORS 200

DO YOU KEEP YOUR FIREARM IN YOUR VEHICLE WHILE YOU'RE AT HOME?
.... 203

87 MINUTES AWAY 204

CHILDREN IN THE HOUSE 207

CHAPTER TEN - *Essentials* **210**

WHAT IS SITUATIONAL AWARENESS? 211

WHAT IS CASTLE DOCTRINE, STAND YOUR GROUND, & DUTY TO RETREAT?
.... 213

PURCHASING YOUR FIRST FIREARM 214

WOMEN PURCHASING FIREARMS 217

YOUR EVERY DAY CARRY (EDC) LOCATION 219

CLEANING & MAINTENANCE 220

THE DAILY ROUTINE 223

BUILD YOUR OWN TARGET STAND 225

CHAPTER ELEVEN - *Tips and Tricks* 226

COVER AND CONCEALMENT 227

DRAW-CONFIGURATION: INCREASING YOUR DRAW TIME 228

SILENCE THAT CELL PHONE 234

LOCKING YOUR CAR BEFORE ENTERING 235

THROW AWAY PROPS 236

SMART SHOPPING IN THE FIREARM WORLD 236

DON'T FORGET YOUR FIREARM 239

CHAPTER TWELVE - *Dressing the Part* 245

DRESSING THE PART 246

WINTERS AND SIDEARMS 247

DRESSING UP & GOING OUT 253

HOW TO DRESS AT THE RANGE 254

BELTS, CLIPS, & CONCEALMENT 255

CLOTHES SHOPPING FOR YOUR FIREARM 258

CHAPTER THIRTEEN - *What Ifs* 263

DROP THAT GUN! 264

AFTER THE TRIGGER IS PULLED 265

LOST OR STOLEN FIREARM(S) 271

THE PARANORMAL & FIREARMS 272

CHAPTER FOURTEEN - *Socializing* 275

CARRYING IN SOMONE ELSE'S HOME 276

HUGGING AND FIREARMS 279

DATING, SEX, FIREARMS, & O-FACES 280

BLACK FRIDAY & BEING ARMED AMONGST THE CRAZIES 285

CHAPTER FIFTEEN - *Things You Should Know* 288

FIREARM OWNERS PROTECTION ACT (FOPA) 289

WARNING SHOTS 292

YOUR DEFENSIVE AMMO 293

FIREARMS AND OFF BODY CARRY 294

PURCHASING A FIREARM AS A GIFT FOR SOMEONE 296

WHAT KIND OF CONCEALED FIREARM SHOULD YOU CARRY? 298

CONCEALED CARRY INSURANCE 302

CONCEALED CARRY & GUN SHOWS 308

CHAPTER SIXTEEN - *Firearm Mentality* 309

IT WON'T HAPPEN TO ME 310

DON'T GET COMPLACENT 311

CARRYING IS A 9-5 JOB 313

BEING IGNORANT CAN'T BE AN EXCUSE 316

THE SELF-PROMISE 317

CONVINCING OTHERS TO CARRY 321

KEEPING YOUR COOL 322

WHY CARRY? - THERE WILL ALWAYS BE PREDATORS 324

15 REASONS WHY YOU SHOULD NOT CARRY A FIREARM 327

CHAPTER SEVENTEEN – *Additional Information* 330

IT'S YOUR RIGHT!!! 331

MY EDC (EVERY DAY CARRY) 332

RESOURCES..337

WEBSITES..339

PREFACE

Dear American Samurai,

    I would like to personally thank you for purchasing this book. It is dedicated to you because you decided to make a life changing decision to carry a firearm to protect yourself and the ones you love. You're following a tradition in American history that dates back hundreds of years. Like many of those before you, the decision was made to carry a firearm to protect oneself against harm. Carrying a firearm is for everyone, no matter your weight, shape, or how athletic you are. Even if you can only lift 10 lbs., you are able to shoot a firearm.

    As we have seen in the news, there are some real evil people in this world and those people have no conscience or morals when they decide to harm your or take your life. They know the difference between right and wrong, but they don't act upon it and they really don't care for anyone's welfare, not even their own. This is a reality we see all the time in the news and around us. We hope that it will never happen to us or someone we know, but the reality of it all, it could. And being prepared is going to change the outcome. These kinds of people are very real and if you're not prepared, you or someone close to you can get seriously hurt or lose their life. I am not selling you fear, but a reality check that this can happen to anyone, no matter where in the world they are.

    As a child, there was a neighborhood kid that I grew up with who spent many times in juvenile detention for stealing, breaking and entering and amongst other things that go against the grain. He later ended up in prison when he hit the age of 18. When he was released and on probation, I was playing on the steps of a church in the old neighborhood. I recognized him from many years back. He was a cousin of one of the kids I used to hang out with.

    We chatted and out of the blue he warned me that there are people who will take your life just for the change in your pockets. He had an empty expression on his face when he said this and claimed to have seen this himself. It was kind of a weird conversation. I had no idea what he was talking about since I had been a pretty good kid and didn't get into trouble where the law was concerned. I was a teenager at the time and I could never ever imagine a person who would do such a horrible thing, so I pretty much ignored it. I found out later that he burglarized that same church that we sat on the steps together and he ended up in jail again. The reason why I bumped into him that day, he was canvassing the church property to find an entry point.

Not until I got older and those who I shared the same sidewalk with, did I realize what he was talking about. Some people on that sidewalk decided that they wanted what was in my pockets, not caring that I was a person like them; decided to take things from me through force and violence. Those same type of people broke down the door of my grandparents' home, walked into their house and roughed them up for a few dollars. They were smacked around, they tried to defend themselves (unarmed) and got hurt in the process while trying to defend each other. They were defenseless against these young hoodlums.

After living in a rough neighborhood for many years, I gained my street smarts, but no experience in self-defense. Since I did not come from a family with money, I could not follow my dreams, so I joined the military right after my 18th birthday for the GI Bill to pay for my college.

I had seen a lot in my military career, visited many countries and the violence never changed from one place to another. I always walked around knowing that someone wanted what was in my pockets and they would do anything to get it. I had grown up quickly learning new responsibilities and being trained while living overseas. Thousands of miles away from that sidewalk that I once shared with others.

After my military service, I had a great job, made good money and moved out to the suburbs, away from the crime and the gangs in the cities (but remember, there is crime everywhere). Back in the day I was never exposed to firearms (except in the military - but we hardly used them) in a way that made me an expert. I had never owned a handgun until I was in my 50's.

One summer day at work, a group of guys asked me if I wanted to go to the range. I told them that it has been years since I fired a firearm. They said no problem and we met that Sunday morning at the firing range. When I arrived, there was one of those empty wooden spools for cable, which was being used as a table, which was loaded up with so much hardware, I thought I was back in the military. I couldn't believe what these people collected over the years.

There were rifles, handguns (semi-autos and revolvers) and mouse guns (tiny handguns). I could tell that I was going to get the chance to try them all. And there was a lot of ammo and with everyone's collection of firearms, I knew I was going to have a great experience.

I was told the universal safety rules to make sure I understood them (which I already memorized beforehand for this event so I completely understood what they meant) before I would go out on the range. I was also trained on each firearm before using any live rounds. Each weapon had different safety features and different types of calibers. I did make the mistake of loading the wrong size round into one of the handguns. An easy mistake if you're new to firearms. With so many different types of ammo and sizes, some look pretty close to being the same size.

During our fun time together, I learned that most of my friends from work were already concealed carriers, some carrying for over 15 years. I heard about this "concealed carry" years before in the newspaper when the news media said the streets would be filled with blood (around the turn of the new century) if people were granted a concealed carry permit (of course this headline never came to fruition), but I really never paid attention to it. I was intrigued that you could carry a loaded weapon on your person in the general public, but never gave it any further thought.

So after my exposure to firearms, I decided to research as much as possible about carrying concealed to see if it was something for me.

After reading and watching videos for several months, along with borrowing a replica pistol with a holster from my friend. I learned how to draw and practiced several of the drills found online. After learning more about the crazy world we live in and how violent that it can get, I decided to sign up for a concealed carry class.

My good friend took the time with me at the range and loaned me his 1911 pistol to practice with before taking my first concealed carry class. Researching and learning before my class really benefited me. I felt more comfortable during the training, especially on the range since I was there a couple times in the past week. So certifying on the range was a piece of cake since I practiced beforehand.

I discovered that after an 8 hour class on concealed carry, I believe that some important information was missed, especially the lifestyle of carrying a sidearm. They went through the legal stuff, situation awareness and other information required by state, but I found it lacking in other areas. So after I got my permit, I decided to take notes of my experiences along with what I had learned from the experts on day to day carrying, especially what you might run into outside the house. The material presented inside is invaluable for anyone who is serious about the new lifestyle they have selected and to help them quickly get into the mindset of carrying comfortably.

I wish you the very best in your new endeavors and I hope you learn something new that you can apply to your concealed carry lifestyle.

Be Safe and Carry On!!!

Grandpa "G"
Author and American Samurai

ABOUT THIS BOOK

This book is focused on those who have decided to legally carry a sidearm and it will concentrate on the day to day activities while carrying one on your person. From getting out of bed when starting the day, until the end of the day and going back to bed.

I am going to start out about what this book is not about. This is not a book on how to aim, shooting fundamentals, differences in handguns (single action, double action, revolvers, semi-automatics, etc.), types of ammo that's out there and other topics surrounding firearms.

Since there is already a lot of information out there on these topics, there is no reason to create another book about the same thing that is already available. I would rather go in another direction by providing information around the lifestyle of carrying concealed, introducing real life situations that you will run into and how to handle them.

This is a book for those who conceal carry a firearm every day, no matter what gender or age they are. It will hopefully answer many of the questions you have about concealed carry. I believe that everyone should be able to defend their loved ones and themselves in this crazy world in which we live in. For thousands of years, violence has existed in one form or another and I don't imagine that it will change anytime soon.

As we have recently started a new millennium, we all imagined a changed world, one of hope and prosperity with the advancements of technology. We thought as a world we matured to a point to remove a lot of violence in our lives. In other words, we thought a lot of this silliness would go away, but in reality things have not changed. Many think as a society, we are digressing instead of moving forward as a whole. The reality of it all, I don't imagine for the next 2,000 years that this would change very much. Like many countries around the world, violence is on the rise, especially in the way of terrorism. People are people and over the generations, society's mindset slowly changes.

September 11th, 2001, was an eye opener for the United States and other countries around the world. The acts of terrorism on our home soil has changed the way we live forever. From shopping malls, schools and Universities, airports, to crowded streets. We have to be more than ever aware of our surroundings and we need the tools to protect ourselves and our loved ones.

In the past decade or so, concealed carry is something new to many of us. In several states, we can now apply for a permit to carry a sidearm on our person. Before it was available to businesses (owners and employees), politicians, the rich and famous (celebrities) to name a few. Over the past decade, much has changed with concealed carry.

Before I got my permit, I decided to do dive into the world of concealed carry and research as much as possible before and after I got my permit and practice many of the techniques learned by others. Since this is a major lifestyle change, you definitely have to be very responsible in your actions. You really need to take this stuff very seriously. If not, you will end up in prison or dead. It's a lot to think about.

There is so much available information, it can make your head swim. And as you become familiar in this area, you will discover misinformation that is out there and you must be careful not take it as gospel on the Internet. Especially in some of the blogs. It just makes me cringe on how people spew so much crap online and those new to this area take their advice. I saw one post saying that shooting someone in the back while they were running away (the assailant was several yards down the street) is a good idea, or firing rounds in the air to warn people is also okay to do. This is horrible advice and it will land you in a jail cell with a new roommate, on a long vacation in hell.

Plus, if you've never fired a gun or have never been around them, then you can easily get lost in all the lingo and get the wrong information from others in this field.

There are also a sea of acronyms describing the same thing around carrying a concealed weapon. Here are a few examples: EDC (Every Day Carry), CCW (Concealed Carry Weapon), HCP (Handgun Carry Permit), GFL (Georgia Firearm License), LTCH (License to Carry Handgun), CHL (Concealed Handgun License), CWP (Concealed Weapons Permit), CFP (Concealed Firearms Permit), CPL (Concealed Pistol License), CWL (Concealed Weapons License), etc. In your state it may be one of these or a different acronym. From here on out, I will just use CCW (Concealed Carry Weapon).

I was never exposed to guns while growing up. No hunters in my family. The only time I saw a gun was with my parents when they bought a revolver for the family business. It was tucked away in the dresser drawer (center top). I happened upon it one day as a child looking for socks in dresser drawer. I just looked at it, never touched it and never thought twice about it. Unfortunately it was not locked up and the folks never gave any training to the children. Not even warning us not to touch it. They presumed that children don't get into things, so they hid it in a drawer thinking we would never find it. We were lucky we didn't play with it and someone got hurt (like my siblings or a childhood friend). The bad thing about it is that many people who do have a gun never lock it up with children around or ever provide proper training about them.

As an adult, I never got involved with handguns until I was in my 50's. I never had an interest until I discovered that several of my coworkers carried and the reasons why they did. Mostly to protect themselves and their loved ones. When first introduce, I had many weak areas on how to use a firearm, like how it works mechanically, how to do preventive maintenance, what types of ammo there is and what is best for me. It was confusing, but my friends were very patient and took me to the range to teach me. While I was learning (before I purchased my first gun), I kept notes and also purchased several books on the subject of handguns, concealed carry law and about concealed carry. There were very few books that had the basics of how a firearm worked, what the difference was between calibers and what type of gun I should buy. In this book I will not discuss these, but really focus on helping you understand the day to day things you may run into when you carry.

    I could not find anything that really introduced me to the basics of carrying concealed. I did not want to take the word of people who taught me, but rather validate what they had shown me. I did not want to get misinformation and if I ever taught someone else, I would be passing along this incorrect info. So every time we went out to the range, whatever I learned, I would research it and sometimes learn something new. Like the difference between a clip and a magazine. These terms are used interchangeably, but are referenced incorrectly.

    It can get complicated, especially about what type of sidearm to purchase and what accessories to add to it, like holsters, belts, mag pouches, etc. There is a lot of marketing and selling in this area since it is a multi-billion dollar business, but some of the stuff you purchase, you end up thinking to yourself, did they actually test this out in the field? On a very limited budget, I researched to make sure I bought the right equipment so I would not end up with something that I did not like, or would have to return and lose money on my investment. I love referrals from people who have actually used something they purchased for a while, tested it and it passed with flying colors. Purchasing things in the gun arena can be very expensive and you could end up with many holsters (for example) that do not work for you.

    I have taken notes of my experiences since the very first days of getting my permit and purchasing my first firearm and decided to put it into a book format and share it with you. As I travelled with my sidearm, I took note of any problems I discovered, or any tips that would be helpful to my readers. What you will find here are the day to day activities of carrying a firearm in the great old US of A. Daily things like shopping, going to the barbers/hair dressers, driving on the highway, visiting public restrooms and other activities that we commonly share daily.

I am hoping that the information contained in this book is helpful for those who are new to concealed carry and to those who have mastered it. My goal here is to bring you to a comfort level of carrying in our society without being noticed and how to carry in some abnormal situations. If you're looking for techniques on how to improve your aim, how to defend yourself in different situation, or what equipment to choose, I have left that up to the reader to gain this knowledge elsewhere and to get training.

I have also provided some excellent resources that I and many others have used, some that are used on a daily basis. Like state reciprocity, how to pick a holster, what to do at the airport when you check in a gun, how to pick the right insurance if you do end up using your sidearm to defend yourself, links to videos about self-defense while using a sidearm and much more.

After reading this book from cover to cover you will discover a whole new world and how to work within your environment. I am hoping the information presented here will be of great value to you.

This book is a great resource, but remember, get trained and continue your education in handgun self-defense.

NOTE TO CRIMINALS

Since the general public has access to this book, I just wanted to inform the criminal community about who they are about to rob and try to do harm.

If you read this book thinking that you will learn how to spot concealed carriers out on the streets, think again. I am going to enlighten you on the subject. Why, oh why, would you want to pick such a hard targets known as concealed carriers? If you think age doesn't matter, think again. By the time you're reading this sentence, another elderly person has strapped on their carry concealed handgun. If you think a person in a wheelchair is an easy target, think again. In the past 24 hours, another disabled person has gone through a training course on how to defend themselves in a wheelchair. They are armed and know how to use it.

If you still don't get it, let me ask you this... How many wars have we gone through in the past 50 years? How many of those people have been trained, especially with a firearm? Millions? Oh yes. Millions. They do not forget their training and many are Special Forces. It doesn't matter their age either. "Once a marine, always a marine". Ever hear that one before? No matter what service they joined, they have been trained and we all look like everyone else. You cannot spot us.

Would you as a criminal take a risk of robbing one of our military veterans? Do you value your life?

Every day, this country has thousands of people who get their permit (depending on their state if they constitutionally carry) to carry concealed. In my state alone, one out of every four people are armed (Concealed Carry Permits). Other states may have more. So your odds of being killed have increased exponentially if you decide to rob one of them. The news media hardly reports on concealed carriers when they stop a criminal using their firearm. If they did, I am sure crime would drop since the criminal element would be informed of the possibility of them meeting their own maker when they take on an armed citizen. They usually eliminate this important part of the story since many news agencies are anti-gunners. So you will hardly hear about it. On a daily basis, someone in this country uses their firearm to protect themselves or someone else.

While you are thinking about harming someone, there will be other concealed carriers nearby. Once you do your dirty deed, you will be full of lead since other concealed carriers will see you as a threat and they will put you down to save the innocent. Or you could take another path and be out with your friends, maybe seeing a movie, or being with your loved ones, staying out of trouble and leaving people alone. Or if you want to risk harming others and thinking that this type of lifestyle will get you somewhere... you will end up in a pool of your own blood, gasping for air as life slowly drains out of your body, while you go through such a horrible, excruciating, painful experience. Is this what you want as a career criminal?

It's going to be around 50% or more of people in this country that will be armed in the years to come. So that's one out of two people who will be carrying. Remember, they are not police officers, so shooting as a civilian is considered self-defense. Your chances of being shot by an officer is low, but the actual concealed carrier you would be robbing, your chances of losing your life is over 90%. They will be armed and trained for such situations.

With so many people being trained around criminal attacks, your chances of survival are slim. Seriously, if I were you, I'd find another profession. An honest one. You'll live longer, maybe hit your 50's someday and enjoy those you love around you. Being a mentor to others to help give them a better chance in life than you did. To get the chance to grow old and die in your sleep, instead of having a violent death while trying to attack a concealed carrier for a few dollars. Wouldn't you want a better life for yourself? Fall in love and grow old with someone. Maybe have kids of your own that can go to college someday and live a better life.

Why lose your life or do hard time over a few lousy dollars? Even using a fake gun is considered a felony and as concealed carriers, if you draw a fake gun, you will lose your life. Is it truly worth it? You're worth more than that. So put down this book and leave this life of crime and make a better person of yourself and make better choices in your life.

If you wish to continue down the criminal path, then I have four words for you....

"You have been warned!!!!"

If you are part of a terrorist organization, you may have noticed in the news that our citizens are armed and not afraid to defend themselves. They have the same weapons or better than you have. So I highly recommend that you do not attempt any terrorist activity in our country. Concealed carriers have stopped terrorists in the past and they will do so in the future.

You also have been given a courteous warning.

THE AMERICAN SAMURAI

American Samurai (Grandpa G's definition): *a new generation of responsibly armed American's of any age, ability or disability, who have chosen the lifestyle to carry a concealed firearm to protect themselves and their loved ones. This armed-citizen goes through periodic training and education, year after year, living and walking the path, learning the way of the concealed carrier. An armed individual that carries every day (when legally possible) and lives by the Concealed Carry Creed.*

The Samurai warrior originated in feudal Japan hundreds of years ago and even though they were abolished in the 19th century, their spirit lives on. Their stories have been passed down from generation to generation. You've seen them in movies, cartoons, games, books and many other forms which continue to breathe life into these historic warriors.

I find that there are some similarities between the Japanese and the new American Samurai. Like the Japanese, many of our responsibly armed citizens continuously train to defend themselves through education and training. With the advancement in weaponry, instead of a sword fight these days, it's now a gunfight. Instead of unholstering a sword, we use a firearm. Like the warriors of past, we carry our weapon at our sides, ready to be unsheathed when trouble arrives.

Many flavors of martial arts from around the world have migrated to the United States over the decades and some of our American Samurai have been trained in the arts of hand to hand combat to defend themselves. Similar to the Japanese Samurai, they learned from their masters in self-defense, using empty handed skills along with wielding a sword to protect themselves. They used weaponry to defend and they were trained and very well disciplined like most of our responsible armed Americans.

Our 21st century American Samurai are more of an independent kind of warrior. They aren't servants to a Daimyo (a lord), they don't belong to a clan (except to their own families), or participate in a military cast system like the Japanese Samurai did. I would consider them more of a Ronin; someone who is a wandering Samurai with no lord or master.

The Japanese sword has been the symbol of the Samurai for many years and it is a proud iconic symbol of Japan. The blade and metallurgy have been perfected, the sword is next to impossible to break during combat and it's so sharp, it can sever body part with one swift stroke. Our firearm manufacturers, like the sword-smiths of Japan, continuously improve the quality of their weapons, a trade secret that is passed on from generation to generation - from Master to student.

Now I wouldn't consider all concealed carriers as American Samurais since some think that just having a weapon is all they need and no training or education is necessary beyond that point. They are a separate group of people with a different mindset, one of not wanting to excel themselves in self-defense. They believe their current skillsets are adequate to save them. They lack respect, responsibility, honor and discipline. They would not qualify under the definition of an American Samurai.

But, there are those who go above and beyond just carrying a sidearm, no matter their age, gender, or ability. And they understand that education, practice and training are perishable skills if not used frequently. They do ongoing education, training and daily disciplines to enhance and maintain their skillset. These are the ones that I would label as the American Samurai (aka American Ronin), a modified version of yesteryears Samurai. Since you are reading this book and decided to you continue your education and training, consider yourself one of our American Samurai.

Did you know there were female Samurai? Yes ladies, women who were warriors participated in battles next to their men. At one archeological site, where the battle of Senbon Matsubaru took place, around the 1580's, DNA shows 35 women warriors were buried there. One of many great untold stories in Samurai history. There is also a story of a village that was attacked, where Takeko and Yuko Nakano (they were sisters), risked their lives and fought for their clans independence after they were invaded. So if you wanted to know if there were any ladies who were actually Samurai, now you know. Women over the centuries from all around the world have fought alongside the men in battle, which I think is pretty awesome and should not be forgotten.

The firearm has leveled the field in the way one defends themselves. And because of this new type of technology, bringing a knife or sword to a gunfight was useless after its invention. Instead of having a Master to learn the way of the sword (which can take years of experience and discipline to master), with a sidearm, you can become proficient in a shorter period of time with the proper training. And you don't have to be in any great physical shape, like the Japanese Samurai.

With a firearm, you can be any age to successfully defend yourself and in almost any physical condition. You could be struggling with a disability, ailment, or be elderly (weak or even frail) and unlike a sword, you can defend yourself with a firearm. Back in those days before the existence of firearms, people were unable to defend themselves with a sword due to their limited mobility and lack of strength. But with a firearm and proper training, now our elderly, disabled or those with medical conditions, can easily defend themselves and take down a life-threatening enemy.

With the advancement in firearms, we have been given the great opportunity to defend ourselves and others and like the Samurai, constant training is available. We can find an assortment of gun-masters who can teach different techniques in wielding a firearm. There is so much versatility today compared to the Samurais of past.

Over the millennia, we still have evil that walks the earth; still robbing, raping, killing and causing harm to the innocent. They have become soulless and more violent than ever before. For thousands of years, the world has not changed much in people needing to defend themselves from those who care not of us and our wellbeing, but instead care in what we possess. But our defenders are a different breed of people, consisting of not just men, but also women of all ages. These people are you and me, honest hard working people trying to live a decent life, trying to fulfill our dreams for ourselves and our families. The world in which we live in has created the American Samurai, defending the innocent against evil.

GRANDPA "G's" CONCEALED CARRY CREED©

"I have made the choice to not to be an average person, but to be a silent warrior that walks upon this earth. I am a mother, a father, a son or a daughter that respects this precious gift of life that we have all been given. I never reveal my weapon to anyone unless it is my last resort to protect myself or others. I am the protector of the innocents until help arrives. I am the gray ghost that is always on alert, never judging others, never looking for trouble, but remaining silent in the background, never sharing my secrets to the masses. I am just a shadow, blending into the landscape, never broadcasting that I am a victim.

Perseverance and discipline are my best friends, ever moving forward, always challenging myself to improve my skills through constant studying, training and practicing while obeying the firearm universal safety rules. As a warrior, I do not seek trouble, but instead avoid it, knowing that I am not a coward, but wise in my decisions. I try to avoid situations that would put me and others at risk and in a position to use lethal force. I am not a superhero, or immortal, nor do I seek heroism. I am but a humble person. I am the trained warrior that will protect so we can all live another day, to live life to its fullest and cherish the ones we love.

I am a law abiding citizen, never taking the law into my own hands. I am non-confrontational, always deescalating the situation and responsible for my own conduct. If others are rude, I just smile and move along, never getting involved with petty nonsense. Daily I will make efforts to be kind, gentle and be a loving person to others around me.

I am the lovable watchdog on the porch, ever aware of my surroundings, never revealing, but springs into action to protect those in harm's way. I am the silent warrior, never wavering, but remaining ever quiet like the calm ether. A lone warrior, a Ronin, an unsung hero who will protect when evil decides to unmask itself with a mission to do harm. I am a good witness, taking note and calling for help when needed.

I am the responsible armed citizen, the silent American Samurai!"

CHAPTER ONE

The Basics

"The only thing that is ultimately real about your journey is the step that you are taking at this moment. That's all there ever is."

Eckhart Tolle

PREPARE BEFORE YOUR FIRST CLASS

There is a lot to know when it comes to firearms and if you have never been exposed to or have had limited time with them, then I highly suggest you learn about it before taking your first class. If you're just going in to take a gun safety or concealed carry class, it would be in your best interest to learn about firearms before your class. Folks sometimes get intimidated by something that is new to them. Like computers. For such a small thing, there is a lot involved with it. The hardware, the software, how it communicates, how it interacts with other computers and basically how to use it. And there is a whole new set of terminology behind it which can get you lost when having conversations with others.

It took almost 4 months of studying about concealed carry, the laws, how a gun works, types of bullets to use, read several books on the subject and memorized the 4 universal firearm safety rules. I took notes in my notepad to reference what I learned or to research more on those topics, watched many videos and read blogs that went back several years about concealed carry. Then when I felt comfortable on what I knew, I took my first concealed carry class. I will share later on about these resources that I thought where really good, some you would benefit from them.

When I took my first concealed carry class, I felt very comfortable in a room of people who were very savvy in this area to those who were completely new to the subject. I understood over 95% of what was being talked about by the instructor and the other 5% I asked questions. It was a very quiet classroom with about 20 people in it. I think some felt intimidated and afraid to ask questions but they felt relieved when someone asked the question that they were thinking of.

I hate to see others who are struggling with any subject. So I would recommend that you pick a date for your class (if a permit is required in your state), go back at least a month or two before it starts and begin learning about the topic. You will definitely feel more comfortable in class and may end up sharing what you learned with your fellow classmates. If your state does not require a permit and you think you need to know more about the topic, then pick a date you will purchase your firearm (if you don't have one). Then go back a month or so and learn more about the topic. When you think you have a deeper understanding about firearms, drills, the law, etc., then pick up that firearm, go to a range and practice. Either way, you're starting your training and you will have to continue training until the day you have to retire yourself from using a firearm.

ALWAYS THINK T.A.N.K. SAFETY ©

As a concealed carrier, you need to memorize the four universal firearm safety rules. Memorizing is important, but following through and living by these rules will save your life, others and also eliminate death or injuries. Live by these rules. For myself, acronyms help me remember important key points. They help me burn important information into my mind. I can't stress enough how important it is to learn these rules.

I use the acronym *T.A.N.K.* to help me memorize these important rules. Why TANK? It's easier to remember and besides they are pretty cool to drive. They also shoot very large projectiles and the person firing the shots should also be following the same safety rules.

You will find similar safety rules in books and on the Internet, but I will share mine with you below.

4 Universal Gun Safety Rules.

Treat all guns as if they are _always_ loaded and when you pick one up, _always_ do a physical and visual clearance check for ammo.

Always be sure of your target and what's behind it.

Never point your gun at anything you're not willing to destroy and _always_ maintain muzzle discipline.

Keep your finger and objects _off_ the trigger and _outside_ of the trigger guard until you have acquired your target and have made the decision to shoot.

Let's go through each one:

_T__reat all guns as if they are _always_ loaded and when you pick one up, always do a physical and visual clearance check for ammo:_

The reason for this rule is that people forget if they have a loaded a weapon or not. It's true. It also gets harder to keep track when you have more than one firearm. When someone hands you a firearm, even though that person has inspected it, it is also your responsibility to check it. I have seen people do a visual check, hand it off to someone, that person receiving it figures that they don't need to check it and when the trigger is pulled, the gun fires a bullet (remember to muzzle discipline). Never do buddy checks on a firearm (letting the person handing you the firearm to check it for you). Check it yourself when you pick it up or when someone hands it to you. This completely insures it is unloaded. I recently saw a video of a man with a shotgun at the range. He leaned it up against a stand. He walked toward his target, the stand fell down and shot him in the back. Treat all firearms as if they are loaded.

_A__lways be sure of your target and what's behind it:_

When you pull that trigger and that bullet leaves that barrel, you are responsible for it. When you are at a range, make sure there is nothing breathing behind that target. We're talking animals (like pets for example) or humans, especially the little ones. You must imprint in your mind that something or someone could be behind that target. For example, there was a shooting in Argentina at a store that was getting robbed. A mother and her child were getting ice cream. They were both unaware of the masked man behind them. The store owner shot at the robber, missing the little girl, but hitting the mother and she was killed in front of her child. The mother was unaware of the events unfolding behind her. The store owner did not follow the rule of making sure of what is behind his target and made a child motherless in less than a second.

<u>N</u>ever point your gun at anything you're not willing to destroy and <u>always</u> maintain muzzle discipline:

    This rule applies to every firearm, loaded or not. From purchasing a firearm at a gun store to loading your sidearm on the range, always keep that muzzle pointed away from anyone or anything that the bullet will destroy. I remember seeing a gentleman that was having a problem with his laser beam on his pistol and it would not turn on for him. He was at the range trying to troubleshoot the problem. So he pointed the muzzle at his hand and pressed the button to see if the red dot would appear to make sure it was working. When he tested it, he shot himself in the hand. I can't make this stuff up, seriously, this does happen to those seasoned in firearms. He didn't maintain his safety discipline, he became complacent and then put himself in danger and possibly those around him. I am sure he will never forget those safety rules again after he left the hospital, but it costed him a good hand by not following these simple rules.

<u>K</u>eep your finger and objects <u>off</u> the trigger and <u>outside</u> of the trigger guard until you have acquired your target and have made the decision to shoot:

    This one of the most important rules of all, keeping your finger off the trigger. Guns do not go off by themselves (it is very rare, but it has happened to some cheap and crappy firearms). The only way they go boom is when the trigger is pulled or if you are re-holstering and something like the edge of a holster itself (poor quality holster) or piece of clothing get caught in the trigger. Many sidearms also have internal and external safeties to prevent accidental discharge, especially when the gun is dropped. That's why you keep your finger away from the trigger and point your finger forward towards the muzzle (you'll see a picture of this later).
    People who grab their firearm when they suspect a prowler in their house, with their trigger on the finger, may end up shooting a loved one, themselves, or have an accidental discharge. You may slip, lose your balance, or fall and pull the trigger, before you have even acquired your target. Or someone in your house is binging at the fridge and you already have your finger on the trigger and accidentally get surprised

and the gun goes off. Believe me, this has happened to household members accidentally being shot. That's why we keep our finger off the trigger, until the target is acquired and you have made the decision to shoot.

This one is rare, but it did happen. I wanted to share a story about a man and his dog on a boat. The man was going out to hunt, he brought his faithful friend with him. He had his rifle loaded and on the deck of this boat all ready to go. While driving the boat, he was shot. How did this happen? His faithful friend put his paw on the trigger and the firearm discharged. Can you recognize which rules should have been used in preventing this incident? Keep your paws off the trigger for example? Can you think of any others?

Following these rules will eliminate accidents happening to you or someone else.

Remember, the greatest safety of all is between your ears. Use your brains and common sense. Create a habit of these rules and you won't run into any problems.

Newsflash: "ABC NEWS: Gun brought to St. Paul school by 7-year-old student goes off, no injuries (November 2016)". This just popped up on my screen while I was writing the previous paragraph. This is very shocking to me. How could this happen? As a responsible gun owner, you must keep your firearms locked up so something like this would never happen. You should also train your children about gun safety, even if you don't own a gun since firearms are very common in homes now.

Depending on the age of your child, they should know what to do when they are near a firearm (like leave the room and inform an adult), what to do if they are at a friend's house, especially if one of their friends pulls out their parents gun. Children are curious and most likely they think that it's a toy. If your child gets a hold of your gun, you may be prosecuted to the fullest extent of the law.

Growing up as a teenager, one of my friends was shot in the face with a handgun. His friend was playing with the firearm and did not know it was loaded. The bullet went through his left cheek, through his throat and lodged itself near his right jugular. He was going to play professional football (he was that good), but is now limited to lite duties. The bullet cannot be removed by surgery since it is too close to his main artery and it could kill him if he hurts his head or neck. He was very lucky to survive.

In the case of the 7 year old, he brought it to school in a classroom full of children, he was showing it off and the trigger was pulled. The bullet went through the floor. It could have been much worse. I am sure legal charges will be filed against the parents. Plus, think of all the news media coverage they will be getting and the friends of the parents whose children were in that classroom. Will other parents continue to be friends with the gun owner? Will the parents allow their children to play with this child ever again? Would the parents of the children in the school file a lawsuit against the family? What does that child think now after taking the weapon to school? What kind of damage has this created for this child? Maybe scarred for life?

It's going to be a real mess and they may be forced to move or have their child attend a different school. This incident has changed their lives forever and it could have been easily prevented. But this gun owner was irresponsible and may end up bankrupt, losing their home and possibly divorced. Don't let this happen to you. Follow the safety rules.

If you never heard of the Eddie Eagle Gunsafe® Program, here is the website to visit to learn more about teaching your children gun safety. EddieEagle.NRA.org

Additional Safety Rules When Passing a Firearm to Another Person

Along with following the universal firearm safety rules, there are others to follow when handing a firearm to someone.

While following the universal rules - TANK (above), include the following below...

- For semi-automatic pistols, always eject the magazine (loaded with ammo or not)

- Rack the slide (upper receiver) to eject the round from the chamber. For revolvers, pass it with the cylinder open.

- Visually and physically inspect the upper receiver (the slide) to be absolutely positive that there is no round inside. For revolvers, check the cylinder for ammo.

- And then pass the firearm, grip first, muzzle pointing down the range, to the other party, while maintaining eye contact with them while the person receiving the firearm uses verbal commands stating that they have control of it (Thanks, I've got it!, for example).

- The party receiving the firearm should always follow the universal safety rules, especially checking to see that the firearm is unloaded. Always assume that it is loaded and double-check it (The "**T**" in **T**ANK).

Don't let an accidental discharge happen to you. Follow the rules and you'll be just fine.

BE AN AMBASSADOR FOR THE REST OF US

If you didn't know, you are the ambassador of the conceal carry community. Congratulations!!! You now have a great responsibility to yourself and those around you. You'll realize that you're not going to be the average person and having a sidearm with you, puts you into a higher category than those who do not carry. You will have to raise the bar and actually be on your best behavior, if not, you may make a mistake and end up in prison with a felony charge. Again, it is a great responsibility and it's your duty to keep up to date with every changing law in your state or those you visit.

You are now representing millions of people who also carry a sidearm in the US for their own protection.

When I was in the military, every country I visited, I was reminded that I was an ambassador for my country and to basically follow the local laws, stay out of trouble and keep a low profile. If I screwed up, others in that country may not be as forgiving and I could be in some hot water and possibly in the news. Remember Michael Fay? The 18 year old kid from the US who was sentenced to caning in Singapore for theft and vandalism. It turned into international news. And our country had to get involved with that mess. Perfect example of not being an ambassador of your country.

While being an ambassador for the rest of us, you have to be very careful while at home and in public.

While in the military, I used to teach foreign prisons to other military personnel while I was stationed overseas. Since my students were also military, they also needed to know what consequences they would suffer if they decided to step out of line. With proper training, this reduced the amount of Americans in foreign jail cells and prison. But there are those who decided to be dumbasses and commit a crime and end up in prison. Remember that you're an ambassador for the rest of us in the concealed carry community. Get trained and educated on the subject of concealed carry and you'll be just fine.

On a side note, there are those who have been fighting a good fight against those who believe that good people like us should not carry a sidearm to defend ourselves or our loved one. These people who write laws against those who carry would rather keep innocent people as victims. Those who have written these insane laws (like limiting how much ammo you can have), their poor decisions has kept the bad people armed while giving them more rights than those of us who are lawful citizens.

For example, in some states, they do not have Stand Your Ground laws. So this means that someone who breaks into your home, threatens to kill you and you shoot them, you are liable for a lawsuit. No kidding. They can sue you (or their family) and you can end up in bankruptcy court. You can lose a lot, including your home and life savings. A criminal who threatens to kill you and your family has more rights than you do. None of this stuff makes sense anymore, but there was a time where anyone could carry a firearm – no questions asked and those who committed violent crimes actually paid for their crimes. And it was like this for hundreds of years. Times sure have changed.

I would like to personally thank those who have been fighting for our rights to protect our lives so that we can carry concealed to defend ourselves and our loved ones. Someday this silliness will be a thing of the past, but for now, be on your very best behavior and an ambassador for the rest of us.

BEFORE YOU CARRY

Before hitting the streets, make sure you test your Firearm at the range. I have heard of people who purchased a firearm and start carrying immediately. They have no idea what state their sidearm is in since they never fired a round through it. This could be a serious problem if you have to use your weapon and you have no idea what state it's in. Unless you like to take risks and be surprised at what's happening around you and discover it's no longer in your favor.

You're newly purchased sidearm may have a recall, like a malfunction where the ammo constantly jams. My neighbor just bought a new handgun, took it to the range and it failed every 3-5 rounds. Then he found out that there's a recall on it. So go out to the range and make sure you put at least 250-500 rounds of ammo through it. Some folks put over 1,000 rounds to thoroughly test their firearm. If your gun fails a single shot or more at the range, investigate the reason behind it. Is it the ammo you are using, is it the handgun, or is it you? If you think it is hardware problem, seek a gunsmith immediately.

You don't want to start carrying and discover during a firefight that your weapon is malfunctioning. You don't want to fail yourself or others that you care about. So don't carry a sidearm if it has never been tested. If you do discover that you have a faulty sidearm, don't use it for defensive purposes. It may cost you dearly.

So before you decide to carry, you're going to want to keep the number of people who know you have a firearm down to a minimum. As in a game of cards, you don't want to show your hand, but keep your cards close to your chest. You want the element of surprise on your side. Showing your cards (telling those around you that you carry) can make you lose the game. You want to be the winner, especially when the chips hit the floor. People talk. They love to gossip. You don't want someone to challenge you because you carry.

I don't even tell my closest unarmed friends I carry. The only people who know that I carry is those I live with of course and those who are also concealed carriers, whom also don't broadcast to others that they carry. It's nice to know those around you are carrying since you may all be out one day having a good time and someone decides to ruin the fun by using deadly force on you or others. It's nice to know that someone has your back in case you get hurt or pinned down in a gun fight.

I don't want a situation to escalate when someone who knows I carry makes an announcement to everyone around us that I have a firearm. Especially when trying to de-escalate a situation, or trying to avoid one, then one of my peeps thinks it's a smart idea to threaten someone because they know I have a gun. They think that the other person will back down if they know someone is armed. Let's say there is an argument and it is about to get into a punching match. Next thing you know, someone calls 911 and says you threatened someone with your gun and you had nothing to do with it and your gun may have never left its holster. It's their word against yours. But when police search you and find a gun, you may be going to jail, even though you did nothing.

A friend of mine was hanging out after a movie with one of his closest friends in the theatre parking lot. Someone called the police on them. The officer came by to find out what was going on and asked for ID and my friend produced his driver's license and his permit. His friend of many years had no idea he carried. And that's the way he wanted it. His secret is used for good reason, to protect himself and those around him.

Don't draw attention to yourself. The less people know you carry, the safer you are and those around you.

KEEP YOUR CONCEALED CARRY SECRET AND PRIVATE

What's the big deal in not letting people know you carry?

The more people know you carry a firearm, several risk factors increase around the safety of you and those around you.

When someone knows you have a firearm, there's a greater possibility of events going sideways and we'll go through some of these. For example, there have been multiple instances where people who knew a person who carried a firearm ended up calling the police because they are pissed at them, they didn't like people with firearms, or they just wanted to be dicks about it. They will lie to law enforcement, saying that you brandished your sidearm and next thing you know, you get arrested for something you never did.

What about those that open carry? Well, I personally shy away from exposing myself in public and for good reason. For one I am a concealed carrier and I don't like to let people know that I carry. I enjoy my freedom and don't want to be bothered, asked questions, or be a target for criminals. Let me explain.

If you decide to open carry, criminals will want your sidearm and will attempt to take it from you. Or if they want to rob a place and they see you with your firearm, they may to decide to eliminate you first because you will be a threat to them. An ambush comes quickly and it is never announced. Having your gun out in the open, you basically lost the element of surprise and possibly your life. If you don't have any type of holster retention, then kiss that sidearm goodbye.

I have seen someone open carry at a fast food restaurant, a person came up behind the carrier in line, took their sidearm and ran out the door. The guy didn't notice it for a few seconds, then ran out the door to chase him and the guy fired back at him in the parking lot with the carriers own firearm.

I have heard of people who are totally against those who carry openly and they go into idiot mode and try to grab their gun out of anger to try to prove a point. Someone could lose their life in this situation. Avoid becoming a target.

At the time of writing this book, a man was arrested after an argument with another guy in a car. The guy had a gun in his holster (exposed to everyone), he approached the car and an argument ensued. The carrier walked away to deescalate the situation. The guy in the car called the police and said that he pointed the gun at him. So he was arrested, even though he never pulled out his gun. But the guy he argued with saw the gun in his holster and decided to get even with him by calling the police.

I've heard discussions around Open Carry, like it deters bad people from doing bad things while out in public. You have your sidearm open to everyone and some bad guys walk in, sees you and maybe decide to leave or come back another time with more criminals. The flip side of that, they may see you as a threat and put a few slugs in you so you don't stop them during the robbery. There's money or valuables at stake here and depending if the robbery has been professionally planned, or just dumb thieves who walked off the street and wanted to take a chance, they both have the same agenda. One may decide taking your life is worth the money. Open carry eliminates surprise which should be on your side and not on the side of those who want to commit crimes. Your biggest advantage is secrecy. Don't throw that away.

I was in the parking lot of a Farm Fleet today (Midwest stores that sell products to farmers) and I saw a women wearing an OWB (Outside the Waistband) holster with a very large 1911 sidearm. She looked very serious and obviously making a statement. I noticed that she did not bother keeping her head on a swivel (situation awareness). I guess she thinks that she has the upper hand and no one would bother her. I noticed that several people were staring at her with that big gun strapped to her hip.

But in my mind I am thinking that this person is putting herself and others in danger. Anyone can walk up, relieve this woman of her sidearm and either decide to wreak havoc on those around them or just plainly steal the weapon which could end up on the black market or be used in a robbery. I was running scenarios in my head if someone did come up behind her, what would I do? If they did get her sidearm, where is the nearest cover? Do I have my cellphone on hand to make the call and be a good witness? If something did happen, this person is putting me and my family into a situation that could have been avoided.

This person lost her advantage right away (not having her sidearm concealed) and is now the number one target for someone who wants that handgun and they will do anything to get it and quick. Keep the advantage and keep your firearm hidden.

I know people want to make a point by slinging an AR-15 over their shoulder and having their handgun at their side (open carry), just to prove to the public they can exercise their constitutional right. But what's going to happen? People will call the cops. Yeah, you're getting attention now. Maybe you'll be on TV or in the newspapers. Good for you. They will ask you for your permit and licenses and you may refuse since you are not breaking any laws, but guess what? You're wasting their time. Those officer that are there to protect and serve may be needed somewhere else more important than being with you. An accident perhaps where people are hurt, or a concealed carry friend of yours that needs their help because of an incident where he/she were protecting themselves. Don't waste law enforcements time by proving a point. We all get it. Let them do their jobs to help others in need. You may save someone's life if you don't waste the time of local law enforcement.

If you think you need to bring awareness about open/concealed carry, then get together with others and do something nice for the community. Feed the poor on thanksgiving, collect toys for children whose parents can't afford them, deliver hot meals to those in need, clean up a park or road, do lawn maintenance for the elderly, work with disabled veterans, etc. Make a statement by doing something really kind towards others. And do this frequently and for years to come. Don't just do it once. You want to continue giving and giving to the community. This can change the perception of how people think about us as a group. Do something really kind for others. This is one of the things we must do as concealed carry citizens, we have to raise the bar higher and set an example for others to follow. Do something peaceful and fun by giving back to your community.

I am not here to tell you that you cannot exercise your 2nd amendment right, but concealed carry will protect you and those around you. Don't put a target on your back. Letting others know you carry will get you attention in the way that you won't expect. Word could spread and criminals looking for a sidearm may start looking for you. This could end up really ugly and you or someone you care about could be in danger. If criminals know you carry they will make attempts to get it away from you either in person, or coming to your home. Remember, avoid conflict at all costs. Don't advertise. Stay concealed and maintain that element of surprise. If you wish to open carry, that's your choice, but not one I would recommend.

NEVER TRUST YOUR MEMORY

This is one of my major personal rules that I follow when working with firearms. I never trust my memory. Sometimes you get distracted, have something on your mind, or you just may forget what state your firearm is. It's like when you forget where you put your keys, or when you are working on something and a tool ends up missing. You have your tools lying around and you just can't find what was in your hands a few seconds ago. It happens to all of us. I also correlate this with firearms (another tool).

Is the chamber loaded? What state is it in? If you have been working with more than one firearm, do you know which one has a round in it or not?

There will be times where you may have more than one firearm you're dealing with and you may not remember if it is loaded or not. You may have to visit places where firearms are not allowed and you have to leave it at home or in your vehicle, locked in a safe. Do you have a round in the chamber when you put it in a safe? Where you in a rush and decided to just put it in the safe without removing a round? Then after a long day, you come back to your firearm, but do you remember what state it's in?

People do forget, we're all human after all and it gets sketchier when you are dealing with multiple firearms. So always follow the four safety rules every time, even if you think your sidearm is in a certain state (loaded or not). You will experience this, especially when you're in gun free zones. In some states, it has to be locked up and unloaded. Other states are not specific if your firearm needs to be unloaded, but as long it's locked up, you should be good to go. It gets a little crazy when you're traveling through states and getting out of your vehicle multiple times because the law says you have to have your firearm locked up. On these long trips, you may forget if there is a round in the chamber.

So always check your sidearm, no matter if you left it somewhere for a short period of time or not. This will save you from any embarrassment of an accidental discharge and shooting someone. I remember an interview of a gentleman that was in a wheelchair. When he was a teenager, his father always took him shooting. He would display his firearms on his wall when he was not using them. One day this child wanted to take a look at one of them and accidentally shot himself in the neck and was paralyzed for life. His father forgot to remove the ammo from that firearm. He thankfully survived, but this person who shot himself accidentally takes the blame since he did not follow the 4 firearm safety rules.

GRANDPA G's FIVE RECOMMENDATIONS FOR KEEPING SHARP AND BEING SMART WHILE CARRYING CONCEALED

1. **Ongoing Training:** Keep improving your skills by taking classes frequently to increase your knowledge about firearms, safety, self-defense and any other training that will enhance your experience.

2. **Continuous Safety:** Always follow the 4 Universal Rules of Gun Safety.

3. **Invest in Yourself:** Read as much on Concealed Carrying as possible. Read blogs, magazines, watch YouTube videos, talk with others that carry. Things are always changing and there are always ways to improve.

4. **Learn The Laws of Concealed Carry (CC) in Your State:** You are responsible in learning the laws in your state around CC. Check out the laws a couple times a year on that states website for any changes or updates.

5. **Constant Practice:** You've learned many things, now go practice them. Keep your sword sharp and don't let it get rusty. There is a lot of muscle memory involved and this has to be maintained on a daily practice. If not, 3-5 times a week (live or dry-firing) should be good enough, but more is better.

WHERE TO CARRY YOUR SIDEARM

Depending on which hand is most dominant and what basically feels best for you when you draw your weapon, there are several on-the-body places to store your sidearm.

In the diagram below, you will see the human body as a clock. The front of you is the 12 o'clock position, the rear is 6' o'clock, the right hip is the 3 o'clock position and the 9 o'clock position is the left hip.

The body is facing the 12 o'clock position.

There are several places to carry your firearm on your body. At the waistline level, chest/arm level, the ankle, the thigh and your pelvic girdle area (your front pockets). Just remember, the closer the firearm is to your hands, the quicker access you will have.

Our bodies are all different shapes and sizes and this also contributes to where you can comfortably carry your sidearm. Also keep in mind where the muzzle is pointing while in the holster and also when it leaves the holster. For example, if you have a shoulder holster under your arm, most likely the muzzle would be pointing behind you. So if there is an accidental discharge, those behind you would be receiving the bullet. When unholstering your sidearm, the muzzle would no doubt be in the path of your arm (unless you raise your arm). If you accidentally pull the trigger while unholstering, you may shoot your arm and hit a major artery (brachial artery) and bleed to death. Always maintain that muzzle discipline.

If you carry in the appendix area (11 - 1 o'clock position) without a holster (like they show the bad guys doing in the movies), you risk pulling the trigger and shooting yourself in the leg, another major artery (femoral artery). And if you're a guy, chances are good, you'll end up giving yourself a sex change. If you do have a flimsy holster (like the Sticky Holster - one of my favorites), remember that after you draw your sidearm and you want to put it back into your holster, remove the holster and reinsert your firearm back into that holster. Then slide the holster with the sidearm back to its original position. DO NOT slip your sidearm back into your flimsy holster while you are wearing it, you risk the chance of having an accidental discharge.

If you carry a firearm in your pocket, <u>ALWAYS</u> use a holster. You risk the chance of shooting yourself when you reinsert the sidearm without a holster, or if you have objects in your pocket with your sidearm, it could pull the trigger. <u>ALWAYS</u> use some type of holster that will protect your trigger while in your pocket. And again, after you pull out your sidearm from your pocket, remove the flimsy holster, reinsert the firearm into that holster and put it back into your pocket. You want your trigger covered and protected at all times. If not, you are risking the chance of hurting or killing yourself.

GUNS SCARE ME

I hear comments from people who have not been around firearms and they express that they have a fear of guns. That's one of the reasons why they don't have one. That's completely healthy and nothing to be ashamed of. Yes, you should be scared in some respect and that's normal. This is a deadly weapon which can harm or kill someone. If you don't have some kind fear or caution while handling a firearm, then there will be a time where you will become complacent and don't follow one of those universal firearm rules and something bad will happen.

When you become too comfortable and your awareness drops in handling guns, accidents can happen. I don't wish people to be scared or fearful of guns, but having some kind of stimuli that keeps you alert of the destruction and the deadly force that a firearm can have will maintain your awareness. Keep in mind that this is a deadly weapon, the rules of safety must be present and when you keep this in the back of your brain, no one will get hurt.

It's no different than working with any other tools, like those used in woodworking. Yes, if you're not cautious, you can seriously hurt yourself and loose body parts. Same thing with driving a car, it can be destructive and can harm or kill someone if you don't follow the safety rules. Or a kitchen knife while preparing food. You don't stand there playing with a sharp knife, you know it can hurt you, your cautious and also know not to run with scissors in your hands.

It comes down to common sense. If you don't have any common sense, then you shouldn't be operating any equipment or vehicle that can be harmful to you or others, especially a firearm.

My point is this, don't be afraid, use caution every time you're around a firearm and never drop your guard by not following the universal safety rules.

If you can do all this, then it's completely safe and you shouldn't have anything to worry about. Yes, I was a little scared at first. I memorized and followed the universal safety rules for firearms, but this fear turned into caution over time and it has been engrained in my soul ever since. It has turned my fear of guns into respect for them like any other tool I have worked with in the past. A firearm is no different than anything else, you just need to proceed with caution to protect yourself and others. By educating yourself on the subject and using common sense you'll be just fine and safe.

GIVING IT THE FINGER

You can tell when people are trained on handguns by the way they hold them. One of my favorite shows is SG-1 (StarGate 1). In this television series, you can tell that everyone has had some sort of firearms training. The soldiers (actors) in the show correctly place their fingers on their firearms, outside the trigger guard. This is rare in Hollywood, since they usually show people with their finger always on the trigger, even your famous cop shows. But at least in this television series, they are putting their fingers in the right position before they're putting rounds on target.

When you have a firearm in hand, you will always keep your finger off the trigger and outside the trigger guard, unless you're going to fire. The example picture (below) is how to place your fingers on a handgun before you decide to fire.

Position for right-handed people.

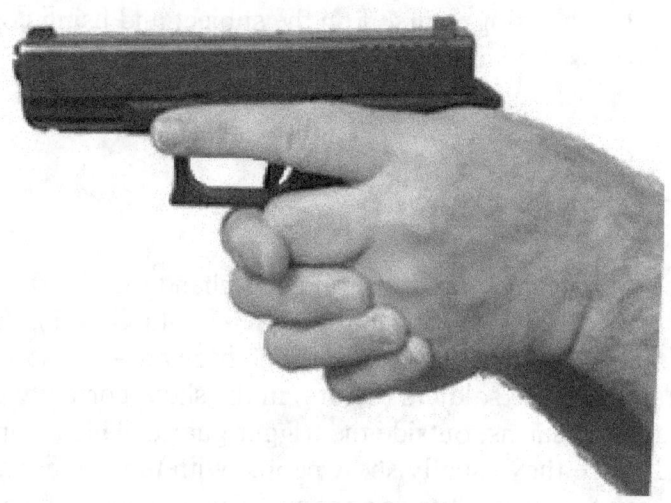

Position for left-handed people.

Always keep your finger off the trigger and outside the trigger guard until you are sure of your target and ready to fire. When you draw, your finger should always go to this position automatically before you place your finger on the trigger. If do not have your finger outside the trigger guard when you pick up a firearm, you will shoot yourself or someone else, especially if you're drawing a sidearm out of your holster.

Incorrect way to hold a firearm when not ready to fire.

This position (above) is incorrect if you have not made the decision to shoot. If you put your finger on the trigger when you pick up a handgun or when you draw, your changes of firing an accidental shot is very likely. Remember, you are responsible for EVERY bullet that leaves your gun. Again, ALWAYS follow the universal firearm safety rules.

NOMENCLATURE OF A SIDEARM

As gun owners, we should educate ourselves on the different parts of a firearm. I have provided a couple of pistols showing their nomenclature as an example to help educate you if you're new to pistols. All pistols are not the same, like the striker fire semi-automatic pistols. They will not have a hammer since most of its components are internal, like its safety features.

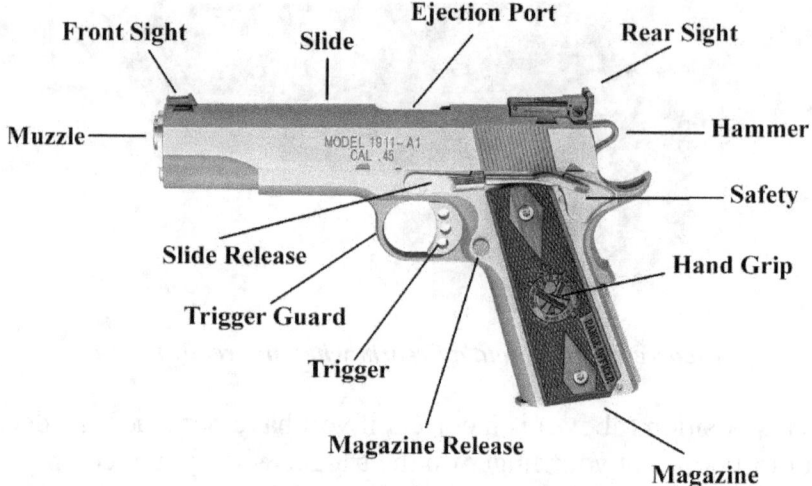

Springfield Model 1911-A1 / .45 Caliber (Semi-Automatic Pistol).

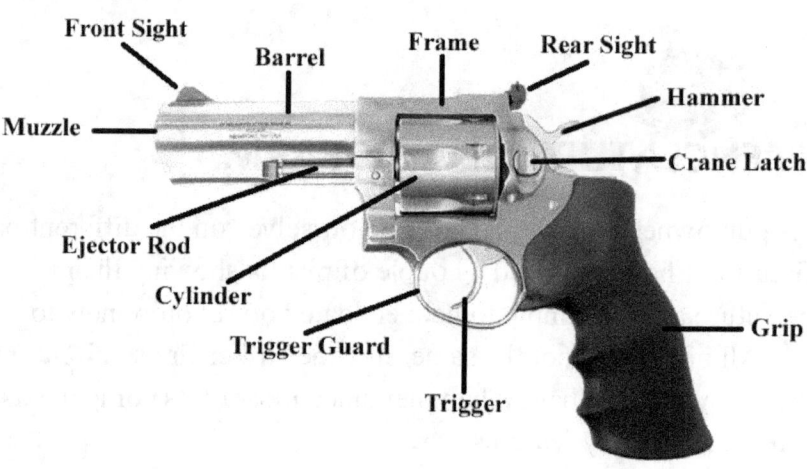

Ruger GP100 / .357 (Revolver Pistol).

PICKING OUT YOUR SIDEARM

This is one of the most controversial issues, picking your sidearm. I am not going to tell you what type of sidearm to purchase, but I am going to help you find the right type of pistol you should be looking for. Everyone is different in their needs so there is no one single pistol that will do it all. Just keep in mind that you're carrying to defend yourself in almost every situation possible.

You obviously want to choose a sidearm that will give you plenty of ammo in the magazine. The more ammo the better. If you do ever end up in a gunfight, you obviously don't want to run out of bullets. Get a sidearm that has a minimum of 15 bullets, this would be your best bet. If you're in a state that limits magazine sizes (10 bullets is the max for example), then get the largest size magazine you can carry, but have more than one magazine (if the law allows).

Weight is also important in a sidearm, the lighter the better, but you also want to have less muzzle flip when you pull the trigger. There are sidearms with polymer frames, which helps reduce the weight of the gun.

Grip size is also important. You want a sidearm that fits in your hands, not one that's too small or too large to handle. Comfort is important because you want control of your firearm. If your firearm is too large for your little hands, or your hands are too large for the grip, your accuracy is going to suffer.

Rear sights for semiautomatic pistols are also important. You should be able to use the rear sight to rack the slide on you handgun. When you're in a situation where one of your hands are out of commission and you need to rack the slide on your pistol, you need a rear sight that can catch on a solid object and put your gun back into battery. You want a rear sight that is at a 90 degree angle, so it can easily catch on other objects that are around 90 degrees.

Using counter top to rack the slide to load a round into the chamber.

For example, you can use a table, place your rear sight on that edge, push it down to rack the slide back and put your sidearm back into battery. You can even use your gun belt, your boot or shoe, or any other object that is close to a 90 degree angle and solid enough to rack your slide on. Some firearms don't have enough height on their rear sight to rack it against an object. With my rear sight, I can even rack the slide on my steering wheel and put it back into battery if I the situation calls for it. Make sure the sights you use will not break (plastic for example). I use iron sights so they will withstand the brute force.

Reliability is very important in a firearm. You don't want one that will break down when you need it the most. Do a lot of research on the sidearm that you have an interest in. There are a lot of YouTube videos showing people testing the reliability of different types of pistols. For example, I saw one of a pistol that the gun owner had buried in his backyard, which it was unearthed a few years later. So he unburied it and took it to the range after he poured water through it. They put hundreds of rounds through it and it didn't fail. Others have soaked firearms in salt water, put in a bucket of mud, buried it in sand, and left it in a creek for days and other crazy things. With such torture, some of these firearms still fired rounds. So do your research. A very reliable firearm will be able to shoot thousands of rounds and doesn't fail.

The size of the firearm is also important. You want something that can be concealed and not print through your clothes. The larger the handgun, the more difficult it becomes to conceal. Look for a compact or subcompact. Printing is when your firearm is showing through your clothes. So if you have it on your hip and you have tight clothing, you can see the outline of your sidearm.

Price is also a key factor for self-defense and daily carry. Don't waste your time spending over $1000 for a sidearm for self-defense. The reason behind this is that if you are involved with a shooting, your firearm will be confiscated and now the police will have a very expensive tool that they may have for several months or longer. It's best to invest in a sidearm that is reliable and at a price range that is affordable to you. So if you spend $500 for a defensive gun and it gets confiscated, at least you can go out and get another around the same price and not worry that someone has your $2000 gun. And now you have to find a replacement for it to continue to defend yourself until they release your confiscated pistol. Are you going to spend another $2000 to replace the one you had?

Caliber is also something to consider. The smaller the size, the more bullets you can have in the magazine. If you consider a 45 ACP, you might be limited to 9 bullets in the magazine. If you go with 9MM, then you may end up with 15. You also want a caliber that you can afford and one that is readily available at any place that sells ammo. I use 9mm critical defense ammo. It can be found anywhere.

Another thing to consider is the recoil. If you have too much recoil (kickback after you pull the trigger), you may end up missing your target. Make sure there is little recoil as possible so you can get on target.

Is the sidearm easy to operate or is it too complicated? Make sure that you're familiar and comfortable with your sidearm. You don't want something that you have to figure out before you shoot it when you need it most. It should come down to point and shoot when in a stressful situation. This could cost you your life. Some criminals do not know how to use a firearm. Sometimes they'll put the wrong ammo in it, don't know how to put it into battery, can't clear malfunctions, or the safety is on when they try to shoot. Don't put yourself in that same situation. Know thy firearm. Get something simple. Point and shoot is what you're looking for.

Interchangeable magazines is a must. If you decide to carry more than one sidearm, then consider having firearms that are interchangeable with the same magazine. If you have a compact and a subcompact, make sure that both magazines will fit in both guns.

Let's say that you have a subcompact that has a single stack and a compact with a double stack magazine. During a struggle with a bad guy, your compact (main defense weapon) gets knocked out of your hand and you don't have access to it. You've fired rounds out of your subcompact and have ran out of ammo and you need another magazine. Since your subcompact is your backup gun, you don't have an extra single stack magazine for it. You only have an extra double stack magazine. Will your subcompact be able to accept that type of magazine and get you back into the fight?

 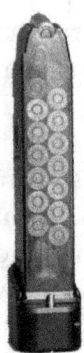

Single stack magazine (left) and double stack magazine (right). These two magazine come from different sidearms and would not be interchangeable.

There are handguns that are interchangeable with magazines. I would suggest finding a pair that will work together without any problems if you are going to carry more than one firearm.

If you want a backup gun, get one with the same caliber as your primary in case you have to share bullets.

STOP TOUCHING YOURSELF

Once you've strapped on that firearm, that's it, it's going to have to stay in its safe place. You will be walking around throughout the day and it will always stay in its holster, unless your life is threatened. You will get to a point where you won't notice it unless you bump into something and it hits it, you put your hands on it over you clothing to support your arms, or someone gets near you and you change positions so no one attempts to grab it. While you're wearing your firearm, just leave it alone. I see people fidget with theirs in public. Don't do this. This will make people curious or alert those who are wanting to invest themselves in a new firearm - your firearm. If you think there is a problem with your sidearm, find a private place and investigate.

If you're constantly touching yourself, you need to find out what the problem is and resolve it quickly. Is the holster or firearm rubbing against you and it's getting your attention? Is it too uncomfortable? Is it pulling down your pants? None of these should be happening. You should have a quality gun belt to hold up you sidearm (if you have your holster attached to it), it should feel comfortable and not digging into your body, or you may need to replace your rig (holster) if it is not doing what it's supposed to be doing. A firearm is nothing to be fidgeting with since it may accidentally discharge.

There was that one young man who was at the Salina Central Mall Theater in Salina, KS. He was dinking around with his sidearm during the movie and it discharged. He shot himself in the leg and he yelled out something like "Oh my god, I shot myself and I just got my concealed carry permit". This is a perfect example. If he was having a problem with his firearm/holster, then he should have gotten up and found a private place (like a bathroom) and took care of it.

A firearm is a deadly weapon and your main concealed carry sidearm should be living in a holster 99% of the time (1% out of the holster for maintenance or range practicing) if you carry daily. You should have complete control of your weapon at all times. It's on you for defensive purposes only, not something you whip out and display to people. Concealed means concealed and it should remain that way. Keep it in your holster at all times and stop playing with it before someone gets hurt.

Again, seek a private location, check out why you keep touching yourself and find a solution right away. You don't want to expose yourself (that didn't sound right) to the public and broadcast that you're carrying a firearm. Keep it concealed and stop playing with it (yep, still sounds funny).

CHAPTER TWO

Holsters

"Life is a journey. Time is a river. The door is ajar."

Jim Butcher

HOW TO FIND THE RIGHT HOLSTER

    I have come up with a list of bullet points on choosing the right type of holster for yourself. I am not going to recommend a particular brand to choose from since everyone is different for what fits for them. But I am going to give you an idea what to look for in a safe holster. There are thousands of holsters on the market, some are alright and some are pretty awesome. Holsters need to be at their very best, meaning, they have to be of top quality to endure the test of time. If you get a cheap one, it may not be safe and could cause an accidental discharge. I understand that you spent a lot of money on your sidearm, but you also need to spend extra money on your holster. Give your firearm a good home to be carried in. Get yourself a really good holster and it will last you a very long time.

    To be honest, there is no concrete industry standard on holster retention levels. So you will see different retention levels that have been put out there by different manufacturers. So a retention level 1 for one manufacturer, might be a retention level 0 for another. I am just going to share what I have put together as a standard for this book. It's a great guideline for finding what fits your needs. I am just going to share the basics for those who conceal carry. You will not need anything more than a molded holster for concealed carry, unless you need more retention due to the environment you work in (rock climbing, climbing telephone poles, testing out roller coaster rides, security guard, etc.).

    Holsters generally consist of either leather, nylon or a plastic/polymer (like KYDEX) or a combination to make them more accommodating for the carrier. For example, my holster has a combination of KYDEX and leather wings on it which makes it more accommodating and comfortable for the carrier. Nylon is becoming rarer as a whole holster and is not as popular as the plastic/polymer type of holsters. But you might find a mixture of this material combined with leather and other plastics/polymer.

Grandpa "G's" Concealed Carry Holster Retention Levels:

Level 0: These holsters have no retention what so ever. You can slide the sidearm into them, but if you held it upside down, it would fall out. Nothing is holding the firearm in place. These would be your flimsy holsters.

Level 1: These types are molded for specific firearms (most common for concealed carriers). When you slide your sidearm into them, the tension from the plastic mold for that particular firearm holds it into place. If you turned it upside down, it will not fall out.

Level 2: These types of holsters use a release lever or a top strap that either your thumb or finger is used to release the firearm.

Level 3: These holsters contain additional retentions (top strap, rocking release, release lever, etc.) since the environment these people work in need extra security since they may be dealing with some bad people (common among law enforcement) and want to prevent their firearms from being taken away from them. Or what you're doing needs a high retention, like climbing or crawling on the ground, since you don't want your sidearm to slip out while performing any of these. Level 3 holsters are for more rigorous activities.

You will find other levels listed by other companies, but for the concealed carrier, these are not needed.

You must find the balance that best fits you. Remember, that if you choose high retention, your ability to present your firearm will add additional time in drawing. If you wish to have the ability to draw quickly, then a lower level holster is what you need. You can't have both. That's why concealed carriers are at a level 1 for low retention and fast drawing.

If you have to carry different types of sidearms that require different holsters, make sure you have the same type of retention for all of them. With muscle memory, if you decide to change things up where one holster is a level 1 and the other is a level 2, your mind might not be able to distinguish between the two during a time of stress. Your mind may forget that you are wearing a level 2 and your hand is trying to pull the firearm out of its holster, but it has a release lever which is still engaged. Keep the same level of retention if you're switching between sidearms so when you actually have to draw to save your life, you're not wasting time trying to figure out which holster you brought to a gunfight.

When we talk about muscle memory, our muscles actually do have a memory. Your body's muscles, after several repetitions of movement will build a memory around it. For example, a child that learns how to walk, they don't do this automatically after birth, they have to teach their new legs. They have not been programmed to walk yet, so teaching them over and over again builds that muscle memory. Then after a while, you unconsciously know how to walk. It becomes an automatic response. You don't have to teach your legs anymore, you do it so often that the muscle memory takes over. So with drawing a sidearm, you will repeatedly draw from your holster until it becomes automatic. You are teaching the muscles in your hands, arms and shoulders. It will be slow at first (like having new legs) but after constant practice, you'll become an expert.

So you should always practice when you get a new holster before you take it out for a walk. You want to make sure it works and no surprises. While practicing, you may have to make adjustments to the holster. Always practice before you take it out into the public and make sure it's safe to use.

GRANDPA "G's" GUIDE TO FINDING THE PERFECT QUALITY HOLSTER

The old adage "Carrying is supposed to be comforting, but not comfortable" used to be the way when carrying a sidearm. With the advancement in technology, it has totally changed. Carrying a firearm these days are becoming not just comforting, but comfortable. When I carry, I completely forget that I am wearing a sidearm. It fits perfectly and it doesn't pinch me.

I no longer get the old dimple above my waistline from the holster pushing up against my side. Some of us may still have that callus spot on our hip where the holster was digging in. Just today, at a restaurant,

I forgot that I had my sidearm and I took off my jacket (which was covering it) and then I put my jacket on the chair. Then the lightbulb went off in my head "hey dummy, your showing your sidearm", then I quickly put my jacket back on. It was so comfortable, it felt like it was a part of me and I didn't notice until my mind alerted me to it.

Since my sidearm is black, along with the pants and shirt I was wearing that day (the Johnny Cash look), it blended in perfectly and those who looked at me never noticed it. So I didn't worry about someone complaining to the management and then being asked to leave since I would be making their customers nervous.

You want to find a holster that is very comfortable. If you don't, it will be a pain in the ass and you'll just either suffer through it or just leave it at home. No reason to suffer or leave it at home. So let me help you pick out your holster so you can feel both comfortable and comforting while carrying a sidearm.

Here is what to look for in an on-the-body carry holster.

- **Perfect Fit:** Avoid generic holsters for carrying. They will not hold the tension and your sidearm can slip out. Make sure your holster is molded for your sidearm. The material should perfectly wrap around your firearm and when you insert it, it should click or snap into place for retention and not feel lose inside your holster.

- **Safety:** Make sure your trigger is protected at all times when you carry and safe from accidental discharge when reinserting back into your holster

- **Retention:** Make sure the retention matches your needs and the environment you work in (level 0- 3).

- **Concealment:** With your sidearm and your holster, when you pull a shirt over it, can it be seen printing through your clothes? The goal here is concealment. You don't want any big bulges.

- **Comfort:** After wearing your holster with your sidearm, does it bother you? Does it rub up against you? Or do you not notice it at all while moving around in your environment? I don't notice mine and you shouldn't either.

- *Material:* Is the holster impervious to chemicals, moisture resistant (like sweat and humidity), water and other elements?

- *Ease of Drawing:* The draw should be smooth and not using extra muscle strength to remove it from the holster.

- *Durability:* Will the material last a long time? Will the belt-clips break? Will it also hold onto you during a scuffle, or will it fall off or break off?

- *Ease of Reholstering*: Does it take only one hand to reholster? Or two? Do you have to force your sidearm into your holster? It should be smooth and easy to reinsert your firearm.

- *Adjustability:* Is the holster adjustable? Does your holster give you the option to angle (cant) your sidearm to different degrees? Some people like to angle their sidearms for easier access. Or is it just straight up and down? Adjustability is great since you can find your sweet spot when drawing.

- *Clips:* Always choose metal over plastic. Plastic will break over a period of time. I have had some that already broke and it put my holster out of commission until I ordered another set.

- *Quality:* Does your holster use metal or plastic rivets? Metal will last you much longer than plastic. Avoid cheaply made and overseas holsters, always buy American with excellent quality.

- *Lightweight:* You don't want a heavy holster, having something that is very lightweight is key in comfort. You don't want to be packing a lot of weight.

- *Ready to Go:* You want a holster that is ready to go and not material that requires a break-in period (like leather). For self-defense, you want it ready at all times.

- *Hard Material:* Kydex material has become very popular with holsters. It is hard and light. The only drawback is that if you get dirt or sand inside of your holster, it can scratch your sidearm. So make sure you keep your holster clean. Otherwise, it's the most perfect material to mold around your sidearm at this time. You don't want a holster that will collapse due to skin (love handles) rolling over the holster. This can prevent you from drawing properly since part of the holster may flop over your sidearm.

- **Flexibility:** Ability to switch between IWB and OWB (**I**nside the **W**aist **B**and and **O**utside the **W**aist **B**and). This is a great cost savings so you don't have to purchase more than one holster for carrying. Remember with IWB, you may have to wear one to two sizes bigger on the waistline of your pants to accommodate your sidearm and holster. My IWB can be converted to an OWB. My IWB also allows me to also tuck my shirt over the firearm and into my pants so it is concealed if I don't wear a jacket. Only the clips show, so make sure your belt or pants have around the same shade so it doesn't pop out and get noticed by others.

- **Exposed Bottom:** Some holster are cut off at the bottom to allow drainage for dirt, moisture, gun oil, sand, etc. You don't want something that will collect crap at the bottom of your holster, it could clog your muzzle and create rust.

- **Test of Time:** Will the holster loosen with age? Leather will stretch over a period of time. Plastic/polymer holsters will hardly ever change with age or stretch over the many years of use.

- **Versatility:** Does your holster give you multiple options to adjust so you can customize it for yourself? Just having a static holster may not be a good fit for you. But something that is dynamic in where you can make several adjustments to match your clothes and your belt is excellent.

- **Seated Position:** Can you pull out your sidearm from your holster while you are sitting? If it is tucked too deep into your pants, you may not get access to it whatsoever or it may delay your draw time. Your sidearm must be at the ready at all times.

- **Low or No Maintenance:** You should really have no maintenance performed on your holster. The only thing that you would usually do as maintenance is tightening loose screws. You should not be taking the time in applying any chemicals to clean the holster. Just using a damp cloth is all you should need.

- ***Closeness to Your Body:*** Is your sidearm nice and comfortable near your body or is it loose and flops around. You want to have your sidearm as close to your body as possible, but not to a point where it would be uncomfortable.

IS THAT A HOLSTER IN YOUR PANTS OR ARE YOU GLAD TO SEE ME?

So where do you put your holster on your body? Everyone is different, depending if you're female or male, if your right or left handed, or if you have sustained an injury. If you struggle from a lower back injury for example, you may have to wear a shoulder harness to take the weight off your hips. Or if you're dealing with some type of disability where you have limited mobility, like being in a wheelchair, you may store your firearm at another location to accommodate your injury. The type of job or duties you perform, will also dictate where your sidearm would be located on your person.

Let's talk about pants/jeans. You finally got your holster and you wonder where to put it. If you are right-handed, most people normally put it in the 3-5 o'clock position. If you are left-handed, normally in the 7-9 o'clock position. Some people will carry in the front (appendix) or the small of their back (5-7 o'clock). You can even have a sidearm attached to your leg or ankle.

Clock Positions.

When you're trying to attach your holster to your pants there are a couple of ways to do this. First and foremost, do not have your sidearm in your holster. Always leave it out while you are attaching your holster to your pants/belt since you will have to make adjustments.

What I usually do is lay my pants on the bed, slide my belt through the loops (attach my everyday carry accessories to the belt), then attach my holster to the pants (not the belt). Then I pull my pants up, adjust my belt, secure the buckle, and then attach the clips to my belt.

In the past I have taken a laundry pen (guys, do not use permanent markers) and marked the inside of my pants indicating where my clips go. It can be different locations on different pants (depending on the location of the belt loops), so you will have to mark them accordingly. Then I can quickly reference the marks, slide my clips on the pants, put my pants on and then clip it to my belt.

When your pants are up and your belt is secured (fastened), then slowly re-holster your sidearm with your finger off the trigger. Some people have discharged accidentally, so be very careful. Make sure there is no clothing in the way when you reholster.

HOLSTER DRAWING & THE CLOTHES YOU WEAR

Before going out into the world armed, you want to make sure that the clothes you wear are adaptable to drawing your sidearm. Your first step is finding those perfect shirts/blouses you will be wearing with your sidearm. Try on multiple shirts/blouses and practice your draw. Depending on the top you're wearing, you may have an easy time drawing your weapon, or it may be a little struggle to being difficult. I have a few Hawaiian shirts that feel silky and when my hands grab it, they slip off. I can't get a good grip on them. So I have problems accessing my sidearm in a timely manner.

So you want to stick with an article of clothing that will give you an easy draw. It could come down to seconds when drawing and your life may be dependent on those few seconds you have. Once you have mastered your draw, practice several times with those shirts/blouses. Since you will be wearing different ones every day, try practicing your draw for a couple of minutes for each article of clothing.

Take note of any difficulties accessing your sidearm. Do you need to make adjustments to the bottom buttons to loosen things up? Can you draw fast and not stall from your clothing? Or is it getting caught or wrapped up on your sidearm? Are the clothes too tight and you can't clear the sidearm from its holster? Once you start going through your clothes, you will also learn about which shirts are the best for drawing a sidearm from.

To draw, there are multiple methods. From grabbing your shirt with your non-dominant hand and raising it to your armpit to clear your pistol, to using your thumb to sweep up the shirt towards the armpit. Then push your hand down onto the firearm's grip, grab it and then draw.

You may carry appendix style, or in the small of your back, but you'll need to practice from this location. Whatever area you choose, you'll need to practice constantly with that article of clothing to be at your very best in case you do need to present your firearm.

Let's say that you carry on your hip (4 o'clock position) and want to practice the most effective draw with the top you're wearing, but depending if your non-dominant hand is free or not, you want to adapt a couple of ways to remove the clothing to access your firearm.

Pretend you're in a convenience store and you have both hands free. Then an armed gunman enters the store. You can either lift your shirt with the non-dominant hand or use your dominant thumb. Now for the same scenario, pretend that this time you have a child in your non-dominant arm. You wouldn't be able to free your non-dominant hand of course to lift up your top, but you would use your thumb instead to pull it up and access your firearm.

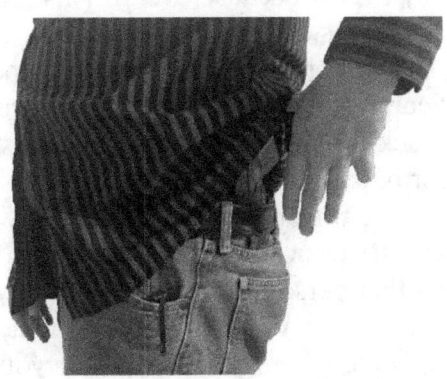

Using the dominant thumb to sweep up the shirt.

At home, I also carry indoors and depending on what I am wearing, I may also have a flimsy pocket holster with my sidearm, kept in my jean pocket or in the pocket of my robe. I would also suggest practicing your draw (without ammo in the firearm – of course) with your pocket holster.

On a side note with pocket holsters, after you draw, remove the holster and grab an area of the holster where the muzzle is not pointing at you or your hands (or anything you don't want to destroy). Then slowly reinsert your weapon into the holster, then put it back into your pocket. DO NOT reinsert your sidearm while the holster is in your pocket, you may get an accidental discharge. ALWAYS remove the pocket holster after you draw, then reinsert your firearm and put it back into your pocket. An unfortunate accident happened to Mr. Phonisay, from Milwaukee, who accidentally shot himself in the groin after reinserting his firearm back into his holster (appendix area) while it was still in his pocket. Unfortunately after the accidental discharge, he died later at the hospital. It's a very tragic story, but a valuable lesson for all of us to learn from.

HIP VS. APPENDIX CARRY

There are advantages and disadvantages with hip and appendix carry. I will briefly go through these. I know that some will agree and disagree, but hey, these are my thoughts on the subject and there will always be controversy over it because everyone is different. That's why there are different takes on it.

I'll start with the hip first since this is the most popular. One of the great advantages of carrying on the hip is that you are able to blade yourself and your attacker will not see your sidearm when you grab it. When you blade your body, you are facing a person, but your body is rotated so that the person in front of you cannot see what your other hand or arm is doing. It's basically facing one side of your body (like your left hip) to that other person, but they can't see your right hip. Try this in a mirror at home. Turn your body to the right, but keep facing the mirror. Get at an angle where you cannot see your right hand. Now move your hand. See, it's hidden from that person in the mirror.

Blading is difficult with appendix carry. There is little to no concealment when blading while appendix carrying. So if you're trying to sneak your firearm into the fight, they will see you going for your appendix position if they are right in front of you. In the mirror turn your hip to the side (blading), double-check again and move your hand to your appendix. Can the assailant still see you go for your firearm? Is it hidden? Concealment is key to your survival. Remember, the hands are the window to people's intentions.

Many people like carrying in the appendix style, but it is not for everyone. If you have a belly on you and it's hanging over your belt, carrying can be uncomfortable, distracting and difficult to unholster your firearm. For some, sitting down, it could be very comfortable and no difficulty in unholstering (especially in a vehicle). Much of it depends on your build and frame. Appendix carrying could be the best option for you and it is the quickest in drawing for some people. You don't have to pull your shirt up all the way to the armpit, but briefly raise your shirt and draw. Plus your hands are in the center of the body, a relative position with your sidearm that could shave off several milliseconds in drawing.

I look at it from a safety standpoint. I personally like carrying on the hip. If my sidearm accidentally discharges, then the bullet would not be hitting any major organs or arteries. Depending on the angle, I might get a flash burn, or lose a very small part of my butt cheek. It may put a hole through my pants (depending if I am seated or not and if it's IWB or OWB), but with appendix, it will be hitting your leg, a major artery (femoral artery) and maybe your private area if it is at an angle.

It also depends on what you're wearing. Are you wearing something on your hip where your firearm would go? Maybe your job requires to have something there, like a work belt. So maybe you decide to carry appendix style due to this fact. Or maybe the clothes you wear will dictate where you would carry your sidearm.

Let's also look at the four firearm safety rules. Are there any rules being broken with appendix vs. hip? I can think of just two that would fit for holsters. Be sure of your target and what's behind it? Never point your gun at anything you're not willing to destroy (always maintain muzzle discipline)? Again, depending on you, which is more comfortable and the safest for you in carrying? This is your choice and I am not telling you how to carry, but for myself, I always look at safety first. Should the way you carry also reflect on the universal firearm safety rules? Absolutely!

CHAPTER THREE

Heading Outdoors for the First Time

*"Today, you can decide to walk in freedom.
You can choose to walk differently.
You can walk as a free person, enjoying every step."*

Thich Nhat Hanh

GOING OUT FOR THE FIRST TIME

What thoughts are racing through your mind when you decide to take your firearm out for a walk? My biggest concern was safety. Should I have a round in the chamber the first time I go out? Will people see my sidearm? Will I walk funny? Should I really be doing this? Will someone notice something that I can't see and become suspicious?

DON'T PANIC - Baby Steps.

I did several things before I carried outside for my very first time. I wanted to be prepared before I went out armed in the wild. While I was waiting for my permit, I purchased some snap caps, a gun belt and a holster online so I can practice around the house after I got my sidearm. When I got my concealed carry permit, with the money I saved for over five months, I finally had enough to purchase my first firearm. Five months? I live paycheck to paycheck (I am sure many of you have experienced this with a family and tight budget). Then came the ammo. For defensive rounds, it was over $1 a round. Since my firearm came with three magazines (total of 45 rounds), I purchased jacketed hallow point (JHP) defensive ammo, which was about $67 and some change after taxes.

Before I went out, I practiced carrying at home. I moved around the home, cleaned, vacuumed, used the bathroom, watched TV, ate at the table, reached for things in the cabinet, picked up things from the floor and did chores around the house. I found that this was an excellent way to get familiar with my new firearm and keeping it holstered. How many times did I find myself adjusting my belt or my sidearm? A few times, but I recommend zero before you go out. So I made the adjustments to my holster and my belt (adding an extra hole in the leather to make my belt just one notch tighter), so that it would not move from its spot, but still felt comfortable.

If you've never carried concealed before, practice carrying around the house and check yourself. Is the quality of your belt good enough to hold the weight of your sidearm? Is it digging into your side? Do you have the feeling to touch your sidearm to make sure it is still there? Whatever it is that is making you check yourself, you are making a target of yourself if you do this in public. Make the adjustments, get a quality gun belt or holster and stop touching yourself, especially when you finally make the leap and carry in public.

Walking around the house was also a great way to test out my new Kydex holster to make sure that the weapon was secure and did not move around, or sag when I am doing normal activities. I also had snap caps (dummy rounds) in my sidearm. I inserted my magazine with snap caps and racked the slide on my semiautomatic. Since the trigger is set I can now test my holster. By the end of the day, was the trigger pulled while just carrying? Did you hear the sound of the trigger snap when you were doing something? If the trigger was pulled, investigate what happened. If it's the holster, then you need to replace it.

If it was a live round, your gun would have fired. It is best to get every idiosyncrasies taken care of before you walk around with a live sidearm. Also test out your holster with snap caps. Put one in the chamber with the trigger ready to be pressed. Practice getting in and out of your car. See if the trigger pulls while removing or inserting your firearm into the holster. I have seen pictures of a person's car with a bullet hole in the seat and through the floor of the vehicle. The leather on the holster was weak and the leather pulled the trigger and fired his gun while he was inserting his firearm back into the holster. Make sure you have a really good holster, your life may depend on it.

Once you feel comfortable, then go ahead and take your new best-friend for a walk. You can put the ammo in, but if you're not ready yet, go ahead and leave a round out of the chamber. For some, it can take days or weeks before one feels comfortable in carrying, especially having one in the chamber ready to be fired. I would want you to feel comfortable and not nervous while carrying before heading out into the world. Others may wonder why you're sweating so much, acting nervous, or touching yourself. You want to get away from these feelings, but again, for some it may take some time.

When I felt ready, I took my rig out for a walk. I made sure my shirt was long enough to conceal my firearm and I did a short walk in the neighborhood. Said hello to people on the streets, but nobody noticed. I finally decided to carry in a local Walmart. Still nothing. Everybody is so busy with their world that they wouldn't even notice if

I did have a bulge bending over trying to pick up somethings off the floor.

My sidearm holds 15 rounds and I can really feel the weight on my hip. Adding ammo makes a big difference. I did not have a round in the chamber for the very first time since I was new to this whole experience and very safety conscious. After I was confident in carrying and I knew my holster was glitch free, I started to carry with a round in the chamber.

After you feel comfortable, from here on out, keep a round in the chamber. I highly recommend this for everyone. If your firearm is not in the ready and something happens where you need to defend yourself using deadly force, you may not have enough time to rack the slide and pull the trigger. You could end up hurt or dead. If that person is robbing another and you need to pull out your sidearm and you're forced to rack the slide or cock the hammer…. They may hear it and you may get a bullet in you before you even pull the trigger. Always have a round chambered ready to go at a moment's notice. It will save your life.

FIRST TIME CARRYING

If it's your first time around a handgun, you're in for a treat. For myself and many others, we were never exposed to guns before. I have shot one with my uncle when I was a kid and shot a rifle once in the military, but never really had the opportunity until I was in my 50's. Yep, I was a late bloomer. There were no hunters in my family and no one close to me who shot guns. So starting out late in life is just as acceptable as starting out young. I just have a little catching up to do, but once you get involved with a lot of reading and training, you will catch on.

If people treat you like an idiot because you're new to firearms, ignore them and find those who will accept you and also learn from them. Don't be embarrassed, always ask questions if you have one. Others would be more than happy to teach you. If someone is not willing to teach you, find someone else. But if you notice those around you who are not following the four rules of gun safety, then it would be your best interest to find someone else to learn from.

I learned from my friends who were very safety conscious and they were willing to teach me. I had a ton of questions and they would either show me or point me to a resource. Those who are "know-it-alls" and treat you differently because you are new to firearms are not the type of people to associate with. Don't let their smugness deter you from learning how to use a firearm or defend yourself. These are the people who will get themselves into trouble, they will teach you improper things about firearms and this will also get you in trouble down the road. If necessary, find yourself a really good instructor. Check out their credentials, see how often they teach class and don't be afraid to ask for references. You want to make sure you have a great instructor so you can learn some really cool stuff and of course learn how to defend yourself and use your firearm.

PACKING ON THE WEIGHT

An idea came to mind today. How much weight am I carrying when carrying? I decided to weigh myself, stark naked that day. Yeah, calm down, nothing to see (insert whistles here!). I recorded my weight and then put on my clothes. I did not include my boots, but just wore the socks, pants, unders, t-shirt and a long sleeve shirt.

Then I put on my gun belt, holster, sidearm with ammo, knife, flashlight, extra magazines with ammo, multi-tool with pouch, magazine holder strapped to my belt, car keys, wallet (with credit cards) and money. Then I weighed myself again. Total weight added....10 lbs. Now if I added another sidearm, loaded, with spare ammo, another holster and possibly a light or laser (or both), you are looking at an additional 5 lbs. or more.

I just found this interesting. I was thinking to myself that the next time I visited the doctors, I would be up 10-15 lbs. or more. So when I schedule my next visit (without the gear), I would be praised for my hard efforts (down 15-20 pounds). I should reward myself with a nice ice cream Sunday for such an ingenious idea. Hmmm....

So the logical thing to do is to make sure you balance the weight with the gear and what you wear. Try to keep it even on opposite sides of your body so that you don't lose your balance, especially in a physical fight. Having more weight on one side can also cause back pain later on in life. Your muscles will strain on one side with all the extra weight bearing down on it. Police officers also have muscle strain injuries, especially back problems over the years due to all that gear they carry. If possible, try to keep the gear weight down. Maybe your knife, sidearm, or light are too heavy. Maybe downsize in length or a lighter alloy, not skimping on reliability and durability. Do the best you can with what you have.

SPARE MAGAZINES (MAGS)

I would recommend carrying extra ammo for your firearm. Either extra magazines for your semi-automatic or speed loaders for your revolver. Since I have different clothes for different occasions, some of my clothes have an extra pocket I can use, some specifically designed for my magazine. If I have a pair of pants that do not have anything to hold my magazine, I have a magazine holder that I can put on my gun belt. There are some people who use a magazine holder that can be placed in their pocket. It has a metal clip on it, which attaches to the side of the pocket.

Why the extra ammo? You will hear law enforcement say that they don't have enough bullets when a gunfight ensues. So if you only have the bullets in your firearm and you have fired all your rounds, you're in a really bad position. Your next move is to get the hell out of there if rounds are still coming your way. Having spare ammo will help you stay in the fight longer when you need it most.

With semi-autos, another reason to carry a spare is that you can have a mechanical malfunction and when you do, you may need to switch to another magazine. Just think of Murphy's Law. Be prepared. Having extra rounds increases your chance of survival.

KEEP YOUR GUN HAND FREE AT ALL TIMES

When you are out and about in public, you want to make sure that you keep your gun hand free of any objects. Say that you're going to load groceries into your car. Use your non-dominant hand while loading the bags into your vehicle (plastic bags work best for this). If you're busy with both hands, remember, it would add an extra few seconds in reaching your sidearm and unholstering since you have to get rid of the objects in your hand(s).

If you're in a situation where both hands are holding something and someone is about to assault you or a loved one, you will have a few limited choices. You can drop the object(s) from your hands and draw. You can run for cover immediately (and don't forget your family member if they are there). Or use that object in your hand(s) to protect yourself. If you have a small child or baby, keep them in your non-dominant arm. Or if you are holding their hand, do it with your non-dominant one.

If you are unable to drop what you have in your hands/arms, make sure you are in situation awareness mode and know where to take cover and know where exits are in case something does happen. Don't take any risks. Always keep your head on a swivel.

While keeping your gun hand free, it is also important to keep your hands empty when you're accessing your sidearm. Multitasking with firearms is a very real danger. If you're not focused at the task at hand, an accidental discharge can also happen. The human brain can only focus on one task at a time and multitasking is not possible with humans, it's been proven. Should the four universal firearm safety rules be modernized and multitasking be added to the list since this too can also be dangerous? Hmmm...

Speaking of multitasking and groceries, I remember seeing a video of a person who was in an elevator carrying groceries with one arm and at the same time, fidgeting to adjust his sidearm with the other hand h(multitasking). End result, he accidentally shot himself. You can see this for yourself on YouTube. He took it out of his holster (with groceries still in his left arm, which he should have put them on the floor while fidgeting), then his jacket got in the way when he tried to force his firearm back into his holster. Then the accidental discharge occurred. Please, please, if you ever need to access your sidearm to make any adjustments, put everything down, don't multitask (this is a bad habit to get into) and put your full attention on your firearm with both hands free.

I have made this mistake in the past. I had my pistol in my floppy holster (not Kydex, so no retention) and put it on a stack of laundry that I was carrying upstairs. I was trying to kill two birds with one stone – what an idiot I was. The gun slid out of the holster, hit the ground and went down the stairs. I didn't have one in the chamber, so it was not ready to fire. Now you're probably thinking of that movie "True Lies" with Schwarzenegger and Jamie Lee Curtis, where she dropped the firearm down the stairs and it shot all of those bad guys that were after her and she never got hurt. Well, that's just Hollywood after all.

Honestly, I freaked. If the firearm was loaded and ready to fire, it would have discharged if the trigger hit something. It has internal safety features to prevent accidental discharges in situations like these if dropped. But don't rely on internal safety features. Not all firearms have internal safety features. Just recently, one firearm failed its internal safety test and it was discovered by someone outside the company who tests firearms. After it failed the drop test, it was reported and immediately recalled.

So please remember, NEVER MULTI-TASK WITH A SIDEARM!!!!! I would strongly suggest that you always give your sidearm your full attention when you have to access it.

WALKING THE DOG

Many of us have pets and one of them in particular gets walked most frequently, the canine. Everyone's best friend. I used to train dogs back in the day and the traditional rule was to walk your dog on the left side. The reason behind this has been lost in history, but I have been told that it had to do with keeping the dominant hand free (for right-handed people). There are more righties then lefties, so the left side was adopted. The dominant hand was kept free so that the person walking their dog would be able to defend themselves, like a sword or dagger. This tradition was also associated with horses, by keeping the dog on the left side so that if attacked, the rider could defend themselves by drawing their sword from their left side and battle on their right (non-dog side).

So as a responsible armed citizen, I would suggest you walk your pet on the non-dominant side. It doesn't matter in this case which side you walk them on since you need to access your sidearm. If you do end up needing to pull out your sidearm, don't forget to drop the leash so you can get control over the situation and get both hands on your firearm. As a responsible dog owner, keep your dog on a leash. In our city, it is illegal to not have a dog on a leash unless they went through some certified training so the dog listens to commands, like police dogs. It's always best to keep your pooch on a leash.

Remember, not everyone likes dogs. Some people are scared to death of them because they may have been attacked by them in the past. I always keep my pet on the leash, law or no law. It is a courtesy to others and I have complete control over my pet. Strangers do not know your pet. If someone else is carrying and they get scared because you don't leash your dog, your pet may get shot. For the love of your pet, always keep them on a leash and always pick up after them (my public service broadcast message).

I have been seriously attacked about 3 times in my life because of idiot dog owners. Their pet was not on a leash. Sometime ago, I was attacked by two Rottweilers at the same time while I was just minding my own business. I was walking down the street and I was not armed that day. My clothes were torn, I was bleeding all over the place from the puncture wounds in my leg and arms. And the dog owner told me that she was sorry and kept telling me that her dogs were friendly. I don't know this lady or her dogs and apparently she did not know her dogs either.

You DO NOT have control over your animals. They think on their own and will act on their own. They can become dangerous. For everyone's safety, keep your pet on a leash. Your pet also has bad days and one day they may turn and bite someone. I've seen it multiple times with friendly dogs. Try to avoid situations with pets and strangers. You may end up trying to deescalate the situation because someone doesn't like your dog or you didn't have it on a leash.

CHAPTER FOUR

Lifestyle Changes

"Zen does not confuse spirituality with thinking about God while peeling potatoes. Zen spirituality is just to peel the potatoes."

Alan Watts

BEING THE GRAY GHOST IN A DIGITAL AGE

    The gray ghost is a person who blends in the background of their environment. They use covertness, produce a low profile and are inconspicuous. They remain unnoticeable and don't stick out as targets, especially for criminals. They just wear plain clothes that don't grab attention to themselves. They immerse themselves in their environment like an undercover agent, going unnoticed. So many of your concealed carriers live this way, being the gray ghost. They try to stay off the radar so they can move freely without being detected. You can find a lot on the Internet about these people and the gear they carry with them.

    Now these days, it doesn't just mean being the gray ghost out in the general public, but it also means being undetectable on the Internet. So in an age where everyone is now being tracked online, everything you put out there on the Internet is there FOREVER!!! Anytime you connect online, the software that uses your Internet connection will leave a trail of breadcrumbs back to you. Even the word processor that you use, in the document or spreadsheet has information that can be traced back to you. Your emails are traceable, the websites you visit, and just about everything you share is traceable back to your computer and you. If you didn't know, many of your printers put markings on the papers that you print, also traceable back to that printer. You cannot visibly see them, but there are techniques online that teach you how to find these invisible markings. No way!!!... Yes way!!!

    Did you know that the Internet is also backed up? Yep, it's true. I can go back and find information that has been removed online. I recently did a search on a post I did back in the early 90's and that comment is still there today. It has been captured by google and other search engines. I can go online and even search snapshots of the Internet since its birth of every webpage and every post made.

    So as a concealed carrier, you will have to be very careful of what you post out there. Not only are your friends and family able to see what you posted (including pictures), the general public, including thieves will see it. If you ever end up in court due to a shooting, those prosecutors will also search information you posted online. I have seen people who post pictures of themselves at the range, hunting, or just showing themselves holding up their sidearm trying to look badass. Remember, every time you go online (including your cell phone and tablets), your information is traceable and it's not private.

If you wish to remain the gray ghost and not let people know you have firearms, don't post information related to guns online. You don't want anything pointing back to you. It's so easy now these days to find information on anyone who has any type of digital or paper trail. Like your computer, cell phone, any bills you pay, mortgage, taxes, bank info, police reports, your credit card purchases, filling out surveys, giving grocery stores your personal info for discounts, etc. Any retailer that has a computer and you give them your personal information, its fair game now. Wonder why your cell phone or home phone is always called by people trying to sell you something? That's because most of the time you gave it out.

Now many of your high tech cars will give your location and information about your driving. Their onboard computers record everything you do. Your speed, where you are (if it has GPS), when you applied the brakes, what turns you made and much more. All of this is trackable. Any one of them will lead back to you. So if you don't want to be a target for thieves, avoid posting anything about yourself and firearms online. If you feel like you want to post something out there, be careful of what you post online (like Facebook, Twitter and other social media).

I have seen people post about going on vacation, they even upload their photos while on vacation. Some have returned home discovering that their house has been robbed. As a gun owner, you should of course have every firearm locked up and inaccessible by thieves or at least very difficult to steal when you step out of your house. So be a responsible gun owner and don't post things online that can alert criminals of your activities and that you're also a gun owner. Remain the gray ghost and be safe.

There is software on the market that will cover your tracks, so you should look into these programs. There are also ways to hide your computer on the Internet. There are ways to be stealthy and never be traced back to you, but this technology is always changing so you will have to research this for yourself. I am not suggesting here that you should use these techniques to be malicious, I am suggesting that you need to protect your privacy.

GETTING INTO THE HABIT

    Habits are forming and with sidearms, especially so. I was at a business conference several years ago and the speaker said that it takes an average of two months to form a new habit. Hmmmm.... So it takes over 60 days to program your brain to create a newly formed habit? They gave an example of a trash can at your desk. If you're right handed and your trash can is on your right side, move it to the left. Watch how many times you throw the trash on the floor on your right side. Your muscle memory is set for that one side where you put your trash into the bin. It will take some time to reprogram your muscles and your mind to throw trash into the left bin. Especially programming your non-dominant hand to do this new action. It could take an average of 60 days.

    I decided to take that challenge. I wanted to incorporate a new daily routine into my life. I tested this theory for myself years ago. I tried it and guess what, it worked. I now do a daily exercise/meditation routine, every day, for over five years now. Let me tell you, it was a hard habit to form in the beginning. As we all know, life can be crazy at times and there are always some sort of event that derails your day and it's usually waiting for you right around the corner. But I didn't let this get in the way of my daily routine. My life troubles are common and no different than anyone else's, but the key to my success was perseverance. This is definitely required in the beginning to keep you going to help form your new habit.

    I created a list of routines that I wanted to accomplish daily and checked them off my calendar as each day passed. I would do this every single day and I would not miss a day. If I did miss a day, I would penalize myself and start the clock all over again. It took several tries to get myself to stick to a routine. I failed several times, but kept going. After two months, the routine stuck and it has been part of my lifestyle for many years. Believe me, there were days that I just hated doing it, I came up with so many excuses, but I knew that it had to be done. I wanted to prove to myself that I could. My routine has now become a part of me and part of my life.

The same thing goes with safety and firearms. You must get into the habit of following those universal safety rules. If you carry, you must follow those safety rules daily. It's going to have to be part of you and your lifestyle. Like checking your sidearm, even though you know that it's empty. ALWAYS follow the safety rules, even though you are 110% sure that the firearm is unloaded. Why? There will be a time in your life where you will get distracted and forget that the gun is loaded. You will swear up and down that it was unloaded, after it discharges.

If you decide to partially follow the safety rules, then that awful day will come where somebody will get hurt or killed and your life will be changed forever.

Get into the habit every damn time you are near a firearm. Four simple rules can save you a lot of headaches. I am sure that you don't want to get into a situation where you will have to explain why your sidearm accidentally discharged to law enforcement and to those around you after the incident. Especially in a public place, oh the embarrassment. But if you accidentally kill someone, your life is going to change forever.

Start today for the next 60 days, follow and practice the four universal safety rules until the day you take your last breath. Get into the habit right now!!!!

A CHANGE IN LIFESTYLE

When you decide to conceal carry, this is going to be a life changing experience for you and those in your family. You're going to have to add carrying to your daily routine (yep a new habit). You will have to be more on alert (heightened awareness), limit yourself on where you can and cannot carry (schools, shopping malls, hospitals, federal and or state grounds, etc.), study up on the local laws of that state/city/county, possible changes in the way you dress and changing your attitude. Whew, that's a lot of responsibility.

When I say changing your attitude, I mean that you're going to have to be extra nice to everyone, including those on the highway, you know, those that cut in front of you on the highway and those that like to tailgate your vehicle. You're going to have to be extra nice to deescalate situations from here on out.

Any time you travel out of state, you will have to know the laws of those states you will be traveling through and visiting. You may have to put your sidearm in your trunk (locked up), because in some states your permit is not valid. It's going to be a pain in the ass. In one state, you are allowed to carry in bars, in others you cannot. Maybe that favorite restaurant you frequently carry in is different in another state which does not allow firearms. "Gun Free Zone" signs are laws in some states and in others they don't hold water. Some states you have to immediately tell the officer that you have a permit to carry and others you do not.

So it's very important and your responsibility to know the laws in other states, even cities or counties of those states. Gun laws are not universal across the Unites States.

You may work at a place where firearms are not allowed, not even in the parking lot. You may be shopping on the opposite side of town from your home, but your job is somewhere in the middle. Since firearms are not allowed at your place of work (not even on the property), you may have to drive all the way across town to go home, then lock up your sidearm, then drive across town again in the opposite direction to get to work. It is a real waste of time. I have had to do this several times to avoid breaking laws. If this is the case for you, you will have to rearrange your personal schedule to accommodate for the extra travel time.

If you're allowed to carry a firearm in the parking lot, but not inside a facility, you will find yourself locking up your sidearm frequently. This is a problem, especially if thieves are watching you do this in the parking lot.

So there could be a whole slew of things that you have to do while you're carrying concealed. Above all, you have to follow the law in those states, or you can get yourself into real trouble. It can end up being a felony with time. It will cost you money and time away from your family.

You wardrobe will have to change to accommodate your new lifestyle. Those skin tight tops may have to go away for a while if you carry on the hip. You don't want people seeing the bulge of your sidearm. There are going to be a lot of changes, but once you get start doing this for a while, it's going to be second nature.

CHANGING THE WAY YOU DRIVE

Now that you're carrying and you are out on the road, your habits will have to change. If not already, you're going to have to be very respective towards others, especially if they're not to you. If you're an aggressive driver, where you like to speed, not stop at stop signs (roll right through them), weave in and out of traffic and have no patience… It's time to make an adjustment to your driving. If someone cuts you off, let it go.

If you have problems doing this, take several deep breaths by inhaling through your nose and exhaling through your mouth three times. If you still feel a little pissed, do it a few more times until you feel okay about your aggressive driver. While taking these deep breathes, clear your mind of the incident. This should help you calm down. This works really well for me on the highway when I have one of those stressful days when there are a lot of crazy people on the road. Your Zen deep breathing exercise should help you deescalate the situation in your mind. Once you've mastered this, you won't care about these people. You'll just let it go and it becomes second nature.

Remember to slow down and do the speed limit. Don't turn into one of those jackasses on the highway. You don't want to get pulled over.

I have read numerous stories of officers that are not very well informed about concealed carry law, or they are against civilians being armed. There was one officer in Florida (Florida Highway Patrol) that was informed by the driver (who was a bodyguard) that he had a permit to carry. She informed him that it was illegal to have a loaded weapon in the vehicle and on his person. He disagreed with her and cited the laws of concealed carry in Florida. She disagreed with him. After he spoke to her supervisor, she resigned from the police force. I have nothing against police officers. Some of my relatives are in law enforcement and a few of my friends are former officers, but you might bump into one that is unaware or lack training on the laws of concealed carry.

You will find plenty of videos posted on the Internet by concealed carriers being pulled over and then things go sideways due to officers being misinformed or they have a chip on their shoulder about civilians who legally carry. This is very scary, so try to avoid breaking any traffic laws. Be the best citizen in the world by avoiding situations where trouble may brew.

If someone is a real pain on the highway, let it be. If you think they're endangering others, then call 911. Give the plate number, any description of the vehicle and persons involved, along with the direction they're traveling. Don't follow them. There are news stories where the armed person follows that aggressive driver on the highway, the person in the other vehicle feels threatened and now you are considered the aggressor. And sometimes a gunfight ensues. These days, the first person who reaches 911 is considered the victim and the other person is the aggressor, even though they are completely innocent. Avoid being the aggressor, or you may end up in the news because things got out of control and a confrontation followed. If you're a hot head, let that person go, call the authorities, pull over and calm yourself down. Otherwise, we will be hearing about you in the news, being the aggressor where you were actually trying to be a good citizen.

TYPE OF SHIRTS/TOPS TO AVOID

I love Hawaiian shirts, especially the ones that are silky or smooth to the touch. They feel really great to wear. Unfortunately, these are difficult to grab and lift while in a hurry to get to my holster. My wife bought me one of those SPF 30 shirts and the fabric is very smooth to the touch. When I pull it up to grab my firearm, I have found that it works about 70-80% of the time. My fingers slip on the fabric and I find it difficult trying to lift it up to gain access to my sidearm. I want access without difficulty 100% of the time when it comes to grabbing my shirt and you should too.

If you have your shirt/blouse hanging out over your holster, you may find that when you have it buttoned all the way down, it becomes very restrictive around your hips and you're unable to pull it up to your armpit. I find that it catches on the butt of the gun or around my waist. There is no play with the garment.

If I unbutton the bottom of my shirt, it gives more leeway and I can get to my firearm. Depending on the shirt, sometimes I end up unbuttoning up past my navel, which I really don't want to do, but it might be fine for the ladies. I avoid wearing any type of tops that are restrictive when I am carrying. So before you go outside, make sure you test your shirt/blouse when you practice drawing. I have set a aside a bunch of tops in a designated area of my closet that are easy to draw my sidearm with. This keeps things simple, especially if I am in a rush. Now I know exactly what shirts to grab when I wear my firearm.

DON'T TALK GUN SMACK

Gun owners, please be careful what you say around people. Some of my friends who carry sometimes say things in a jokingly manner, for example: "Putting a cap in someone's ass". "That guy just cut me off, I should have just shown him my gun or just sent a few shots in his direction. That would've taught him a lesson." Or, "Next time, when that asshole gets in my face, he'll be looking down the barrel of my .357 magnum, wishing he was never born".

Comments like these could be disastrous. You never know whose listening.

I would advise against making comments where you are verbally threatening someone with your firearm. You know that it's a joke, but others may take it seriously. You should reconsider and stop doing this. People overhear conversations and if you do end up in a gunfight and the prosecutor gets wind of this (or find it online), it can be used against you. This could look bad in a court of law and you may end up looking as the aggressor and not the victim.

It may be all fun and games to you, but people these days take things too seriously and you're dealing with a politically correct society. Your chances of winning your court case may be difficult.

I am sure some of you will disagree with me on this one, but crazy things do happen in our society and for myself, I like to be a responsible gun owner, online, offline, in public, or with those I hang with. Threats done jokingly can be misinterpreted. Again, you're going to have to be extra kind to people if you carry.

ADVERTISING T-SHIRTS

We all like to wear shirts that express how we feel about things, or wear some of our favorite brand names and logos. Nike, Harley Davidson, I am with stupid, shoot them all and let god sort them out and so forth. But as concealed carrier goes, do you think a t-shirt would make you a target for the bad people who are looking to arm themselves?

I was at a comedy club one night and I saw this 20 year old with t-shirt that had the English crown it.

Side note: As Americans, why are we wearing something with the English crown on it? Didn't our ancestors fight for their freedom from these people? How soon we forget. Ok, I digress.

On the back of the t-shirt it had the royal crown of England on it, it said "Remain Calm, Carry Guns!" And on the front of the shirt it said NRA.

Now think people, isn't this an advertisement that you may have a gun? As a criminal, I would probably think to myself that you're a gun owner and you may have a gun in your car or in your home. And of course, you may be possibly carrying. A criminal would probably get reinforcements (most of the time they work in packs) and try to get your gun, your truck and maybe take you to your home. This is a big payout for these crooks.

Maybe you were just heading out to the range to practice and you got jumped at the gas station in complete daylight because your shirt was advertising something about guns, which gave you away. Now you no longer have the upper hand. You've lost your concealment and you no longer have the element of surprise. This is not going to end well for anyone.

Please, do not put yourself into this situation. Why risk your life or others over a t-shirt? You're more valuable than a slogan or advertisement. Remain concealed, remain alive, be the gray ghost!

LIVING A RESPONSIBLE CONCEALED CARRY LIFESTYLE

Once you've decided to carry a sidearm, your entering a world of such great responsibility and with that, you will have to change your lifestyle. If not, your chances of going to jail and adopting a new lifestyle are very likely and you won't be able to defend yourself in a cell with your new roommate. Carrying does not make you a badass and if you think it does, get this out of your mind. That's an irresponsible gun owner and thinking this way will get you into trouble.

When you're carrying, there is so much you have to know, but once you get the hang of it, you'll be okay. The number one thing is knowing the laws in your state. Can you carry in businesses, schools, state grounds, bars, restaurants, movie theaters, shopping malls, grocery stores, banks, state capital, etc.? This is what I mean in a change of lifestyle. Depending on your state, you may not be able to go out and enjoy yourself while you're armed. You may end up locking it up in a safe in your car. So get very familiar on where you can carry. Yes, it can become a pain in the ass, but it's the law.

You'll also have to increase your situational awareness. You'll hear this all the time as a concealed carrier. You will have to be on the alert all the time when you're carrying. If not, your weapon can be taken away from you in a heartbeat by those who want to steal it from you. And your life will depend on your situational awareness. When you use it, you'll notice that you're probably the only one looking around for danger compared to those who have their faces buried in their phones.

Traveling out of state is another ordeal. If you decide to go on vacation, what places can you visit that will allow you to carry concealed? Can you carry concealed at all in that state? You will definitely have to find out the laws. What if you're flying? Is the state you'll be visiting allow you to be armed? What if you're driving? The states that you're driving through allow you to be armed, or only allow you to carry but only locked up in a safe in your car? You will need to check the laws in those states before visiting.

How about being out with friends and family and there is a situation where someone in your party picked a fight with someone.

Since you're armed, do you intervene? What about yourself? When someone is calling you or your loved one bad names and this upsets you (or your loved one), do you take the challenge or deescalate the situation? As a responsible gun owner, you will have to deescalate the situation and avoid at all costs in getting involved. So in other words, as a concealed carrier, you will have to be on your very best behavior. And for some, this could be a major lifestyle change.

You'll also have to keep secrets from those around you, meaning you're not going to advertise to everyone that you carry a sidearm. There are only 1 family member and 3 other friends (who are concealed carriers whom introduced me into carrying) who know that I carry concealed. That's it. My own son, his wife, children, or any of my siblings have no idea that I carry. It's not that I don't trust them, but they have different viewpoints than mine on firearms. My best friends that I have known for over 20 and 30 years have no idea I carry. Loose lips sink ships is how I look at it and I am keeping this ship afloat and protected. They don't need to know and I don't need to explain to them why I carry a sidearm. But if a situation arises while I am there with my sidearm, I have their backs.

Change in clothing will be another factor for some. You're going to have to wear clothing that allows you to conceal your sidearm. I wear an IWB (Inside the waistband) and have to wear pants that are an inch or two bigger to accommodate my holster and sidearm. If you're going to carry a sidearm on your waist, you will have to upgrade to a gun belt. Women will also have to find clothing to conceal their equipment and also the ability to access it quickly. Some wear extra clothing underneath that is designed to conceal a firearm.

You'll also have to secure your firearms to prevent children and thieves from getting their hands on them. So training people in your home is important. This is going to be a different lifestyle change for those new to firearms. Yes, you will have to keep your stuff locked up when you're not home, in case there is a break in. You don't want your firearms stolen and be used in a crime. So as a firearm owner, you'll have additional responsibilities that non-gun owners have.

Just to recap, your lifestyle will change and that's okay. You just have to adjust to it and its worth it since you'll be protecting yourself and those you love from a violent crime. For some, the lifestyle change will be adapted quickly, for others it could take a month or more of frequent carrying to get used to it.

GUNS AND CAMELS JUST DON'T MIX

I thought I would add this just to make you think about what you may run into during the day, especially things that you will never expect. You never know where you'll end up. My grandchild and I went to a place that was like a county fair. They had rides, a petting zoo, slides, corn mazes and your proverbial camels. We were in line to ride one of these beasts and I am thinking out scenarios in my head of what could happen around me (remember to always play out scenarios of "what ifs"), including that camel. What if that camel bucked us off and started to attack? Then there are the other camels, would they follow suit and now we have a stampede? Would I shoot to defend myself and my grandchild (obviously - YES). None of this happened, but something else did that I never expected.

On these camels, to keep people from sliding off, there is a metal bar that goes three quarters of the way around the camel. Since I was sitting in the back, the bar would be on my right side and behind me, pressing up against my back. The bar behind me on the camel relieved my gun more than halfway out of my holster when the camel started to walk.

Every time that camel moved, the safety bar would hit my sidearm and partially push it out of the holster. I found myself struggling with my pinned down shirt on the bar and my sidearm, along with holding the child in front of me. I finally had to move myself partially forward and push the gun back down into my holster, but then it got pushed out half-way again.

Now since the firearm is loaded and had a round in the chamber, I did not want this to hit the ground or the trigger get pressed against my shirt while I pushed it back into the holster and a round fires. This would obviously cause a panic and start the camel running. Or the round may end up in the back of the camel and then things would get worse from there. It was driving me crazy. I finally got control of the sidearm until the ride was over.

So, just a fair warning, you can't think of everything. Just keeping it in the back of your mind that if you go on rides, obstructions around you may cause you some problems.

I probably wouldn't recommend going on a roller coaster ride, the log flume, or something that gravity (being upside down in the roller coaster) would relieve you of your sidearm. You're just asking for trouble. Avoid these situations (or have a family member who can carry for you legally - hand it to them in the bathroom), or disarm yourself so you don't lose your firearm. You don't want to have an accidental discharge in public on one of those rides.

If you're going to do some serious jostling of your body, like being upside down, going on rides with some added g-forces, then you may have to consider a level 3 or higher retention holster. I am sure many of us don't have that kind of holster, these are usually used by military or law enforcement, but as civilians, you can still purchase these items.

So we have to find other ways to keep our sidearm safe and others too, when circumstances change in how we must carry. The higher the retention level you go, the larger the holster size will be due to the retention of the sidearm. So if you go outdoors and drive an ATV or do some serious four wheeling, you also may want to consider a higher retention holster. Level 3 or higher are not common amongst conceal carriers since the holster is larger, but if you are doing activities that can relieve you of your firearm, you may want to consider the higher retention to keep everyone safe and eliminate an accidental discharge of your weapon or losing it completely.

Always expect the unexpected when carrying a firearm. You never know where life will take you.

CARRYING CONCEALED IN YOUR DREAMS

If your frequently reading, researching and training on firearms, then you'll notice that in your dreams you may be carrying a sidearm.

I have those dreams of protecting my family when things go sideways or if I am just out and about. I get them more frequently as time goes by and they're very interesting scenarios. For example, I had a dream where I was lost in a city, took a wrong turn while walking and then I was approached by six people who started to quickly come upon me, threatening me with words. I asked them to stay back in a very loud voice, then one came after me with a lead pipe and another started to go for his firearm.

After all the gunfire, I woke up with my heart pounding and I found myself doing the old situational awareness in my room. I remembered what happened and critiqued the situation on how I did and what I could have done better the next time to improve myself. I noticed in my dream that I didn't find cover. I should've gone with my gut feeling and not take that street. My sidearm did jam during the fight, I tried to clear it quickly (tap, rack and roll) since it wouldn't fire. This did not work, so I dropped the magazine and went for my spare, inserted it, racked the slide and then it started to fire. You may have these types of dreams and this is completely normal. Your mind is trying to train itself and it's trying to work out possible scenarios you may run into.

If you experience dreams like this, write it down as soon as you wake up. I usually have a notepad on my nightstand and start writing frantically of key things that my mind is feeding me while I am still a little sleepy. This is the best way so far that I know of that helps retrieve those dreams soon after you wake up.

Then after I have written as much as possible that I can remember, I start taking what I wrote and piece the dream together. Keep track of these and reference them as much as possible. Try to keep these fresh in your mind and critique them. How would you have done it differently? Are you lacking in an area that you need improvement on? Did you move off the 'X' while shooting? Did you seek cover or concealment? Where you shooting with one hand or two? Did you delay your reholstering in case there were more than one bad person? Did you continue to look around after you thought the threat was over?

Concealed carry becomes a part of your fabric and inner being after you start carrying, practicing and learning more about it. This is a good thing. You're retaining what you've learned and applying it, not just to your daily routine, but also in your dreams.

This means that you're becoming more aware of what's going on around you but it also heightens your situational awareness. You may even notice that you're playing scenarios in your head while you're out and about. Since you're playing these scenarios, they are also appearing in your dreams.

It's nothing to be scared of and this is completely normal. Your brain is trying to work out problems while you're asleep. I remember when I was a teenager, working at a fast food restaurant and flipping burgers, I noticed that I was also doing this in my sleep. I was flipping burgers all the damn time. It was annoying but it ended after I perfected the grill. These dreams (or nightmares of flipping burgers and making them) never came back after I felt like I had control over the situation. But the dreams did help. The constant burger making in my head quickly became second nature in real life. So don't quit training.

Having real-life scenarios in your dreams is also a good way to critique yourself in how you can improve in real-life threatening situations.

Several months of learning about concealed carry (practicing and educating myself frequently), I have noticed that over time that I am no longer a victim in my own dreams. Since carrying my sidearm has become my daily routine, it has carried over into my dreams and now I find that I have the ability to defend myself in them. In my dreams, I am always carrying, so now it has become not only part of my fabric, but also my inner being. I still get the occasional "Where's my clothes?" routine in my dreams and surrounded by a crowd of people, but I guess everyone has those types of dreams. Or do they? Hmmmmm.....

I AM TOO OLD FOR THIS SHIT!!

Getting old sucks. Those younglings have no idea what's in store for them. When you start hitting your 30's, you might notice that your body is slowing down a bit. Then in your 40's, just a little bit more. It seems that each decade that passes, you just start slowing down. Since your body went through the ringer over the years, the badges of painful honors (those accidents or joints wearing out) will start taking a toll on your body as you get older.

And then you'll try to hang onto to that old saying "You're only as young as you feel". I have sustained several injuries over the years and when you hurt something and it's not taken care of right away, it will creep up on you as you get older. Joints start hurting, your flexibility declines, arthritis sets in on those old injuries and when you get to the top of the stairs, you have to collect yourself and notice that you're out of breath.

Yes, some of us are out of shape and I am not here to change your habits, or convince you in what foods you should eat. Yes, you may need to take a little better care of yourself, but it is what it is. You're the only one that can change your lifestyle and carrying a sidearm, you may want to rethink how you live your life, even if you're young.

When it comes to defending oneself, I would recommend doing exercises to help put back the flexibility in your shoulders, legs, arms, hands and back. Since there are a lot of muscles used to draw your weapon, you need to be at the top of your game. Over the many years I have learned a martial art, yoga, qigong, tai-chi, meditation and other modalities to help flex and strengthen the mind, body and spirit. If you're young, this is a great time to pick up some of these health tools and form a lifetime habit of using them, especially stretching. Your body will thank you when you start hitting your 40's.

If you have stiffness in the arms, shoulders, or wrists, you can find many techniques online to help reduce or eliminate that stiffness. Maybe a stretching class would be good for you. You can usually find classes at a community center, school, a park, healing center, etc. There are more and more of these types of classes that are popping up all over the place. If you're in a rural area, a search online would probably be your first choice to find something that can teach you how to be more flexible. Even buying a DVD that does exercises would also be helpful. Start your exercises now, your body will thank you. Remember, it's the only vehicle that your soul occupies and there is no replacement.

PREGNANT AND ARMED

You found out your pregnant, you know things are about to change in your life and you wonder what to do with your sidearm. First, I would like to say congratulations to you and your family. It's a very exciting time for everyone.

When you discover that you're pregnant, you'll have to start planning for the entire pregnancy and also after the birth of your child. You'll have to make a decision on what you're going to be wearing and how to adapt to your new concealed carry style. Don't wait until the last minute since you may need to order things online, or visit a store that sells clothing/holsters that will accommodate you during your pregnancy. Also keep in mind how many hours a day you'll be carrying a sidearm.

Think to yourself….Is the weight of the firearm going to be an issue or it's location on your body? Will it be comfortable for eight hours or more a day? Should you retire your sidearm until the child is born? Or should you continue to carry?

These questions that are not uncommon for pregnant women who have been carrying or those who are new to it. Since you'll be carrying a child, things are going to get uncomfortable at times. With the extra weight due to your child growing and carrying additional weight on top of that (your sidearm, etc.), can produce additional pains to the body.

If you carry a big gun, you'll have to downsize to a smaller size handgun. There are some pretty good subcompact firearms that will be far less in weight compared to a full size handgun. Make sure you find one that can hold enough rounds since you may not be able to carry an extra magazine. Remember, some states have a limit on how much ammo you can carry in a magazine.

Your lifestyle and the way you carry are about to change. For example, if you wear a belly band type of holster, this is going to be useless after a few months of your pregnancy. So what do you do?

Your body is going to change and you're going to notice that you'll be moving your firearm around according to your shape, plus you'll run into some additional challenges. You'll also want to make sure that you're not printing in the new outfits that you're purchasing. As you're moving through the trimesters, you want to make sure that carrying is comfortable and not force your holster/sidearm too tight up against your body. You don't want to put any more stress on your body or your baby.

Clothing is also going to change and many of the maternity clothes will not allow you to wear a belt, especially one designed for a sidearm. You're going to have to be creative in this area. You may think of an ankle holster, but bending over to gain access may be difficult and too strenuous on you and the baby. Plus your ankles will swell and it may outgrow your holster.

Appendix carry is definitely not an option after a while. Off carry might be an option, but if you have other children, especially if you have to carry one in your arm, digging into a purse with one hand may be impossible if you need it in a hurry. Another problem here is that with children and having a firearm in an off-body carry bag, this could end up disastrous if the child starts digging into your bag. I am not a fan of off-body carry for several reasons (discussed later). There are also bras that are designed for concealed carry, but this option may also change as the weeks pass by.

Unfortunately, you're going to have some very limited options in carrying and as time goes by, you will have to keep changing the way you carry.

Keep your sidearm very clean. Since there are chemicals from the powder after being fired, some of it attaches to your firearm, so make sure you give it a real proper cleaning. Remove as much powder as possible. If you can, have someone else do it for you. That would be great since you and your unborn won't get exposed to it. I would also recommend that you don't go out and practice at the range. When you pull the trigger, you will be exposed to lead, even inhaling it. So put this on hold for now.

You can still practice while you're pregnant, but doing dry-firing instead. Dry-firing can assist you in determining where the best place on the body to draw your firearm from. Plus it will help in continuing your training. Again, over a period of time, you may be moving your holster to a different part of your body to adapt to the challenges while being pregnant.

The weather will also have an impact. If it's winter time, having a jacket with a holster inside one of the pockets would be a good option. But when you go to places where you take your jacket off, it might be challenging. It will be out of reach when you need it (jacket hanging on the back of a chair for example). You probably don't want to wear your winter jacket inside some places since it might overheat your body. If you're in other weather conditions, having a jacket may be an option to carry.

Breastfeeding while carrying is another thing to consider. After your child is born, you'll have a lot of stuff to drag around with you; a stroller, a diaper bag, bottles of formula, talcum powder, etc. Where is the best way to carry while traveling with all this stuff?

If you decide to use a shoulder holster, this could be an option, but after the child is born, you want to make sure that it is not accessible by the child while you carry or breastfeed.

Some women have claimed that they carry in the 3-6 o'clock (right hand) or 6-9 (left hand) position while they have been pregnant, but everyone will be different.

After your child is born, DO NOT multitask with your child and your firearm(s). ALWAYS keep them separated. Always follow the universal firearm safety rules!!

The holster that you will be using will have to completely cover the trigger guard to keep little fingers from touching the trigger. Children are fast so having the trigger and guard completely covered is utmost important and make sure that firearm cannot slide out of your holster. Having some type of retention with little fingers around might be a good option. Your child will be hanging on to you all the time, so toes and fingers may hit the sidearm, but the trigger must always be protected so you don't have an accidental discharge.

Having a sling for your child is one of the best options when carrying a firearm. You will have access to your firearm on your hip. If you need to draw and since your child is secured in the sling, you will be able to use both hands. If you end up using one hand, you can place your non-dominant hand over the ear of your child and press their little head against your chest to cover the other ear to protect their hearing in case you have to pull the trigger. This is something that will need to be practiced. You may want to practice with a pillow in your sling to build that muscle memory.

Here are some suggestions on carrying while you're pregnant. Again, you will be changing from one bullet point to another depending on your situation. While being pregnant, it is going to be a real challenge in carrying, but here are some ideas to help get you started.

- **Shoulder Holster**: If you decide to do this, make sure the opposite side of the holster is holding spare magazines. This will help you balance out your pistol on the opposite side. Your boobs and your belly during pregnancy may get in the way, depending how big they get.

- **Off-Body Carry:** I would not recommend for reasons mentioned in this book, but if your options are limited, then practice, practice, practice with the off-body bag/purse. You need to get your firearm out of the bag/purse as quickly as possible. It will add additional seconds, especially if you're carrying your child in your arm. Off body carry would also be appropriate at the doctor's office since they would be examining you.

- **Customized Clothing:** There are clothing that are designed with holsters built into them. You may want to consider this, but you may outgrow it over the trimesters. Bra holsters may be an option for some, but this also depends on the size of your breasts. It may be difficult to reach for your firearm.

- **Hip Carry:** If you can carry a holster on the hip (and this may change with trimesters), then this would be a great option, but remember that comfort is important. If it's too tight against your side, then you may want to look for other options.

Why carry when pregnant? Pregnant women are not immune to crimes. There are some weirdos out there that have gone after pregnant women for their babies, even while it's still inside them (like the case of *Dynel Lane). So you must protect yourself and your baby - at all costs. So as a mother or father to be, be aware by keeping your situational awareness on.

Again, congratulation to the addition to your family.

---

*Dynel Lane of Colorado (a certified Nurse Aide) was convicted in February of 2016 for attempted murder. The pregnant women answered an ad on craigslist for baby clothes. When she arrived, Dynel decided to remove the baby from the 7 month pregnant women. The mother survived, but her unborn child did not.

CHAPTER FIVE
Samurai Self Training

*"To follow the path, look to the master,
follow the master, walk with the master,
see through the master, become the master"*

Zen Proverb

BEING THE STUDENT ARE YOUR FIRST STEPS IN BECOMING A MASTER

Ask yourself this question, would you feel safe around those who purchased a firearm but have no training or experience in using them? Think about it. They have never taken a class on concealed carry or even fired a firearm. They have gotten most of their information on the Internet (if they bothered), but information from those who also have no training or experience, but full of opinions. They lack fundamental knowledge of the law, like castle doctrine or stand your ground. Or they never bothered in furthering their education in using firearms, or even taken the time in knowing the universal firearm safety rules. Could they be a danger to you and your kin?

Carrying a firearm comes with great responsibility and training is one of them.

I strongly believe that everyone needs training. You are not born with the innate knowledge of carrying and using a sidearm. You must be taught by someone or learn on your own. This is a controversial issue with many where people believe that it is their constitutional right to carry and training is an option. When people apply for a permit, in some states it is required to go through a minimum amount of training for that state before you can legally carry a firearm. Even before your permit expires, you may be required to go through the same training again to retain your legal status.

I would disagree with people's thinking that training is not necessary when it comes to firearms. I think training is very important. It keeps you informed, it builds more confidence in people, it opens up new possibilities and expands your horizons. It can also be a lot of fun learning something new. I don't agree that we should be forced into training and those who do not know us want to make those decisions for us. You should get training, but you should be the one to choose what type you need. If you are new to firearms, of course you need to learn the basics. There's nothing wrong with this. This is for your safety and others.

Anytime we are introduced to something new, we must get some kind of education around it so that we can become proficient at it. This could be a new firearm you just got and you need to educate yourself on how to use it and take care of it. For those who are experienced in the world of firearms, it doesn't hurt to relearn the basics ("so boring" you may say to yourself). The basics is the foundation of which you build upon. Every time you learn something new, practice it and retain it. When you do, you're adding another brick to your building to secure that foundation. Like building a home on a slab of concrete (your foundation). Training is perishable and if you don't continue to use it (like the four universal firearm safety rules), you will lose it (forget it).

But there could be a time where that foundation can become ignored which can make you complacent. Ignoring your foundation can get you into trouble. You must repair those deficiencies before it takes over your foundation. If not, then that day will come, without any warning, everything you worked so hard on now crumbles onto that foundation. This can be dangerous to you and others around you.

There are those who have decades of experience in firearms who end up accidentally shooting themselves, or they shot someone else by accident. That's because they started to ignore their foundation, like forgetting one of the basic firearm safety rules. All those years investing in themselves, have now crumbled around them. That's because they became complacent by ignoring their foundation and because of this, someone paid the price. Be a great landlord for your tenants by taking care of your foundation. Get the training you need and continue to train.

Like those who have mastered their martial art. They have spent years and years and years (thousands of hours) training. And when they practice martial arts, they continue to use the basics, this is their foundation. If ignored their foundation will collapse and someone can be seriously hurt or killed when it was not necessary. Avoid accidents, get training and continue your education.

Take a class or two per year, or learn online from a reputable source and practice on your own, but keep it up. Get proficient at it. It will save your life someday. Those who have mastered their martial art don't stop training, they continue it for life and this is what you should also do. Improve yourself, you will thank yourself later for doing so. When you speak to anyone who is considered the master of something, they will tell you that they are still the student and they are always learning, even though they have mastered it. This is wise thinking, something to be practiced and lived by. Thinking differently is unwise which means you still have much to learn.

Training is very important, especially learning from the professionals. If you learn from others who are not as experienced, you may get erroneous information which may lead you down a path where your actions may not be legally justified. Just because you heard about it on an online post does not make it so.

If you didn't know, criminals are also getting training. They are showing up at the ranges, paying for classes and using what they learned and applying it on the streets against innocent people like you and me. Yes, we sometimes see videos of dumb criminals, but some are looking at a lifetime of crime and using what they steel to take classes to improve their skills to successfully rob people. They are not going to have their concealed carry permit, they don't need to in using a firearm. They can get training and go to the gun range with their stolen firearms. No one's going to check people to see if they are using a legal firearm or not. With more and more people carrying concealed, they realize this and want to defend themselves just in case they are robbing one of us. So it is vitally important to keep up on your training. Remember, criminals have the same access to resources as you do. So continuous training is going to be the very best thing you can do for yourself to survive a gunfight.

DRY FIRE PRACTICE

Ammo is getting expensive these days and shooting 500 plus rounds can get costly if done often. Also the time to drive to a range, then waiting for your turn (if there is something available) to practice, it could ends up taking up your valuable time. So most people will practice dry firing at home to save themselves time and money on ammo. Many of your modern handguns will allow you to dry-fire these days, but if you're unsure, then contact the manufacturer. You can also use Snap Caps (dummy rounds) to practice. If you get the chance continue visiting the range to train with live rounds.

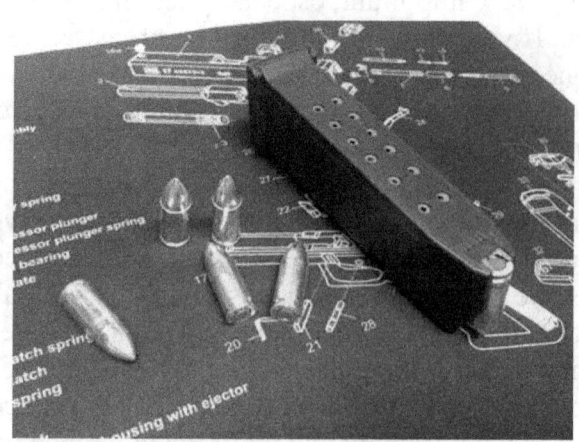
Snap caps and snap caps inside magazine.

Dry firing enables you to practice with your handgun without using live rounds. So if you need to practice drawing, then you're able to do so without using live ammo. You're just firing it with an empty chamber, or using products that you can put into the chamber to allow you to enhance your dry fire experience. Depending on your firearm, you may not need any of these products since you can just pull the trigger multiple times without any manipulation to your firearm. Some firearms may need you to add a specially designed trigger to allow you to pull the trigger without racking the slide.

Snap caps are not only great for dry firing, they are also used to practice your tap, rack and roll to fix a jam in your semi-automatic sidearm. During a gunfight, if you fire your semi-automatic and it goes click and no bang, you will need to quickly rectify the problem. First tap the bottom of the magazine, rack the slide to eject any rounds, then roll the firearm to the side to make sure the round falls to the ground. Then get back into the fight. If the first time doesn't work, then a couple of more times may release the round. If not, release the magazine, slide in a new one, rack the slide again and get back into the fight. Snap Caps are excellent for practicing this type of malfunction and clearing the bad round.

For revolvers, some people just use spent cases instead of spending the extra money for snap caps.

I have a Glock and I had to purchase a trigger reset kit to enable dry firing without racking the slide. Without it, I have to rack the slide every time I pull the trigger to reset it. I have tried putting a piece of thick paper into the top of the slide to move the slide back a little bit (put it out of battery) so the trigger can be pressed and it will move forward again, but the firing pin does not reset. So if I incorporate laser ammo to practice with, it will not work. The internal functions do not allow the trigger to automatically reset when you pull the trigger.

You will have to do research on your sidearm to see what you can use for a laser bullet ammo and if you are able to pull the trigger multiple times without racking the slide.

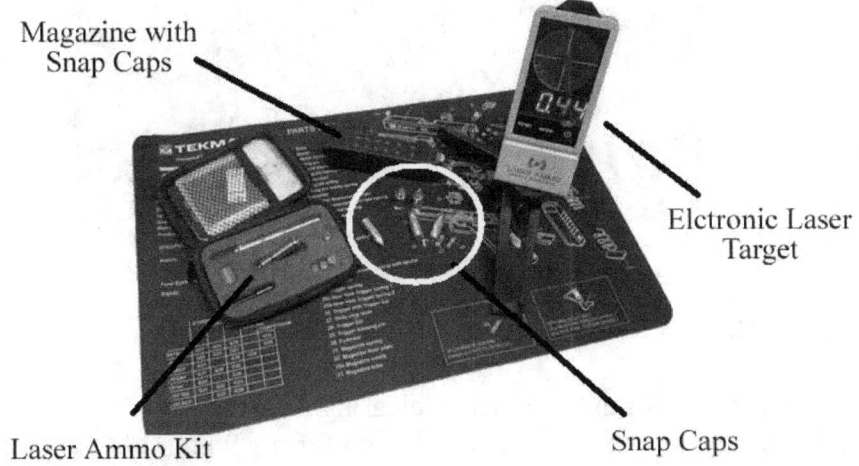

This is my training kit I put together to practice dry firing.

There are many products on the market to help you improve your trigger pull, clear malfunctions, improve your accuracy, decrease draw time and get on target. For example, I use a software program that's downloadable from the Internet that enables me to create my own virtual firing range at home. I can select different types of targets and I can fire at them using my laser ammo. I use my computer with a digital video camera, a target on the wall and I am ready to go. Just do a search online with the keywords "Free Dry Fire Software" and you'll find some downloadable programs.

When you're all setup and ready to go, practice as much as possible on dry firing. You'll notice after a while how much your muscle memory improves and how quick you're at drawing and shooting. You should also practice clearing malfunctions with snap caps (you can't mix laser ammo and snap caps) since you already have a target on the wall.

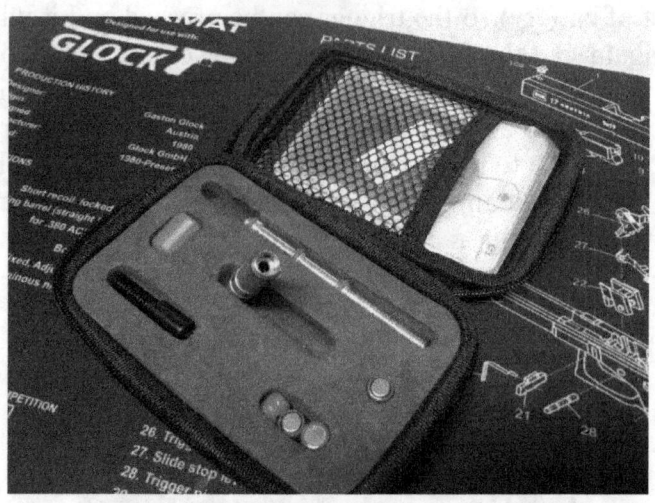

Laser ammo kit that I practice with.

DRILL TIME!

Here is a drill I use to practice clearing malfunctions. I went online and purchased snap caps at about $1 each for my 9mm. I bought 10 of them. You can purchase additional snap caps to keep your training running longer. I also have two spare magazines for my sidearm for training. I make sure there is no ammo in the room and that the firearm is unloaded. I would load up two magazine with three rounds each and the third with four rounds. I would mix up the magazines so I don't know which one has an extra round in it. I also want to pick an area where I won't lose my snap caps. When you eject one from your sidearm, it will travel a distance, so make sure that it won't end up in a floor vent, under the bed, under the couch, in the sink, down the drain, in the mouse trap, the kitty litter box, etc. You want to be in an area where your flying rounds won't get lost.

Once I find the perfect area, I will have my magazines loaded with the snap caps and I'll have two magazine in a holder made out of Kydex on my non-dominant side and access it when I run out of ammo in my sidearm. I will pick an area on the wall as my target, rack the slide and fire at it. I will pretend that there is a malfunction since the gun didn't fire, then I will tap the bottom of the magazine, rack the slide to eject the round, roll the firearm to have the ammo fall out, get back on target and pull the trigger.

I would repeat this until I am out of snap caps in that magazine. Then I will release the magazine and replace it with a newly loaded one (with snap caps) from my hip and do the drill over again. Practice this as much as possible. This exercise will build your muscle memory to clear a malfunction while under attack.

If you're at an outdoor range, you can also use snap caps with your live rounds. Just randomly put a couple of snap caps with your live ammo in your magazines. So when you fire at your target(s) and during one of the rounds that doesn't fire, than you can do the tap, rack and roll. It's a great way to teach yourself on what to do while live fire training.

Types of Firearm Malfunctions:

Failure to Feed (FTF): This is when ammo from your magazine fails to feed the next round into the firing chamber. This can be contributed to not having a strong grip on your firearm (limp wrist) when you pull the trigger, it could be the ammo you are using, a problem with the magazine spring, feed ramp problem, a problem in the chamber, a problem with your extractor, recoil spring, or something else. I would suggest doing the basics on troubleshooting the problem and if you can't figure it out, then you should visit a gunsmith. You may notice that your weapon is not in full battery (the slide is not even with the frame since it will look out of place).

Failure to feed (round did not get into barrel).

How to Fix: Drop the magazine and pull the slide all the way back until it locks. The round should drop out of the bottom of the magazine.

Stovepipe: This is when you fire a shot, the bullet leaves the barrel and the shell casing gets stuck in the ejection port. You will visually see the casing jammed in the port. This is usually caused by holding the firearm improperly, like a dead fish handshake on the grip. Others refer to it as limp wristing. It just looks like a stove pipe sticking out of the top of your firearm.

Stovepipe (bullet fired but casing not ejected).

How to Fix: Remove the magazine and move the slide back until it locks and expel the round.

Squib Load: Squib Loads are extremely dangerous. If you didn't know, Brandon Lee, son of Bruce Lee (the famous martial artist) died on the picture set of "The Crow" due to a squib load.

When you press the trigger on your firearm and you hear a muffled or quiet sound instead of the big bang, you have a squib load. What happens during a squib load is that the bullet does not have enough force to leave the barrel and it gets lodged inside of it. If not checked and you pull the trigger a second time, the next bullet will hit the first bullet stuck in the barrel and it may cause a breach or create a bulge.

If this happens, this can lead to death or being seriously injured. In some cases, squib loads can be caused by reloaded (reloads) ammo that has very little or no gun powder. The definition of a squib is a small firework that burns with a hissing sound before exploding. In this case, there will be no hissing.

Squipload (bullet stuck in barrel).

How to Fix: Immediately check your firearm and verify that there is no round stuck in the barrel. DO NOT LOOK INSIDE THE BARREL!!! Find something that you can insert (non-metal), like a pen, to see if there is a round stuck in the chamber.

Hang Fire: This one is dangerous, but is rare. After pulling the trigger and the cartridge doesn't fire, you may have a hang fire. It is also referred to as a misfire.

How to Fix: If this happens, keep the firearm pointed down range for about a minute. Don't mess with the firearm. Just keep it pointed away in case it does fire. This type of malfunction is caused by the propellant inside the bullet casing slowly burning. If it does not fire after a minute, remove the round. Do not use it again, get rid of it.

HOLSTER DRAWING

To draw from the holster, you will obviously need to get access to it in an emergency. One major thing that will have an impact in how fast you can get to your firearm are the clothes you wear. If you wear a Mumu and have your sidearm concealed inside, it may take you way too much time to gain access to it, like lifting it up and trying to draw. In most cases, you will be accessing your firearm somewhere around the area of the hipline. Your main concerns will be what you'll be wearing for a shirt or top. If you're going to access your firearm below the waist in concealed carry style, like the thigh or the legs, additional practice will be needed. So if you need to draw from your legs (like wearing a skirt) or from your ankle, practice this with clothing that will allow you "quick" access.

For those who commonly carry around the waist-line or above, before you start drawing, you will have to try on multiple shirts/tops and practice skinning that smoke wagon. If you're going to wear a holster under your armpits, you will have to practice with a jacket on. Depending on what you wear, you may have an easy time drawing your weapon, or it may be just a little struggle to being difficult. Stick with the shirts that give you an easy draw. It could be a matter of life and death. Once you have mastered your draw, practice several times with those shirts/tops. Since you'll be wearing different ones throughout the week, you can practice 5-10 minutes per day for each of those shirts, so you can learn how to draw fast from them and not end up fumbling for your sidearm when you need it most.

I have my clothes separated in my closet where I know exactly which shirts will go with my sidearm. I don't have the hassle in trying to figure out which shirt worked the best. It's there in plain sight. So for any clothes that you'll be carrying a sidearm with, keep these in a dedicated area of your closet. There will be times where you may have to dress up, but cannot wear a sidearm, like at a school graduation. So in your closet, you will have an area dedicated for these types of situations.

There are a number of ways to draw your pistol. One way is to cross over your torso with your non-dominant arm to the area near your sidearm and grab your shirt/top from the bottom. Then lift your shirt up to your armpit while grabbing your sidearm and drawing it. This works best when both hands are free.

Another way to draw is using your thumb on your dominant hand to sweep up the shirt towards the armpit and then push your dominant hand down onto the grip of the firearm, grab it firmly and then draw. It works really well if you have your hands in your pocket since your shirt is over your hands or if your non-dominant hand is not free, like holding a child.

If you're using a flimsy pocket holster instead of one with a hard shell, then remember, after removing your firearm, don't put it back into your pocket where the holster is. Remove the holster first, grab an area on it where the muzzle is not pointing at you or your hands, then slowly reinsert your weapon back into the holster. Then reinsert the holster with the firearm back into your pocket. Make sure there are no other objects in your pocket where your firearm is.

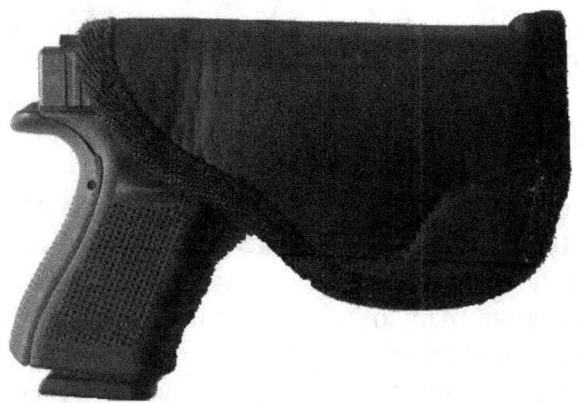

Sidearm inside floppy holster.

You can use the same techniques to draw for the pocket holster. Continue practicing all the time. I practice a few minutes when I put on my shirt before I go out for the day. When I get a new shirt, I will practice for several minutes to get comfortable with it. Just remember to practice with no ammo in your firearm and continue to follow the firearm safety rules.

DON'T STOP READING OR WATCHING VIDEOS

I can't stress this enough. Continuously read as much as you can about concealed carry, watch as many videos produced by the pros and also watch those who make mistakes so you can learn from them. I read at least one article and watch a couple of videos per day to continue my education on concealed carry. If you want to watch amateurs, I would suggest that you search for videos called failed guns or failed firearms. These are video compilations of people who just don't follow the rules and end up being shot, shoot others, damage property, or hurt themselves. Honestly, most of these people need to take a basic physics class. Learn from these people who do not follow the four universal firearm rules. These are perfect examples of what <u>not</u> to do. Quiz yourself on which rules were broken. People laugh at these, but cringe every time and just shake my head. These are real people doing real stupid things.

While you're watching these, you're going to see one out there where this guy pulls the trigger on his rifle and it just goes click. Then he puts the muzzle to his face and shoots his hat off and burns his face. He's so lucky that he didn't blow his head off. Watch these idiots so you can really see what happens when people don't follow the four basic rules.

While surfing online, you're going to notice that things are always changing in the firearms industry since people are discovering new techniques to defend themselves. Laws are ever changing, new gadgets are being made, but many other wonderful things are being created to help our sisters and brothers who carry concealed. You may discover a better way of doing things which could shave off a second or more in responding to a deadly threat. There is so much to learn out there and there are some pretty good videos and articles to review.

Watching videos helps put you in the mindset of "What If?" "What If" is a game that concealed carriers play to improve their mindset in how to handle situations in their environment. It's a mind-scenario-based game of taking in your surroundings and visualizing what a possible attack would be right there and then and think to yourself "What would I do?" First you would look around for exits, figure out where cover and concealment is, then create a pretend situation in which how you would handle the situation. It could be as simple as walking out the exit in some of these mind-scenarios.

Here's an example. When I walk around a mall, I will look up to the other open floors above me and imagine someone walking in with a rifle. Since this is a good tactical position for someone who wants to do harm, I would look around for the closest exits and spy for some cover. That's it. I am programming my mind to be more aware of my surroundings.

Or you see a real situation unfold in front of you (like two people yelling at each other) while you're walking away, you play the "What If" game to pretend that something happens. Like one person is punching the other. What would you do? Call 911? Would you get involved or be a good witness?

When you watch these videos online showing people defending themselves, play the "What If" scenarios in your mind, put yourself in the shoes of that concealed carrier. Did they do it correctly? Could have the outcome been much better? Is this person breaking any laws? Would you have changed something or done it differently if that was you? What about after the trigger was pulled and police want to take you into custody? What would you say? What about being summoned to court? Imagine yourself in court. How would the jury view this incident?

Would they convict the concealed carrier in that situation? Did the carrier do everything possible to deescalate and get out of that situation? Did they try everything possible to prevent it from happening? Let's say in one of these videos, someone was walking down a dark alley at night. Why did they not walk in the lit areas where other people would normally be walking? Could they have prevented this from happening or does it look like they were looking for trouble? I play out the scenario past the incident to imagine how the courts would view this video and if they would convict the carrier or not.

The books, videos and the "What If" game is part of your training. Educate yourself by reading what the experts are doing. You don't have to agree with everything you read or see. Remember to question things. If it doesn't sound right then move on. Research that topic and see what others are saying. Is there a better or safer way of doing it? I have found myself questioning things. Maybe the information was out of date or no longer being used. Maybe it's recommended by some, but not by others. What are the pros and cons of the review?

Let's look at the topic of off-body handbags. I have seen experts say not to use them and others endorse them. When you find confusion, research this for yourself. After extensive research, I personally would not off-body carry for the following reasons… People forget, bags get left behind with guns in them and children also get into them when unattended. They also get stolen while being worn (purses are a target for thieves) and draw times are delayed a few extra seconds where you need that time to get on target. I always consider safety first in a product and you should too. I don't want to deter you from off-body carry and it may be perfect for you.

If the cons outweigh the pros, then don't choose that product. And you also have to keep in the back of your noggin that some of the positive comments may be by the manufacturer themselves. The staff of that company could be posting stuff online under a different name to try to sell their product. So research and see if it makes sense to you. Talk to others who are using the product to see if they like it or not. I always read the 1-2 stars first to really hear what people are saying. If the 1-2 star review has a higher percentage compared to the 5 star or it's close to half or more, then try to find another similar product.

PRACTICING IN THE DARK

With any type of exercises, always follow the universal firearm safety rules. Before you attempt this, make sure you're pretty proficient in drawing your sidearm in the light before moving onto limited to no lighting. Do this with **no** ammo in your firearm and make sure that any ammo is away from you and in another room. I would recommend practicing your draw in low lighting until you're really good at it. If your lights are unable to dim, get some night lights and place them around the room. It would be pretty close to actually being outside in dim lit areas.

It may take you some time, but be patient. It will pay off in the long run. Then when you're very comfortable with the low lightening conditions, then practice in complete darkness with a tactical flashlight. It may be a struggle at first, but keep practicing. Make sure you do it in a carpeted area in case you drop your weapon. You don't want to damage your firearm. If you have wooden floors, you may have to be creative and purchase a plush rug, put piles of dirty clothes from the hamper around you or come up with a better idea. Make sure you have no pets around so you don't trip over them in the dark. Secure the room, don't let anyone bother you and you'll be able to focus on your training.

Just pick a target to draw at and practice. Always start out slow. Remember that slow is smooth and smooth is fast. Once you've mastered drawing and shooting in the dark/low-lighting, then try your non-dominant hand. Get proficient in drawing and shooting in the dark/low-light conditions with your dominant and non-dominant hand. If you need to learn additional skills in this area, find an instructor to teach you.

REPETITION & RETENTION

If you really want to get a better understanding of carrying concealed, then I would recommend subscribing to magazines, reading books and articles online, watch videos, etc. There's a lot of information out there and knowing what to do in situations is top priority. Also get training with an instructor, this will help to reinforce what you've learned. Sometimes you forget about when drawing a gun is considered justified since there is so much legal stuff involved and state laws do change.

If you continue to frequently research and read on topics associated to your firearm and carrying concealed, you'll start getting familiar with it and feeling more comfortable around the subject. The more you dive into it, the more you'll see topics repeated and this will help you build your retention. You will see the basics repeated, but that's okay. You might be in the early stages of learning about concealed carry and find something that you glossed over the first time but remember it for the next.

So if you read something about how to clear a jammed gun, like a squib load for example, you may forget about it later. Gee, I remember the name squib, but can't remember what it was or how to clear it from my sidearm. Then you see a video on it later, then it's talked about in a magazine, or you see someone talk about it online and so on. This becomes very helpful in understanding what you've learned. If you're new to firearms, this is a great way to get familiar with them.

GRANDPA G's WARRIOR WORKOUT

These exercises are geared towards improving your balance during a gunfight. It will also get you into the habit of situational awareness while you reholster. Whenever you practice these, at all times have your firearm unloaded and continue to follow the four universal firearm safety rules.

If you have balance, breathing, or heart problems, do not attempt these exercises. Make sure there is a hand railing to grab in case you lose your balance. When you're practicing your situational awareness during these exercises, don't just look around, seriously look to your left and right and zero in on an object. Pause for a quick second on that object and continue to move your head. Don't just move your head. You want to train yourself to be aware of your surroundings, not gloss over them.

Climbing Up and Down the Mountain

You will need staircases for this exercise. Walking up and down one level of stairs will be sufficient. If you have multiple levels, this will be excellent way in challenging yourself. The object of this exercise is to walk up the stairs and continue to draw and re-holster your weapon.

Start at the bottom of the stairs, pick a point on the wall at the top of the stairs that you'll use to point your firearm at. Walk up a few steps, stop, draw your firearm and point it at the wall, then look left to right and slowly re-holster while you are still looking around. Do this again, continuously until you reach the top of the stairs.

Now do the same as you walk down the stairs. Draw your sidearm, look left and right and re-holster slowly while looking around. Do this at least three times going up and three times going down the stairs.

Climbing Up and Down the Mountain with Distractions on Your Path

This is going to be the same exercise as above except that you'll have an object in your non-dominant hand. So if you draw right-handed, you will have an object in your left hand. You'll be walking up the staircase, drawing and re-holstering while your other hand is busy.

Start with a pillow in your non-dominant hand, press it up against your chest like you're carrying a child. Walk up a couple of steps, stop, draw your firearm, and aim at your target while holding the pillow in the other hand. Look right, left and re-holster slowly while looking around. Do this multiple times as you climb the stairs and then walk back down them again. Do this three times. Three times up the stairs and three times down the stairs.

Advance Techniques

Climbing Up and Down the Mountain on Opposite Side

This technique is great for those who want to strengthen the muscle memory in their non-dominant drawing hand. For this exercise, you will need a holster for the opposite side of the area you usually draw from. So if you regularly draw from the right, then this time, you will draw with your left-hand. If you don't have a non-dominant holster, then use a flimsy pocket holster instead. While climbing the staircase, stop, draw from your non-dominant side, aim at your target, look right to left and re-holster. Do this multiple times as you walk up and down the stairs. Do this three times for going up and down.

Climbing Up and Down the Mountain on Opposite Side of Pathway with Distractions

This is the same exercise as the one above, but this time, yep you guessed it, you will have an object in the opposite hand. So you will have a holster strapped to your non-dominant side, draw from that side, while you have a pillow in your dominant hand. Climb the stairs, stop, draw your firearm, keep the object in your dominant hand, look right to left and re-holster slowly. Again, do this three times going up the stairs and three times going down the stairs.

Clearing Malfunction while Climbing Up and Down the Mountain

There's a lot going on during this exercise. It is similar to the above exercises, but you'll be using snap caps. The choice of weapon will be a semi-automatic pistol for this drill. Make sure there is no ammo in the room and no ammo in your sidearm. Load it up with snap caps. It's pretty much the same exercises that you have practiced, but this time you will be walking up the stairs, stop, draw your firearm, shoot at your target, tap the bottom of your magazine, rack the slide and roll it to make sure the round is ejected. Point again at the target, look around, slowly reholster. Then climb the steps again and repeat. Do this going up and down the stairs.

After doing a few of these, you can use your imagination and change things up.

These exercises will help with balance, increase your heart rate, keeps you focused, helps with coordination and increases your awareness. It also improves your non-dominant hand in case your dominant is unable to function at that time when it is needed most. When you draw and depending on your terrain, you may not be on leveled ground or you may be on an actual flight of stairs.

OUT FOR A WALK

I enjoy the great outdoors, especially walking around in my neighborhood. The sunshine, the fresh air and the people who wave and say hello, it's so joyful to get out and stretch the old legs. While I am out walking, exchanging pleasantries, I still keep my head on a swivel and distance from those I don't know - Just being mindfulness of my surroundings.

Even though you're walking in a familiar area, don't stop your situational awareness. Violence can happen anywhere, like the attempted assassinations of our nation's leaders in 2017 at a baseball practice. They started practice at around 6:30 am and someone decided they wanted to assassinate them. A familiar area, an upscale neighborhood, but that day it came with an active shooter. It can happen anywhere at any time.

So when I walk with someone, we share turns in looking behind ourselves every so often. Having a partner with you makes it easier to expand your radar. Especially if you have neck injuries and it's hard sometimes to look around. Having someone else at your side who also joins in your situation awareness makes it easier for the both of you. So enjoy your walk, stay safe, but have fun.

HOW'S YOUR SIX?

Situational awareness is key to your survival and keeping your head on a swivel is going to be a full time job.

I try to walk frequently in my neighborhood to stay healthy, enjoying the outdoors and sometimes saying hello to the neighbors while sharing the same sidewalk. While walking, there is going to be some activity. There will be cars, bicycles, dogs, people, geese, etc.. So how do you keep your eye on all this activity?

I like to play the situational awareness game of "What If". While it's easy to watch what's going on in front of you, there's also things going on behind you (your six o'clock position). I first gauge how much activity that's going on around me. If it seems too busy, I'll try to pick another place to walk. If I feel comfortable of what's going on around me in my environment, I'll start mapping out my walk in my head. I will pick objects ahead of me on my path that will be a minute or less to walk to. When I reach that point, then I look behind me and around me.

For example, while walking, I'll pick out a sign ahead of me which will be about a minute or so walking time. When I reach that point, I'll glance behind me. Then I'll pick another object, like a light post and when I reach that point, I look behind me again. Then I'll pick a tree, a bush, telephone pole, etc. Then when I reach that point, I look behind me. I stay away from places that people can take cover and sneak up on me. Like hedges, a row of trees, a brick wall, etc. But I will also take note that these places are also good for cover or concealment if needed.

When you practice this daily, it becomes automated and your mind starts picking spots in front of you and you'll start to automatically looking at your six when you reach those points. It will take about a month or so of practicing, almost daily to build that mental and muscle memory. But after a while, your mind and body will start doing it automatically. If you're with someone, the challenge is to continue to do this during conversations. Don't get distracted. Keep setting your marks ahead of you and turn around briefly.

When you're dealing with a sidewalk that is shared with bicycles, this going to be challenging. These people come up on you so quickly, plus they hardly ever give warning that they are behind you (like ringing the bell on the bike or saying something). I have accidentally walked in the way of a bike that was behind me because I did not hear them. So if you're one of those people riding your bike, please let the people in front of you know you're coming.

A friend of mine was walking with his wife one early morning and a teenager on a bike come up behind them quickly, she did not hear the bike, she walked into his bike and got slammed to the ground. She banged her head, was in a coma for over a month and died from the brain injury. All of this could have been avoided by being courteous, signaling ahead of time and going around the person. Just basic common sense. But you're going to run into these types of people while you're walking who think they own the road and don't want to share it with others.

With bicycles, you'll have to cut your time short between spots to see if they are coming or not. Remember, they are traveling faster than you. When I was a teenager, I was at a park and two guys on bicycles, on each side of me, came up on me quickly, they both put their fists out and nailed me in the chest. It was so fast. It knocked the wind out of me. I struggled on the ground trying to get up and people just walked by me, not offering a hand. I could have had broken ribs or internal bleeding. Those two guys just laughed and laughed as they rode away. I was lucky that they did not turn around and decide to inflict more pain or do something worse since I was out of commission and doubled-over. I could have avoided this situation, but did not. Lesson learned.

It's always a good idea to try and keep a 360 degree view of things to avoid something or someone injuring you. There are a lot of idiots out there who just don't get it. I am sure you are nodding your head in agreement right now thinking back to an incident that happened to you.

After a while of doing this, you'll get really good at it and improve your situational awareness. And don't forget to play the "What If" game also during this time.

MEDITATION FOR THE ARMED WARRIOR

This meditation plays off the "What If" situational awareness game. It's called the Grandpa "G's" *S*cenario *A*wareness *T*hought *T*echnique

(**SATT**©). When you practice this, remove all ammo from your sidearm and out of the room.

With any visualization technique, you will need a quiet space so you can focus during your training. This meditation will help you relax so you can play scenarios in your mind in the comfort of your own home. It will help you remain calm and collective in case you do have an incident where your sidearm needs to be presented to defend yourself.

I will go over some of the benefits of doing mediation so you can get an idea what it can do for you. Meditation is practiced by millions of people every day around the globe and what has been discovered is that it helps slow the aging process, it improves your cardiovascular system, increases concentration, reduces stress, improves your immune system and much more. There are hundreds and possibly thousands of different types of meditations and any one of them that is practiced over time will heighten your awareness. Some of these meditation techniques that I will share have been passed down from thousands of years ago, from Master to student and its origins is from the Far East.

I will not go in-depth on meditation since this is not the topic of this book. Plus it takes years of experience to master, but I will share some of the basics. I want to keep things simple for you, the reader and not lose track of what we're trying to accomplish here. Just follow along and try it for yourself. If you want to learn more about meditation, there are many classes and books on the subject. There are also masters out there that can teach you, but it depends on what you're trying to accomplish and where you live. If you enjoy meditating, find a mentor. There are some Masters whom reside in the US, but again, it depends on what you're looking for.

The upcoming meditation is divided into two halves. The first half is similar to the one that I have taught in my veteran classes. It's very calming and has been very successful with releasing stress. The second half was designed just for the concealed carrier and not to be used by those who experience PTSD. If you suffer from PTSD, skip the second half where I begin with several scenarios involving stressful situations. The purpose of this exercise is to get you into a relaxed meditative state, introduce inner awareness, to focus on different types of defensive scenarios and learn to remain calm during them. Do not have your firearm near you when you practice these meditations. Do not do these meditations with a loaded firearm.

So let's begin….

Stress Test Meditation (20-30 Minutes…. Or Longer)

Find yourself a quiet spot where you will not be disturbed. Use a chair that is semi-comfortable. A wooden chair is best. The reason for the semi-comfortable chair is to create a slight discomfort to prevent your mind from falling asleep. You want to do this exercise sitting down, or using a meditation bench (seiza) and avoid lying down. If you lay down, you will trigger the body to go into sleep mode when you become very relaxed. Having a slight discomfort helps with focus and keeps you from falling asleep. You want to be relaxed in the upright position, but not too comfortable that your mind will drift away and you find yourself falling asleep.

During the meditation, your mind is going to be busy. Jumping from one thought to another. It's like TV surfing. You find a channel of interest, it is short lived and you surf other channels. Your focus gets lost and your mind is jumping around. It wants to be entertained and doesn't like to be ignored. You want to slow down this mind jumping to a point of empty mind (no-mind). No distractions.

During my meditations, a trick that I use when thoughts come to me (like a grocery list of things to do) is to imagine I have shelves around me. Once a thought comes, knowing that it must be important, I take it and place that thought on the shelf. I know that it will always be there and I can retrieve it at any time.

For example, during my meditation, a thought comes to me, like I have to pick up the kids at the bus stop today at 2:30 and I cannot be late. It's very important and I cannot forget to do this. I place that thought on my imaginary shelf knowing that when my mediation is done, it is always there for me and I won't forget about it and I can retrieve it at any time. Then I focus on my mediation again. Keep practicing this and you will go further into your meditation. No worries, your shelves are limitless like the universe. So your mind doesn't have to worry and it will not think you're ignoring it.

If you're sitting on a chair, make sure you spine is straight, tuck in your chin (this makes your spine straighter), keep your feet flat on the floor and if you have heart issues (blood pressure problems or a recent heart attack), keep your palms down on your lap or legs. If you don't have these issues, keep your hands up. Now breathe in through your nose and exhale through your mouth slowly. Do this 10 times. With every exhale, imagine any stress in your body as a cloud of smoke and on the exhale, blow it towards the end of the universe, never for it to return.

Now put the tongue on the roof of your mouth behind your two front teeth. Now breathe through the nose. Keep your eyes closed and relax. Take your index finger and thumb and press the tips together and hold this position for both hands. This finger position helps you retain energy and prevents it from escaping. It also prevents others from draining your energy.

In the next steps, take it very slow. Use visual imagery and while you are imagining these things, try to also feel for it. When I say feel it, be part of it. For example, if you are a cloud, imagine that you are, but also feel for it. Feel the lightness, the subtle breezes, the movement of the cloud, the feeling of you moving across rolling green hills, high up in the sky, above the beautiful landscape. Be the cloud, be one with it. This helps in the realism of the exercise.

Take a minute or so to clear your mind. Now imagine yourself in the clouds……. Once you get to the point that you are feeling the cloud, imagine it getting denser and denser. Now the cloud is getting heavier and heavier. And it's getting darker and darker. Now imagine different parts of the cloud turning into rain. Imagine yourself as a single droplet…. And you are falling towards the earth.

Is the wind rushing up on you? How does this feel? As you're falling towards the earth, imagine that you end up in a pond. What does this feel like? Think of yourself becoming part of the collective of the other raindrops and the pond. As you imagine yourself as the pond, what does it feel like when hundreds of thousands of raindrops are hitting you (the pond) at different intervals? Try to feel this sensation and hold this for several minutes.

When you start to feel it, then imagine the sky becoming clear and the sun is beating down on you (the body of water - the pond) and it is heating up. Now the water is slowly evaporating. Imagine yourself as the water converting into steam. You are floating across the water and slowly rising into the air. How does this feel? Can you feel the weightlessness? The sense of slowly rising up into the sky? Now you are rising up past the clouds and then moving above them, leaving earth and above the world….. The feeling of nothingness and weightlessness. And the feeling of being surrounded by stars, moons, planets, galaxies. The entire cosmos is moving around you. Hold this feeling for a several minutes. Try to keep your mind clear at this point.

In this relaxed state, now imagine yourself in a grocery store. You are at a checkout line. Your groceries are on the conveyor belt and you are next in line to be checked out. You are completely relaxed, waiting to be checked out. Your awareness has not changed. You are looking around, paying attention to your surroundings. You don't have a worry in the world, but remembering to maintain your situational awareness.

Then suddenly you hear some yelling and a figure appears in a hoodie wearing a skull mask, with their gun drawn on the cashier. The gun is in their face, the cashier is crying and she is being yelled at to open the cash drawer, but she is fumbling to get it open. There are people behind you, in line and one person ahead of you. What do you do?

Now examine your body during this part of the meditation. Do you notice any tightening in the muscles? Is your adrenaline rushing through your veins? Did your shoulders or neck tighten up? How about your facial expression? Did this change? Did your hands move or the muscles tighten too? Did you go for your firearm? If so, then relax yourself.

Play the scenario again in your mind. Did the same muscles tighten or different set? Play the scenario again. Any changes? If not, try it again. Relax. Don't frustrate yourself. Like drawing a gun, this is training and you will improve as you continuously repeat it. This is muscle memory that we're working with and we are training our muscles to remain calm, but focused and to build our awareness. Doing these meditations will increase your situation awareness and help if you have problems freezing with fear. You may even want to write down different scenarios, pick one out and just meditate on that particular one.

Change it up, surprise yourself. Maybe gunshots rang out. Check yourself again. Any muscles tighten up? Relax them again and play out the same scenario or another over and over again. Don't create all scenarios where you have to pull the trigger. Maybe you are a good witness. Maybe in other scenarios you draw, but you don't fire. Mix it up, maybe you go for the exit when the time is right and escape without being harmed.

Keep doing this and continue checking yourself and correct it. You want to remain calm during these exercises. You want to trick your mind as if it is real, but try to remain calm and collective. After a while, you will feel a moment of being Zen like.

While you're doing this exercise, play out different scenarios in different places. Like a restaurant, a gas station, ATM, hotel, parking lot, walking down the street, shopping malls, drive thru, hiking in the park, on a walking path, on the town with your friends, your children, your wife or husband, etc. Keep changing it up and check yourself.

This is a really good exercise to help you relax during stressful situations, but remain focused of what's going on. Even after the event and your adrenaline is still pumping through your body, taking those 10 deep breaths will help you relax. If not, do another 10. I have done this when someone rammed their car into mine to force me off the road. After the accident, I was pretty shook up and deep breathing exercises helped me calm down.

Go through the scenario in your mind of drawing your sidearm, pulling the trigger, looking for other dangers (bad people usually travel in packs), keep your situational awareness on full and slowly return your sidearm in your holster as you are looking around. Do this meditation multiple times during the week and see if there are any muscles tightening in your body.

Maybe you freeze up when you need to use deadly force. If so, play it again in your mind and see if you freeze again. If so, change up the scenario to see if you freeze again or not. Keep practicing until you no longer freeze. Through meditation, you may discover the reason for freezing.

For several years, I have dedicated 30 minutes of my time to meditate and I do this on a daily basis. I'll do it at home or on my lunch break at work in a private room. It's a great way to clear the mind and release the stresses of the day. On the weekend, I will find some quiet time in the morning before everyone else gets up and create one of the scenarios above. The purpose of these meditative exercises is to program your mind to be calm, relaxed and focused, but remain fully aware. You have to keep practicing frequently to remain sharp.

Lock yourself in a room, hang a sign on the door reminding people that you're mediating so you won't be disturbed. I do this at home, especially when children are present. I have to use earplugs sometimes to keep the noise out. You can even use your ear muffs that you use at the range to drown out the noise.

If you have military experience and have been in combat, I would highly recommend that you either unload the ammo in your sidearm or put it off to the side so you don't have access to it. I would hate to have you draw in the middle of a meditation and discharge your firearm.

I have worked with military vets over the years to help relieve their stress through meditation (Tai-Chi/Qigong). I <u>do not</u> teach them the meditation above.

During one of my meditation classes, one gentleman who was in a deep meditative state suddenly went through the motions of grabbing for his firearm (which he did not have) and then calling out for his sidearm. He was a World War II veteran who saw a lot of action in the war and he slipped back to a battle he was in. One of the nurses calmed him down and then he went back to meditating as if nothing happened.

With the meditation I presented above, I want everyone to be safe. I want to eliminate the possibility of grabbing for your sidearm and presenting it with a live round in the chamber. So please remove all ammo and set your firearm to the side so no one gets hurt.

I have worked with many veterans who have fought in different campaigns and they have gone through a lot, putting their lives on the line to defend our nation and some still continue fighting those battles years after they have left the service. I would like to reach out to all of our service members and veterans and say thank you for all you have done to protect us. This country owes you a great gratitude in keeping our country's freedom.

"NO MIND" SHOOTING

I do meditations daily to relax the mind, body and soul. I have been doing this for many years so it is a habit I have formed. While meditating, one of the goals is to go into a state of "No Mind". It's a very peaceful state, one that just melts away the stresses of the day and the past. There's a Zen expression - "Mind without Mind" and it's called Mushin no Shin. This is where your mind is in a state of no thought or emotions, but a state of heightened awareness.

I have been testing this "No Mind" state with my laser ammo and Laser PET Electronic Target for dry firing. The PET has several options and one of them can be used to time how fast you can draw your sidearm. I average about 1.25 seconds on my draw with my shirt over my pistol. I do have some arthritis in my hands, so I think that it's not too bad for this old man. But what I found interesting is that when I go into a Mushin no Shin state, my best time is .96 seconds. My quickest time for drawing while sitting down on a chair doing "No Mind" was .77 seconds and hitting the target almost dead center. I found this very interesting. It also makes me wonder if I could draw faster without the arthritis.

Before I draw, I just relax my mind, where there are no thoughts, no emotions - just pure awareness. Then when I hear the tone from the PET, I don't think about the target, I don't think about the tone, I just draw, point and shoot without thinking. Then I notice that my seconds decrease per draw. I also notice my mind is clear before the tone. My muscles become automatic and I hit the target every time.

It's like an out of body experience. When I am in this state, I can see my sidearm present itself, it looks slow when it comes out of the holster, then pressing the trigger and hitting the electronic target with the laser beam. Then I look at the time on the PET and I am surprised at how fast the draw was. It looked slower in my eyes than expected and I see the results on the screen - a very impressive time under a second. I am sure some martial artists have experienced this where time has slowed down and the end results are quick and precise with practice.

It's remarkable at how quick that I can draw. I am not into competitive shooting but if I was, this would be something I would definitely practice to see how far I could take it.

When I see that my time has increased, I noticed that my mind was busy and not clear. I was thinking about what I was doing or some other distraction. I noticed that my mind was going through the steps (grabbing my sidearm, looking for my target, checking to see if my finger is on the trigger when I present it, am I off the "X", etc.). A lot of noise and distractions are in my mind. I have seen my time go up to

1.75 seconds. When I purge my thoughts, my time decreases considerably.

If you attempt this and it's not working for you, try doing a daily 30 minute meditation for about 30 days straight without any breaks in between. There are some really great books out there on meditation. I would recommend Tobin Blakes book - The Power of Stillness. This book actually does 30 days of various types of meditation. You might find a few that you enjoy and stick with it. It will help you focus better and improve your situational awareness.

I have discovered that the best time to meditate is before anyone else gets up in the house. Many of us have busy lives, but carving 30 minutes out of you schedule is worth it. So if you live alone, do it before you go to work or just do it early in the morning. If you have kids, then finding a quiet spot before everyone gets up may work out best for you. Having peaceful time to yourself sound pretty good without all the craziness associated with children. The best times for me is around midnight (11 pm - 1 am) since it fits into my schedule and it is very calm around the house and the neighborhood.

I wish you the best in trying this. I would be curious on the results of those who notice any changes while in the "No Mind" state.

GUNFIGHTING & SPIRITUALITY

Are you prepared to die?

Think about that statement for a while. Are you prepared to die? Are you ready spiritually before you leave this plane of existence? Are you prepared for the worse to come?

You planned on going home today, something happened on the way and you never made it. An accident occurred and you're either injured so severely that you are hospitalized, maybe you're on your last dying breath, or you're dead.

Being spiritually ready should be part of your bucket list. So ask yourself again, deep down, are you prepared for the worse to come? It doesn't matter if you have faith, or no faith at all, you should still be spiritually fit. You need to live your life to the fullest as much as you can, every single day. Now is a good time to look around and smell the flowers, build that awareness and notice what you've taken for granted all this time.

Do you have a living will? Does your family have coverage in case something happens to you? Is your funeral paid for, including the plot of real estate your body will be occupying until the end of this world so that your family are not financially burdened? Will your loved ones be financially supported when you depart this world?

Since you might be the bread winner of your family, will they have enough money to cover the mortgage (or rent), food, utilities, transportation, etc., while you are gone or incapacitated? Do you have a health care directive filled out with the state, or with that hospital in case you are on a respirator, the only thing that's keeping you alive? What if you're on a respirator, you're brain dead and your family would like to pull the plug, but the state intervenes and says no because there is no healthcare directive on file?

Your family will still be billed for the time you are still hooked up to the machine. If you're hospitalized, are your bills covered by insurance? Will your family be covered financially while you're in the hospital? Will they be able to protect themselves once you're indisposed?

If that day comes that I kick the bucket, I want to make sure that I don't leave a great burden behind where people are stuck with my bills, my mortgage, or put my family in jeopardy where they can lose everything. I don't feel that my actions should put my family into a position where they have to fight to survive. I would like them to be in a good place financially for the years to come and they can get on with their lives after I am gone.

You should have your game plan ready. Now once the legal and medical stuff is taken care of, what about _you_ spiritually? Are you doing anything daily that tries to make things right in the world for you? You will have to live each day as if it's your last. Don't live in the past or future, but live in the present moment.

Enjoy the hell out of that walk, the places you visit, and the people you're with. Get closer to the ones you love. If you're a negative person, change this around. Don't leave this earth with any regrets. It's also about the state of mind you're in. Do something kind for someone.

Go out of your way for a stranger. Volunteer for those in need and greatly appreciate what you have.

You may just have to seriously sit down with yourself and have one of those inner private conversations. What type of life do you wish to live before your death? Live life. Love life. Treat it as the most precious thing in the world. Treat others as the most precious thing in the world. Dying sucks, but it will happen to all of us, but treat this day as if it's your last.

The secret to living is knowing that death is a reality, it will catch up to you one of these days and knowing most of all is that you can't stop it. You have no control over it. Your body can live so long. It was not designed to outlive the planet we're on. It will age, die and turn into dust. You will never find immortality here in this form. So it's time to move on and be truthful with yourself and get off this thought process that you will live forever. Take the next logical step (that spiritual growth) in your life and do whatever you can to be ready for that day to come. And remind yourself every day to live the most you can, every minute of that day.

There's a lot to think about and prepare for, especially if you're carrying a gun. You may one day have to relieve that iron from its holster and pull the trigger to defend yourself or a loved one. If there is an exchange of gunfire and you're hit, it may be game over for you. Yes, we all have an expiration date, but when that day comes, there will be no email, no letter or announcement, and you will not get any notice whatsoever of any kind to help you prepare. It will just happen without any warning, but hopefully it's quick and painless.

There may be a day where you may lose the gunfight and you may end up dead or seriously injured. I am hoping that you don't, but if it does happen, are you ready for what's to come? I am not going to talk about anyone's belief systems here, but being prepared spiritually is important. You don't have to be a spiritual person, but being in a state of mind that you're ready to move on if such an event happens puts your mind at ease and in a better position than most people. It's good for the soul.

I think of it as not having any ties to this world so I can move onto the next. I have prepared myself and made sure others are also taken care of in case something happens to me. I don't worry about what I haven't accomplished and not worry about leaving my family in a bad situation before leaving this world. I want to feel free without any worries, knowing that I took care of as much as possible to protect those I love.

As a gunman/gunwoman, spiritual fitness should be on your bucket list no matter what your age. It's essential for the current life you live and the one that will come.

If you're not a spiritual person, that's okay. Not many of us are. So what does it mean to be spiritually fit? What does it mean to you? The way I look at it, it's a tool to prepare my soul for this world and the next one to come.

To be prepared, you must forgive yourself for the wrongs you've done. I understand that others may not forgive you, which is okay. They don't have to. But the hardest thing to do is to forgive yourself. Once you do, it'll be easier to live with yourself. Remember, you are a good person. We all make mistakes, but what's really important is that we also need to learn from them. We are not perfect, but we try to be.

To prepare yourself spiritually, set aside some time in a private area and have an internal conversation with yourself. A nice and quiet area so you will not be bothered, a place where you can reflect on things. I personally meditate to relax my mind and body. I put myself in a meditative state to calm my mind and become one with everything around me. Stillness of the mind is what I want to accomplish. It is the language of the universe. It makes me closer to the intelligence of our creator.

When people sit there and have that internal conversation, some focus on their life and the things they have accomplished and what needs to be done to prepare for the future. Others try to connect with their creator, inner self, higher self, the powers that be, the divine, the universal, or whatever or whomever they want to have an internal conversation with. Some will just pray. And there are those that have obtained that level of stillness, no mind. They have set their egos aside and immersed themselves into the intelligence of the universe.

While connecting with one or all of these, some ask for forgiveness, try to find out how to be a better person, do some soul searching, request for something, look for guidance and ask for a sign to be sent to them. Or if they disagree with something, they express their disappointment and there is nothing wrong with this. It's kind of a spiritual therapy. When people do get a sign, they consider this a validation of their conversation. A sign could be immediate, days, or months. So you will have to keep a lookout.

For spiritual fitness, you don't have to put yourself into a meditative state, you just need to change your mindset, knowing that you should prepare yourself. Get things ready. When that time comes, your spirit should have no worries because you know that you've taken care of things and those that depend on you will also have no worries. You can pass in peace knowing that everything will be okay and you can move onto your next transition in your spiritual life.

KNOW THY SIDEARM

It's a big responsibility to carry a sidearm and it's also a greater responsibility to do frequent preventive maintenance on it. Know your handgun inside and out. What I mean by this is to understand all the safety features, how to disassemble it, how to shoot it, how to put ammo in it and know how to clean it. You want your equipment in tip-top performance since this is a lifesaving instrument.

There are many videos out there about your firearm. I watched several for my first handgun since I wanted to know everything about it; how it functions, how to clean it, etc. Sometimes while watching these videos, someone misses a step and on another video you'll pick up on that missed piece of valuable information. You'll also discover some really cool techniques to use with your firearm. Like how to clean some tough spots, like the rails on your slide. I saw a person using a rag and credit card to remove the buildup. What a great and simple idea. Before you do anything with your firearm, always read the entire manual, from front to back. The manufacture will have recommendations on what to do and what not to do. Some things you do in these videos may void your warranty, so make sure that you're aware of this.

You're responsible for your own firearm. Understand as much as possible about it. Watch videos, read books, break it down as much as you can and learn about the parts. What does each part do? How does the ammo feed into the chamber? How do you store it, take care of it, what type of oil and cleaning agents can you use? How do you clear a type 1 or type 2 malfunction?

Understand the basics of this very valuable piece of equipment that you invested in and learn how to maintain it since it will save your life someday. If you don't take care of it, it won't take care of you.

HOLLYWOOD IS NOT YOUR TRAINING INSTRUCTOR

Do you like those action packed movies? I sure do. Protagonists versus your antagonists, the different types of cool weapons used, bullets flying everywhere and the fight scenes that defy all physics. It really gets your adrenaline pumping. The hundreds or thousands of rounds flying all over the place and your hero escaping without a single gunshot wound. These action heroes sure know how to slow down time to avoid every single bullet coming their way. It's a real miracle….

Well, the truth is…. It's all bullcrap. **It's All Hollywood!!** It's not real, it's just special effects. These special effects people really don't take the time to seriously look at the direction when a bullet leaves the muzzle, they don't follow a path along with the marriage of our friend physics and these projectiles should be hitting the hero in the movie. I love those scenes with fully automatic weapons and bullets that are just hitting around our hero and not even one scratches them causing a minor flesh wound.

What you've seen in these movies from all the years past, they are not real and you need to get into the mindset of reprogramming yourself that it's just plainly giving you the wrong information on firearms. You don't want to tell yourself that you can outrun a bullet by running away from cover and that bullets will never hit you when someone is pointing a gun at you. Keep your cover and defend yourself. If you watch those old black and white western movies, they actually used real bullets back in the day. A very dangerous way of doing stunts, but still Hollywood.

Even scenes where people are in cars and they are exchanging gunfire in the movie and nobody gets hit, its pure fiction. Bullets do penetrate cars. I have seen demonstrations of bullets going in one door and out the other. And if you are a passenger, it will either go through you or stop at you. Never take cover inside or behind a car, especially the car door (like you see in Hollywood movies). If you have no choice, put your car engine between you and the bad person. This should hopefully block some of those bullets from reaching you, but do try to find some solid cover.

So the next time you see an action packed flick, keep in the back of your mind that some of it is computer generated imagery (CGI) and everything you're watching is not real. Don't let your mind think that it is. It could get you in real trouble if a situation happens that you must present your firearm or take cover. You will also see actors not following the universal safety rules in the show. You will see their finger on the trigger at all times, when they hand off their weapon to someone else, they don't check it to make sure that it is in battery or make a clearance check. I am sure these movies must drive firearm instructors crazy.

I have limited my action movies since the human brain is like a computer and seeing images like this over and over again could produce a memory that the actions I am seeing are real. I don't want to make the mistake of seeing something on the screen and my mind takes that same action, implements it during a gunfight and I end up the loser because what I saw was not real. When you see these movies, make it a game and try to pick out the many mistakes during the gun scenes. Don't believe everything you see or hear from a show. Even some of your statistics are incorrect that they present to the audience.

If you watch those law enforcement shows (remember these are all drama), pay close attention. Your actors are doing things wrong, like going around a corner with a firearm extended out in their hands, especially when they are clearing a room. They may be using old techniques or making things up. Find yourself a really good instructor and learn the correct techniques. Don't let Hollywood be your firearms instructor, it will get you in a lot of trouble or have you taking the room temperature test.

SAMPLE SCENARIOS

These are some sample scenarios from real stories that have happened with those who have been armed. Some stories have been mixed with other real stories in the news to give you a more interesting situation to make you think more about what you should do. The scenario is laid out, you select the best answer and then read the number you picked for more information about that action. This will help give you a better insight on what to do when something in one of these examples may happen to you.

You are outside, late at night and you see across the street a man breaking into your neighbor's house. What do you do?

1. Get the attention of the burglar hoping they will run away?
2. Pull out your weapon and take the intruder by force.
3. Shoot the intruder.
4. Call 911 and report it while remaining in your home.

If you picked number…

1. You risk the chance of the burglar attacking you.
2. Again you are risking your life. They may have an accomplice that you are not aware of.
3. Using lethal force without cause may send you to prison
4. Calling 911 while the intruder is breaking in will give the police a chance to surprise the intruder, your life will not be in danger, and you are playing it safe and not risking your life or your family members.

Someone is breaking into your car. As you try to investigate they are driving off your property. What do you do?

1. Shoot at the thief while they're driving away.
2. You chase the car thief down the street and empty your magazine into your own car.
3. Call 911 to report a stolen car.
4. Jump in your second car and chase them down the street.

If you picked number…

1. If you shoot the thief, you are now considered the aggressor and if you kill them, you may end up in prison.
2. Running while shooting is very difficult and you are responsible for every bullet that leaves that gun. You may end up hitting innocent people or damaging your neighbor's property.
3. This is the safest option. You are not risking your life, the life of others (and their property) and it's just a vehicle that is hopefully insured anyways.
4. This is not a good option. It could end up in a high speed chase, or they may pick up that you're following them and if they are armed, you may end up in a shootout. Risking your life for personal property is not worth it.

You are at a bar with friends and some guys are making lewd remarks towards the ladies you are with. What do you do?

1. Go over to them and make them apologize.
2. Just walk out of the bar to avoid any conflict.
3. Get up and punch their lights out.
4. Take out your sidearm and ask them to leave.

If you picked number…

1. You may end up in a fight and if they discover you have a sidearm, it could be used against you.
2. If ignoring them does not work, then just get up, pay your bill and leave. You may have to have individuals leave one or two at a time (pretending as if they are getting a drink from the bar), not giving any signs that anyone is leaving, but in reality everyone is. A good option in trying to avoid any confrontations.
3. Getting physical could be deadly (since you are armed), especially throwing the first punch is assault.
4. Since there is no deadly force used by the other party, this will land you in prison and your actions will not impress the women at all.

You are in a store, you reach up to grab something off the shelf and someone sees your sidearm. They approach you to ask you why you're carrying a gun in a tone that may escalate the situation. What do you do?

1. Tell them it's none of their business and walk away.
2. Show them you have a permit to carry and explain the reasons why you carry.
3. Walk away, leave your stuff behind and walk towards the exit without saying a word.

If you picked number…

1. You want to try and deescalate the situation. Telling them that its none of their business may escalate the situation and others may start showing up in your aisle wondering what's going on with the loud exchange of pleasantries.
2. If you are in a state that requires a permit, you don't have to show them anything. They are not the law and it may not help anyways. They may be trying to pick a fight with you over the topic of carrying a firearm. You are not required to show anything or explain why you are carrying to anyone that is not law enforcement.
3. The best course of action is to deescalate the situation by walking away and getting out of there. You don't want a crowd of people showing up either. If they call the police, then that's okay. You can just show the police your permit and explain what happened. You were not brandishing your firearm in the first place. If you think it is bad enough situation, call the police, inform them what has happened so they get your story first before someone else calls 911 and the situation escalates and gets out of control.

You are sitting in a chair during a meeting, you get up and your sidearm pops out of your holster. Do you grab the gun in midair or let it hit the floor?

1. Try to quickly grab it before it hits the ground before anyone notices.
2. Let it hit the floor, pick it up and reholster.

If you picked number…

1. NEVER EVER grab your gun in midair. If your finger hits the trigger, then you will have an accidental discharge and you may shoot yourself, another person, or cause damage to property.
2. Yes, let it hit the floor. Modern day sidearms will not fire if they hit the floor since they have internal safeties designed to be dropped without misfiring. This is your safest choice.

You are out and about and someone stops you. They pull out a knife demanding money. What do you do?

1. Since you don't want to seriously hurt anyone, you decide to shoot them in the leg instead.
2. You decide to shoot in the air to give them a warning.
3. You do a warning shot into the ground because you don't want to kill this person.
4. You aim for center mass and pull the trigger until the threat stops.

If you picked number…

1. Things happen so quickly with an ambush that you will not have time to shoot them in the leg. This is wishful thinking.
2. NEVER shoot in the air, the bullet will come down and it may kill someone. If this person who is mugging you sees your gun in the air, it is their opportunity to take you out, take your firearm and get your money.
3. Again, warning shots will not stop a mugging. If you're not willing to pull the trigger on someone who has a knife and they are willing to take your life for a few bucks, then why are you carrying a firearm? If you're not prepared to shoot someone, then you're not ready to carry a firearm. A firearm is a deadly weapon and if you will not use it to stop a deadly threat, then you will have to rethink your options in carrying a gun. You might as well be unarmed and take your chances. You're next best option is to lay down and play dead to see if this tricks your attacker and see if it saves your life. Yeah, good luck with that!

4. Since knives are very real and they can do real damage to your body and kill you (even more damage than a bullet), then you have every right to use deadly force. You are justified in your actions by pulling the trigger until the threat has stopped.

You are at a restaurant, there are plenty of tables to choose from, as a responsible concealed carrier, where do you sit?

1. Get as close as possible where the register is since it is near the entrance.
2. Find a booth in the middle of the restaurant.
3. Look for exit signs, possible exit points in the restaurant and sit at a table where you can see everyone.
4. Get a table near the restroom.

If you picked number…

1. Registers have money and thieves will target this. If you are near the register and the place gets robbed, your only exit may be the doors that you and the robbers just walked through and you may not be able to get out of there and be forced to use your sidearm. Don't put yourself in this situation.
2. A booth is a very difficult place to draw your sidearm, plus being in the middle makes it more difficult for situation awareness. Avoid booths at all costs.
3. When your inside the restaurant immediately look for exits (kitchen, exit doors, anything else that will get you outside quickly) and find a table where you can see as much of your environment as possible near those exits. It's easier to draw a sidearm from a chair then in a booth. You have less restrictions and you can move much quicker towards the exit then fighting your way out of a booth.
4. Restrooms don't have exits except the one you walked through to get to the bathroom. It is a dead end and a place that would be very difficult to fight your way out of. Avoid getting trapped here.

You are driving down the street and you hear gunshots ringing out and then you see someone being shot at. What do you do?

1. Pull over, get your sidearm out and join the fight.
2. Drive to cover first, then get out of your car to determine the situation and move in closer to get a clear shot.
3. Roll your windows down, head towards the shooting and start shooting out of your window to hit the bad guy.
4. Get the hell out of there, call 911 and become a good witness.

If you picked number…

1. If you decide to pull over and join the fight, who is the bad guy/gal? You were not part of this situation and have no idea what's going on. Do not get involved.
2. Again, you do not know what is going on, you may shoot the wrong person or you may get shot yourself.
3. A bad place to be is in your car during a shooting. Car doors or windows DO NOT stop bullets. It's basically a coffin on wheels.
4. If you hear gun shots, get the hell out of there. Do not get involved, get yourself to safety and when you feel you are out of the danger zone, call the police. Don't risk your life or others by getting involved. You have no idea what's going on, or who the good person or bad person is. Your best bet is to call 911 and stay out of there.

You are driving down the highway and a drunk driver passes you, then hits the car in front of you and it flips over. The drunk driver instead of stopping speeds up to leave the scene. Then the drunk driver crashes their car into the overpass a mile down the highway, but escapes on foot into the woods. What do you do?

1. Drive up to the overpass, chase them through the woods with your sidearm drawn, tracking them down, hoping to find them to bring them back to the scene of the crime and turn them over to police.
2. Just keep driving and not get involved, it's not your problem
3. Pull over to help the person that got hit, call 911.

If you picked number…

1. Unless you are law enforcement, this would not be the best thing to do. You are in uncharted territory - you could get lost in the woods or get hurt. Chasing someone through the woods armed is not a good option. What happens if they jump you and you didn't see it coming? Leave this to the experts. This is a very unsafe option.
2. Some would just move on and not get involved. That's okay. If no one else is around, call 911 to report it. Do the right thing. If there are cars pulling over to assist, the chances of the police and ambulance being on their way are pretty high.
3. Focusing on helping the person in the vehicle would be a good option. You're not in danger, you are helping someone who is hurt and you have an ambulance on the way since you called 911. The police will no doubt find this drunk driver.

You are walking down the street and cornered by two unarmed guys who are threatening you by asking for your money and Jewelry. What do you do?

1. Immediately draw your sidearm, they run away and start shooting at them before they get away.
2. Raise your voice so others can hear you, tell them that you are armed and to back off. If they continue to threat, defend yourself.
3. Start shooting immediately without any warning.
4. Put your gun in the air and give warning shots.

If you picked number…

1. If you decide to shoot them when they are running, you are now considered the aggressor. They decided that you are not worth the trouble and decided to run once they saw your sidearm. If you shoot them while they're running away, you will most likely land yourself in jail.
2. You want to get as loud as possible to get people to hear and see the situation (they will be your witnesses) along with informing

your aggressors that you are armed. If you do pull out your weapon (without firing), chances are that they may back off. If the threat continues, after you fire, hopefully you will have witnesses to back you up. Call 911 right after the incident.
3. Remember, these people are unarmed. If you aren't in danger yet, but decide to start shooting, you will end up on the news and in jail.
4. Again, warning shots will get you in trouble, either by the aggressors or the police. And if someone is hit by your bullet, you may be spending time in jail.

You are at a super shopping center and you notice that someone just filled their cart full of merchandise and start heading out the door without paying. A clerk has also seen the same thing and starts chasing them out the door. What do you do?

1. Since you are armed, you head out the door with the clerk and assist him in case he is jumped by the thieves.
2. You follow the clerk out the door, you notice that the thieves pile into their stolen vehicle and start driving away. You pull out your sidearm and start shooting the tires to stop them.
3. It's not your problem, so you check yourself out and head off to your next destination.
4. You follow the clerk, you notice that the thieves are not complying with the clerk in bringing back the merchandise, you approach them and start exchanging words with them to put the stuff back, one guy reaches for something behind his back, you draw and start shooting. One of the thieves is killed, the other two are also shot, but they get away. You call 911 to report it.

If you picked number…

1. Looks like you want to play the Good Samaritan. But wait, why are you following the clerk out the door in the first place? You don't work there. Is this your responsibility?
2. Why would you start shooting at the car? How do you know if it is stolen anyways? They have not threatened you in any way that

would say your life is in danger. You have also put other people in danger by firing your weapon at a moving target.
3. Seriously, it's not your problem. You are not security at this store, you do not work there, why get involved? You're not the owner of the store. You're just a customer. So not getting involved is your best choice.
4. Why are you getting involved? Again, this is not your problem. You will most likely end up in prison since you intervened in something that was not your issue and you shot someone who may not be threatening your life. You may go down as a want to-be cop and this looks bad in front of a jury. Stay out of it completely and save yourself the court costs and jail time.

You are at a shopping mall. You hear gunshots ring out in the mall. People are running for cover. Remember, there may also be other concealed carriers (the good people) also in the mall. You are currently in a safe area and call 911. You need to get out of there. How do you determine who the good and the bad person are? What do you do?

1. You ask for identification from those who have their sidearms out and see if they have a permit to determine if they are on your side.
2. You draw your gun and look for cover yourself and shoot at anyone that has a gun while you are trying to get out of the mall.
3. You see a 25 year old adult with a rifle shooting at people. You find cover and he is getting near you, while they are up close and do not see you, you draw your sidearm and start shooting at him to end the threat. Then look around for any others. Then call 911 and identify yourself.

If you picked number...

1. This is not the best course of action while there is a killer in the mall. How do you not know they are an accomplice?
2. If you start shooting at everyone that has a gun, you're going to kill innocent people and end up shot yourself since others (legal carriers) may think you are the killer in the mall.

3. If you see someone with a rifle, about 100% of the time, this is going to be your person, especially if they are shooting people. You should also see if other people who have handguns out look like they are frightened and under stress (the guy with the rifle will probably be calm but suicidal), if they are crouching down and looking for the attacker, they are either in concealment or cover trying to protect themselves and they are not acting like an aggressor, but a defender. These people are most likely like you. When the threat has been stopped and there are no other shooters, put your sidearm away so the police do not think you are the killer. They have no idea who is who when they get to the scene. Since they have your description when you called 911, this will help, especially when they will be searching people to find additional armed people.

You're going out to your vehicle and notice someone is inside stealing your property. What do you do?

1. Call 911 to report it and sneak up on that person and hold them at gun point.
2. Find a safe position, call 911 and pull out your key-fob for the car and press the panic button
3. Shoot the person who is stealing from your car.

If you picked number….

1. Calling 911 is a good course of action, but pulling your gun on someone whom you don't know is armed or not is not using equal deadly force. They may also have an accomplice or two hiding somewhere who may be armed. Sometimes these people work in packs.
2. Safety first. Find a defensive position where you can scan the area for other accomplices, call 911 and hit the key-fob panic button to beep the horn and flash the lights. This will no doubt scare them off. Then wait for the police and file a report.
3. Again, they are not using deadly force on you. It's just property anyways and most likely can be replaced. Don't shoot someone over this, you will most likely end up in jail. Take the loss and move on.

THAT ITCHY TRIGGER FINGER

You've purchased a firearm, you carry it all the time, but you want to get more out of it. You sit in front of your TV breaking down your firearm on the table, checking the internal components, trying to figure out how it all works. You've read the manual a few times, building familiarity around your new purchase. You reassemble and without any ammo, you point and shoot (dry firing). You may also have watched a bunch of videos related to your sidearm to fill that void of questions. I say kudos to those who have invested their time in doing their research and building an understanding of how to take care of their sidearm and getting familiar with it.

But for some, with a new sidearm, you want more out of it. Maybe there are no ranges nearby to practice live fire and you're kind of getting that itchy trigger finger with your new purchase. You've invested a lot of money into this but all you've done so far is just carry it, clean it, but have been unable to fire it.

Please don't think of this firearm as a toy that you are unable to use. First of all, it is not a toy, but a weapon used for defensive purposes. But, you also need to get familiar with it and after a while of carrying, it will become a part of you. And the four universal firearm safety rules must always be turned on in your head every time you touch one, which is a great way to train your mind.

Remember, you've made a wise investment, but you will need to get training. Either from a respectable trainer, or if you are in a remote location and there's no one near you, go online and learn from the pros. There are plenty of drills to use online and I would ask that you practice a couple of times a week to keep yourself from becoming rusty. With self-practice and training, this will solve that old itchy trigger finger conundrum.

I would recommend getting some sort of laser ammo and a target to practice with. There are some computer programs out there that you can use with any type of laser ammo. You'll need a computer, a video camera and some targets you can hang on the wall to use with that target practice software. The USB video camera and the targets are going to be pretty inexpensive, but if you don't have a computer, this is going to be the most expensive item (in the hundreds for a cheap computer).

The computer program for target practice will enable you to use your wall targets and when you fire at them with your laser light ammo, the video camera will see it and the application will register the hit by producing a sound. You can use it for fast drawing, checking your time between trigger presses and many other features. You will have to search for these. There are free and paid versions of these programs. You just need a PC. Some may work on a MAC computer, but you'll have to ask if they have software for the type of computer you are using.

There are all sorts of things you can do with your new sidearm at home on a daily basis, so you know you're getting your monies worth and you don't have to visit a range. If you do get the chance, go to the range and practice with live rounds since firing bullets is going to be a different feel than firing with some type of laser light ammo. Plus you want to test your ammo in you firearm. Practicing at home and going to the range will improve your skills and this will also help you in a situation where you do have to present your firearm. In my neighborhood, we don't have the luxury of a firing range. The closest one is over an hour away. So a monthly visit works out, plus with most of the training at home helps me improve at the range.

FIRST TIME AT THE RANGE

In some states it's required to shoot at a range to qualify for your concealed carry permit, so you may want to go out and practice before you qualify. Even if there are no range qualification in your state, I would highly recommend that you take your sidearm to the range and practice. The more you practice, the more you will get familiar with your firearm.

Now every range has different rules in how they want their patrons to conduct themselves, but one set of rules NEVER change and that's ALWAYS going to be the four universal firearm safety rules. If you've never been at a gun range and you've got questions, don't be afraid to ask. Talk to those whom you know that frequent the firing range. Ask them to take you along. If you don't know anyone, then talk to someone who works at the range to help you out. Tell them it's your first time and you want to make sure that you do things correctly so you can walk away with a good experience and return again. They may be willing to work with you or hook you up with someone.

There may also be clubs or events that you can participate in for those new to firearms. Get your feet wet and learn something new. You can really learn a lot from these and also meet those who have similar interests. You can also get together with some of these people you met and head out to the range and improve your skills. You'll have a blast!

If it's your first time at that range, some places offer a safety video to watch before they will allow you to shoot. If you have questions from the video, ask before you go onto the range. Safety is always number one at the range.

I know that most of us feel intimidated by those around us who may know more about firearms than we do, but they too were once in our shoes. They too had to ask questions to get to where they are today in knowing firearms. So what if they know more than you? Good, these are the people to ask questions. If the staff at the range treat you differently (like you just fell off the turnip truck) because you're new to firearms, then take your business elsewhere. It's better to ask questions now then to learn from a mistake that could have been avoided. If you're going to master your sidearm, you will have to ask questions.

A firearm can be dangerous in the wrong hands, especially by those who did not take the time to research, practice or ask questions. They can be a danger to themselves and others. I started out late in life with firearms and it does take time to understand all the lingo, but I took the time to better understand how a sidearm works, how to use it and how to protect myself and my loved ones. You don't have to be an expert by no means in enjoying firearms. If you want to be a master at firearms by knowing everything about them, go for it. But if you just want to learn and be proficient with the basics because your goal is to only protect yourself and your loved ones, there's absolutely nothing wrong with this either.

Like computers, there are so many things to learn about them; the software and hardware, the Internet, networks, servers, printers, etc. If you just need the basics to get the work done, that's what you do. You learn what you need to learn. If all you're going to do is word processing, than that's all you learn. If you want to learn how everything works, then you take your education further and learn as much about it as possible. Same thing with firearms. You learn what you need to learn and become proficient at it.

I love listening to conversations about firearms. I ask questions because I don't understand and I want to learn more about it. There's a lot of passion from people who use firearms and there are some who just want to defend themselves and enjoy firing one. You just choose what side of the fence you want to be on and work with it. But keep up the training on no matter what your decision is.

At the range, there should be a Range Safety Officers (RSO). These folks have been trained to supervise a range to prevent any accidents from happening. They are responsible in making sure people shoot safely and removing those who can become a danger to others. If you are approached by one, stop what you are doing and follow their instructions. If you don't understand, ask questions. Always follow the rules of the range.

All firing ranges are different. There will be indoor and outdoor. I prefer outdoor ranges since you have a lot more room to move around to practice different drills. Some ranges may allow you to unholster your firearm (drawing), but many do not since people have shot themselves when pulling the sidearm out of their holster.

If you choose an indoor range, make sure there is some sort of air quality system that will remove the lead from the air. You don't want to be breathing this in. The indoor range I go to have a really good filter system. You will notice indoor ranges with poor air quality by blowing your nose and you'll see a dark soot. This is from everyone's firearm and you're breathing this into your lungs. Try to avoid these places since you don't want to end up with lead poisoning or if it's the only place in town, reduce your time there. People have died from over exposure to lead from firearms. It takes years, but lead cannot ever be removed from your body. Your bones absorb it.

I will walk you through on what it's like to be at an indoor range. This will vary amongst ranges, especially outdoor ones.

On my first visit at the range, I had to fill out paperwork, which contained the rules of the range. They will either take your driver's license or have you show them one. For one of the rules, no cameras or video recording devices were allowed. I didn't understand the reasoning behind this at first, but after watching people take their phones on the range and record video, I now have a better understanding. This is a distraction and a safety hazard!!! I've seen people shoot a firearm and try to video record themselves, or have their friend do it for them. Then I notice that they are not paying attention and start sweeping people around them with their firearm, with live rounds in it. One guy turned around and pointed his firearm at his buddy that was recording. His finger was still on the trigger and it was still loaded. So don't do this and keep focus on what you're doing.

Then I had to watch a video since it was my first time at the range. It explained the universal firearms safety rules and then the range rules. After the video, I waited in line for my turn to practice and I had to put on my safety gear to protect my eyes and ears. Some ranges require that you provide your own. Then I was assigned a stall. The RSO (Range Safety Officer) inspected my ammo and sidearm.

Ranges inspect your ammo to make sure that it was manufactured by a company and not people using reloads (where spent ammo casings are loaded with powder and produced by the gun owner and not a manufacturer), armor piercing bullets, tracers, etc. Most require that your sidearm be empty and be inspected by the RSO before you start shooting. The indoor range that I used has an electronic display that is used to move the targets to specific distances. The RSO will also teach you how to use this.

When your time is up, the RSO will let you know and direct you to where you have to go. Some places make you clean up your ammo on the ground (sweeping it to the side for the next person), others will do it for you. Some places provide targets, others allow you to bring your own. Some will not let you use human targets. Every place is different. So if you know of people who have gone to a particular range before, ask them about it or have them take you.

So what items do you bring with you to the range? I myself have a range bag to carry all of my equipment. This all depends if you're shooting indoors or outdoors. If you're doing the indoor range, you might not have to bring some of the same equipment as going outdoors. I will share what I bring to the range.

Indoor Range: These are the basics, but you may add to it later depending on what you're trying to accomplish.

1. Range bag to hold all of your items.
2. Firearm(s)
3. Ammo (500 rounds minimum, but more is better). Some ranges may require that the ammo come in its original box.
4. A brimmed cap (ball cap for example) to keep ammo from falling behind your safety glasses
5. Safety glasses
6. Ear protection
7. Extra magazines
8. Gunshot first-aid kit (get some training on using it)
9. Multi-tool (always handy for almost anything mechanical)
10. Permanent markers (multiple colors): Mark up your target after each practice so you know which holes are yours (if sharing target with others), or after each reload so you know during that session which holes were new and which ones were old
11. Batteries: If you have any lights for you sidearm (laser or mounted light)
12. Protective case: If you have more than one firearm, you should have them in something. Some range bags come with a foam insert or something that can hold multiple sidearms. You may have to be creative and either purchase something or create one yourself. Some people use the original case the firearm came in.
13. Lead wipes: You can find hand wipes that remove lead from your skin if the range does not have any
14. A rag: I keep a few to clean up my sidearm or dry my hands after using wipes
15. Gun cleaning kit (optional): It depends if you're near home or not. If I am out of state or will be gone for days, then yes, I'll take it with me. But if I just go home that day, then I just keep it on my workbench and clean it when I get home

Outdoor Range: Include all the above for the indoor range and add the following from the list below.

1. Target stand(s): I have three. I use these for drills or when friends tag along. I have also included steps on how to build one at www.WayOfTheConcealedCarrier.com
2. Targets: These can be purchased online. Get the cheapest since you'll be tossing these away
3. Cones: I use orange cones for doing drills
4. Table: Depending on the condition of the range (wet or snow), a table is very useful and your equipment will be kept clean and dry
5. Binoculars (optional): If you're shooting from a greater distance, it will help you see where your bullets hit on the target and it will help you with your shooting accuracy. Some will even tell you the distance to the target so you know how many yards you're shooting from

I hope your first gun range experience is an awesome one.

CHAPTER SIX

Inside Establishments

*"Not thinking about anything is Zen.
Once you know this, walking, sitting
or lying down, everything you do is Zen."*

Bodhidharma

WORKING OUT IN THE GYM

Before entering a gymnasium, make sure there is no round in the chamber (I'll explain later). No need to do this for revolvers. When you enter the locker room, if no backpack, grab a towel or two. Head off to the bathroom stall. Remove your sidearm and holster (while following those safety rules) and put them into the towel(s). Since there is no round in the chamber, you don't have to worry about ejecting the bullet and chasing it across the bathroom floor. If you want to be extra secure, use a lock on the trigger guard, or use one that goes through the barrel.

Make sure your firearm is securely wrapped up or inside your backpack and put it in the locker without the others being any wiser. Be like a ninja and keep it stealthy. You don't want to come back after a workout and your sidearm is missing. Then you have to report it to the police. Or someone called the police and they are looking for you at the gym because they saw you with a firearm.

When you're ready to go, do the same thing. Carry the towels with your sidearm into the stall and put your gear on. Do not chamber a round. It can be heard and echoed and it may put people into a panic. Wait until you are in the car or in a private area where no one can hear it and then rack the slide. For revolvers, there is no worries in this area.

Also, don't workout with your weapon. People will see it, it gets in the way and you can become a target. Others will know, word will spread and those undesirables will take note and decide that you no longer need to possess such an item. Or people will be unhappy with this and express their opinions to you or complain to the management. Don't lose your element of surprise because you want to be macho, impress others, or send fear across the room. Not cool.

Some gymnasiums may have something in the contract about carrying firearms on their establishment. There may also be a laws on the books for that state, city, or county about carrying in such places.

Weight lifting, boxing, being on a treadmill, yoga, Pilates and any of those fancy workouts you pay money for, is not really a good place to carry. Imagine your loaded weapon hitting the floor during a workout. What if you try to grab it in midair and it accidentally discharges. What kind of mess is that going to make for you? Number one rule of having a concealed carry permit is to keep it concealed. People who see it may challenge you or they may be someone who doesn't mind taking it from you. Don't be careless. If you have a gym bag in a closed room for your workout (like for yoga), then have your sidearm in a holster in your bag, be as far away from the door so no one swipes it and heads out the door. Have your bag where you can reach it if needed.

SHOPPING WITH YOUR SIDEARM

Depending on which state you're in and if you're allowed to carry in a store, you may have to make some adjustments while shopping.

When shopping, select a cart, even if you're only grabbing a few items. The reasoning behind this is that you want to have your hands free. If you decide to pick up one of those baskets, you have only one free hand. I know that I have a list of only a few items in my head and then by the time I am done, my little basket is overfilled. Or a few items are pretty heavy, like beverages for example and I find myself getting weighed down. Then I would be switching the basket between hands since it's getting too heavy. When you need your sidearm the most and you're carrying a basket, your dominant hand may be holding onto a heavy basket.

Shopping with a cart gives you the advantage to get rid of it a lot easier than having a basket in your hand, plus you're not carrying heavy items. You can get away from your cart quickly and head for cover or an exit, or if you have to draw, both hands are free to do so.

Next time you hit a supermarket or any other place that has a shopping cart, utilize it. Keep things simple. If you have to book it out of there or defend yourself, you will be able to do so with nothing delaying your decision or draw time.

AT A RESTAURANT

While in a restaurant, try to keep as far away from the entrance as possible and the cashier. Find an area where you can see everyone. Take note of the nearest exits, like the kitchen and emergency exits.

I notice that families are at their tables surfing on their phones and tablets, completely unaware of their surroundings. Just stay off your phone or tablet, keep your eyes and ears open, but also enjoy yourself. Keep in mind where you can take cover so you can protect yourself and your family.

I would also recommend that you eat lite. Just eat until you're half full and take the rest of the food home with you if need be. When you fill yourself, your energy starts to get pulled from other places of the body to help digest your food. Your energy level feels like it is dropping, you may feel little tired or sleepy and your reflexes start to slow down a little.

The reason for this is when you eat, blood flows to your digestive tract and your body increases its heart rate and constricts certain blood vessels to help maintain normal blood pressure. If you over eat, it takes more energy to break down the food, so you're like an overstuffed garbage disposal, trying to grind down its food.

For optimum performance, don't eat a heavy meal and your awareness will be at peak performance. Avoid alcohol in the restaurant when carrying a firearm. If something does happen and you do end up in court, your answer to drinking alcohol would be a sound "no" and you won't be judged on being impaired during the time you had to draw your weapon. The prosecutors would love to find a "yes" in there somewhere. So don't drink and be armed, even if it's allowed in your state. It's best not to give ammunition to the prosecutor.

I avoid booths at all costs. It is so hard to draw a firearm in a booth. Pick a table with chairs instead. I usually move my chair at a slight angle so the backside does not interfere with my sidearm. If I just sat normally, it becomes difficult to move my arm since it will be hitting the back of the chair. A slight few degrees in pivoting the chair will allow you to draw your sidearm. My pistol grip gets hung up on the backs of some chairs when I get up; it snags the chair and it moves with me. So try to avoid this.

If I am stuck in a booth, then I'll angle my body to a point where I can get access to my firearm. The table will get in my way, my elbow will be hitting the back of the seat and it's a very tight squeeze. If the place is packed and there is limited seating and I have to sit in a booth, I'll sit on the open end of the booth where the server greets and serves us.

I do not want to be crammed up against the wall in the booth since I am basically in a dead end with limited options to escape or defend myself. Plus I'll have people sitting next to me and they could get in the path of my muzzle if I have to draw. When sitting on the open-ended side of the booth with my dominant arm free, my dominant hand will have limited restrictions and I can access my sidearm. But I will have to sit on the edge of the seat to gain some open space for my arms movement since the back of the booth may restrict me.

If I do end up against the wall, I will pull my shirt out of the way of my sidearm. This does expose it, but no one will be looking there anyways and it would be hard for anyone to see. But at least I can access my sidearm quickly without pulling up my shirt and fumbling with it, the table and the backside of the booth when I am trying to draw. And before I leave, I pull my shirt over my firearm again so it's hidden and I won't get any stares. Again, if possible, avoid booths.

SIDEARMS AND FURNITURE

One of the most annoying things while carrying on the hip is that your weapon will sometimes rub up against objects. Seats/chairs is a perfect example. I don't like the wooden chairs that don't have a solid backing. If you have slats of wood behind you (the ribs of the chair), your pistol grip may get wedged or clank against it since there is space between the wood. Or if you turn, it makes a noise while it's hitting the back end of the chair.

Typical ribbed chair where your firearm snags on.

If you have to draw from this position, let's hope that your sidearm isn't stuck in between the wood slats. You may have also noticed that while you're near a corner of a wall, you turn and your firearm hits it. What's really important for safety is that you have an excellent holster that the trigger guard is protected and it has great retention. If your sidearm is hitting objects, you may have to reevaluate to see if changes in the position of the holster needs to be adjusted or maybe change it up and go from OWB to IWB (outside the waistband to inside the waistband).

I find myself sitting a little sideways (depending on the chair), away from the backing of the chair, or I sit a little forward with some space, so that I have accessibility to my sidearm. It does get annoying after a while when it starts hitting the back of the chair. While you're carrying, you'll notice that some things will rub up against your sidearm or it bangs into things. If an adjustment to your holster does not solve the problem, you'll just have to become more aware of your surroundings and just avoid clanking your sidearm against things.

RUNNING OUT OF HAIRCUTS

We all need haircuts at one point or another, but what do you do when you carry concealed while sitting in a barber's chair?

Haircut places have been robbed, even while people are sitting in their chairs. There have been several instances where the bad guys have even shot multiple people (possibly because they don't want witnesses)

and others have been simply executed while sitting in their chairs. It's so sad that this kind of stuff happens. So we must always be prepared for the worse.

So if you're carrying, make sure that your weapon is reachable in a moment's notice. I for one carry IWB and my clothing hangs over my sidearm. So when I sit in the chair, I lift up my clothing, over and out of the way of my firearm, so that I can reach my weapon. Don't fiddle with it while you're in the chair as this may create an accidental discharge. I also move to the far side of the chair (left or right, depending where your sidearm is located) to create more space for access to my firearm. You will not have much wiggle room when you draw, but you will be able to do it if necessary. And this also depends on how much space your body fills in that chair.

Once your haircut is over and before the sheet is removed, just lift up your shirt over your sidearm again.

I was very nervous the first time I carried inside a barbershop. I would think to myself, do people notice if there is a bulge when I am waiting to sit in the chair? Then I continue my situation awareness, not just in the shop, but watching people outside. I have my exits pegged and scenarios are running through my mind - the "What Ifs".

Then I listened to other people tell stories as they were getting their hair cut. I am in the Midwest and we have a lot of people that go hunting. When I listened to some of their stories at the barbershop, I can see that I am in good company since most of them are hunters. So if I do accidentally show my sidearm, I know I won't get much of a stare. You never know who else might be carrying while you're getting your haircut. I would imagine at the rate that people are getting their permits, you will have good company in many places you visit.

ACTIVE SHOOTER TRAINING IN THE WORKPLACE

I just got out of a class that was presented by an agent from one of our government agencies and it was on what to do in the workplace when there is an active shooter. I am not going to say which agency due to security reasons, my clearance, plus I like my job.

Can you guess how long the training was?

Training started at 1 pm and ended at 1:05 pm. Just five minutes. I felt like microwaved food. Just pop me into class, set timer on high for 5 minutes and poof - I am trained to perfection. The government agency I work for just showed a 3 minute video, asked if there were any questions and dismissed the entire class. This was the absolute worst training I have ever received during the past decade since I have worked for this organization. Our last training on this topic was several years ago and at least this class was 30 minutes long.

Due to the spread of terrorism around the world, it's having an impact on us at home, in public places and at work. Because of the real threat, companies have decided to put some type of training together for its employees. But there's no guarantee that it's going to be good quality training. Employees are only going to be good at the amount of training they receive. And training is a perishable skill. If you only get training once a year, you'll forget about what you've learned after a while, especially if you don't do it again until years later. There should be continuous training around this topic, not a one off since it's becoming more common place.

At my place of employment, what was really disappointing was that they never really explained in detail on what to do during these active shooter situations. There was no real dialog between those training and the employees. A DVD was thrown into a player, showing a cartoonish video, where the character on the screen had flashbacks to their active shooter training class on how to handle that particular situation.

It was apparent that this cartoonish character had more training about active shooters than we did. It reminded me of the duck and cover videos during the Cuban missile crisis - providing information that was useless in saving your own life. The training we received was not thoroughly thought-out and provided no value at all.

I wish they would have provided us with a survey instead of me writing about it. If you work for a government agency, then this may not shock you at all. The video I saw at work was geared towards putting more fear into people (loud gunshots and screams in the background) then actually training you on what to do. It would have been nice to talk about real-life situations that have happened, what was learned from those shootings and provide us with real-life success stories on what people did that saved their lives. You could tell that a lot of money went into this 3 minute video and upper management was proud of it, but not much money was placed into our safety (budget cutbacks?).

Why not talk about how people usually react during a shooting, like the Ft. Lauderdale airport shooting. Many people just stood there and didn't find cover. This happens all the time where people just stand and watch as bullets fly, thinking it's not real, until they get wounded or lose their life. People just get so curious to see what's happening around them, like drivers watching a stranded car on the side of the road and everyone just has to slow down to see what's going on. A phenomenon in which I don't understand. It causes headaches and safety issues for everyone.

Let me bullet point on some areas that was missed in this class:

1. Know your exits and how to get outside.

2. Situation awareness, what is it and how to use it daily at work and everywhere you go.

3. Drop everything and get the hell out of there. No need to go back and grab your possessions.

4. What conceal and cover is? Knowing the difference and what to look for in your surroundings during a shooting to save your life.

5. Don't move wounded people, unless they are in danger.

6. Try to avoid rooms where there is no escape (like a bathroom, office, or conference room).

7. What to do to defend yourself. Give examples of what objects to grab in the room and to use in self-defense.

8. What to do when police arrive (all they mentioned was keep your hands up), but there's more to that.

9. If evacuation is not possible, what to do.

10. And more....

What was covered in the video?

1. Don't activate the fire alarm.

2. Yell at people to get out of the area and out of the building.

3. Keep your hands up when police arrive.

4. Barricade the doors and if someone comes in with a gun, fight them.

5. Have flashbacks to your training so you can get out of your situation.

6. Keep your phone silent and call 911 when you are safe to do so.

Here is what we were told to do when there is an Active Shooter:

- **Call Out!:** Yell out at people to get out
- **Get Out!:** Get out of the area of the shooter
- **Hide Out!:** Find a place to hide

This is completely different from the FBI's & Homeland Security's Active Shooter version:

- **Run:** Basically get the hell out of there
- **Hide:** If you can't get out, find a place to hide
- **Fight:** Fight for your life if it comes down to it

Now I am very concerned that our government agencies are training differently from each other on what to do when there is an Active Shooter. Why aren't we all on the same page? I did a search online to see what was presented to us and it's like a hacked version of what some schools are teaching to their students. So only three was picked out from the list that is being taught in schools and the rest was left out (which I would consider as important). After some researching, I found what was missing: "figure out, keep out and take out". I can't find the reasoning behind not adding these to the list since it is also being taught.

So let's break it down in order of what is being taught and I am going to assume that this is going to be the order of priority since it was presented this way during training. I guess we are supposed to remember the three bullet points during a high adrenaline situation.

(1) *Call Out:* I am supposed to tell people to get out or direct them somewhere during the shooting. I am not sure why I would be calling out to people and giving away our position to the shooter. First of all, if shots are being fired and people are running everywhere, should we all stand there and start organizing people and telling them where to go? Now I for one, would rather RUN and get the hell out of there and not spend time yelling at people trying to convince them that "Hey, there's some guy with a gun, can you hear the pop pop sounds down the hallway, maybe we should leave or something?". I am not going to become a target using this methodology. It's their own responsibility to take action and not mine to try and herd cats. This is very dangerous, especially giving away your position.

(2) *Get Out:* Common sense here, yes I would get out, so not sure why this is not the first one as a priority in their list.

(3) *Hide Out:* This should have been the second thing to do in the list if people are unable to escape outside. And what's kind of funny (not ha ha) here is that there is no mention of defending yourself either in this list.

So going through the list in order, I am just supposed to risk myself trying to beat common sense into people and warning them about pending doom, then find a place to hide and wait several minutes for help (which many lives could be lost before the police arrive). Now I know they mentioned defending yourself in the video, but they never really got into how to do this. I guess you're on your own to figure this out during the time someone is trying to take your life.

I like the FBI/Homeland Security version where you run, hide if necessary and fight for your life and not sit around waiting for death. This tells me that they thought it through and took the time to study real active shooter situations.

So is this is the quality of training that is going to be offered by some of our government agencies and possibly in the work place? Especially during the time where terrorism is on the rise. The training offered to me and my peers, it earned a grade of **F–** in my opinion.

So if the decision makers are going to offer unrealistic active shooter training, or no training at all, folks need to be given the opportunity to defend themselves. They should be allowed to carry concealed at their workplace, even for those working on government property and take their chances with a terrorist. It's just common sense. This is their life and their responsibility to take care of themselves, not others making decisions on their behalf and coming up with some justification in not allowing people to defend themselves. I am an advocate for carrying everywhere you go.

The world is ever changing and we need to be proactive and not reactive and base senseless results after the deaths of innocent and defenseless people. Then politically fight about it on who is right and wrong. Remove the politics and place yourself in these real situations. If you are unarmed like many of these people have been, would your outcome be any different? Would you too (Mr. and Mrs. Politician) not lose your life also since you are not allowed to defend yourself in using equal deadly force? Put yourself in their shoes. If they were armed, trained and given the chance to defend themselves, I am positive that more lives would have been saved in many of these terrorist acts in our country. It's just common sense.

One good example of governments making the right decisions and allowing people the choice to defend themselves are the ones that allow people to carry concealed at their state capital. For many years, in my state, it is allowed to carry concealed in the state capital and there has never been an incident of a responsible armed person shooting up the place. So apparently this is not a problem at the local government level and it would be nice if the Feds followed suit.

Depending on what your job is, employees in the public and private sector (especially on government property) will be completely defenseless. With the increase in violence, along with most of your criminals and terrorists being armed, most of our lawful citizens are siting targets since they're not allowed to carry at work. The odds are against us good people and in favor of those violent people. Terrorist have attacked schools, hospitals, malls and businesses, but no one is armed, except the active shooter. These places are considered as soft targets and they will be at the top of the list for terrorists. Why wait for this to happen when it can be prevented? Again, as a nation, let's be proactive and not reactive. Let's do the smart thing and allow the option for people to carry concealed in all places.

So why not let those who have gone through the background checks be armed at work? I believe that people should have the right to defend themselves, no matter where they are. Crime has no boundaries, but we continue to make these imaginary (make believe) lines thinking that everyone else is not going to dare cross. These establishments claim that being a gun-free zone is for the protection of their employees, but if you don't offer the right kind of training, then what's the point of giving training at all? They're creating an unsafe work environment for their employees.

If you're afraid of everyone being armed, how about designating people to be trained on using a firearm and carry one (like teachers are doing in some schools to protect the children) at the workplace in case something does happen. Or just allow your concealed carry people who have passed their background checks to carry inside the building. Government and private property are not immune to acts of violence. These are "Gun-Free Zones" and we all know what that means. It doesn't stop the bad people from entering a building and harming or killing people. They should be "Violence-Free Zones". A warning to the bad people to move on and telling them their chances are slim to none in acting out their violent aggressions in these zones since responsible and trained people will be armed.

If your workplace doesn't take the time to work with you on a good quality active shooter training, than they really don't care about you. They're just worried about meeting minimum standards put in place by the organization instead of providing quality training that can save people's lives. As long as they can show that they did provide training to their employees (no matter how many minutes - like 3 minutes in my case), then they can check this off of their list. And if there are complaints or a shooting later, they can say they provided the training to cover themselves. If this is the case, then this company really doesn't' have concerns about your safety, they don't take it seriously and they're putting your life in danger.

I would highly recommend that your company hire an expert who trains people on what to do in an active shooter situations, not someone who plays a video, dismisses the class and really has no experience in this area.

If you think you're getting poor training at work, than seek out someone who has experience in this area for yourself. So if that day ever does come, you will be prepared and have some skills and training on how to save your life and possibly others.

If your company is doing any active shooter training, ask them if there is an emergency medical kit just for gunshot wounds, in case several people do get shot. Are there any bandages, tourniquets, chest seals, something to plug holes in a body? Will they provide some type of training for medical emergencies on gunshot wounds?

If you're one of the managers at your company who makes training decisions for your employees around active shooters, imagine yourself skimming on this training. There is no medical kit or first aid training around employees that are wounded. Then one day, it happens. A disgruntled employee decides that he wants to vent his anger on management and the employees. Then there are shots fired.

What if you're one of those people who was shot and there is no one around to help you since there was no good training provided? Would you not want to have your employees attempt to save your life? Or would you rather risk the chance of waiting for an ambulance, that's minutes away? Or wait for the paramedics that are delayed entering the building because the shooter is still in the area. They will not go into the building until the police have secured the area and this can take a long time. If there are hostages, then this can take hours. By the time it's all over, I hope you were spiritually prepared and your family would be taken care of after you've met your maker.

If you're still not convinced, do a search on the Internet where employees have been fired and they came back to murder people. There are plenty out there and after reading these stories and watching any of the videos from these shootings, then hopefully reality will set in. Like John Robert Neumann Jr. He was fired from his Job in Orlando, Florida and later came back and shot 5 people. He singled out these people. These people had no warning whatsoever. What if the employees had some sort of training and could have alerted others and provided medical attention to those in need? What if the employees were armed? Could there been more lives saved?

It's unfortunate that people think it would never happen to them and when it does, it's too late. If you're a decision maker at your business, make the wise choice and get your people trained properly. It can save a life someday and it might be yours.

CHAPTER SEVEN

Involvement with Law Enforcement

*"Before enlightenment; chop wood, carry water.
After enlightenment; chop wood, carry water"*

Buddha

WHAT NOT TO CARRY FOR A DEFENSIVE SIDEARM

I am sure your attention just peaked with the title of this topic. Well, I am not going to tell you what type of firearm to carry, but I'll tell you what to look for.

Let's say that you're involved in a shooting and being hauled down to the police department. They've confiscated your 1911 handgun as evidence (worth over $1,500). After you have been released pending a court date, now what? Go out and buy another? Would you be able to come up with another $1,500? My recommendation on the type of handgun you carry, is obviously something very reliable, but one that will not hit your pocket book. Unless you can afford to go out and spend another grand or more for a sidearm to replace the one that was confiscated.

So when you first decide on a firearm to carry daily for protection, think about the above situation. Purchase yourself a reliable sidearm that you'll use for defensive purposes, one that is agreeable to your budget, but one that you can afford to lose. But remember, the more accessories you add (sights, laser, light, etc.), the more money you'll be spending.

There are some reliable firearms that start around $300, so you're not breaking the bank. I paid around $565 for a new Glock 19 with no extras. Then replaced the sights with a set of TriJicons filled with tritium (a radioactive isotope of hydrogen) that keeps the three dots glowing in the dark for about 12 years, priced at $86. So my defensive investment, with critical defense ammo came to a total around $700 including taxes and shipping. That's about half of the price of the 1911 example used above. I have nothing against the 1911s, but it is not my main defensive weapon. I wouldn't want that beauty in someone else's hands anyways, especially the police.

But if your gun gets confiscated, then you'll have to go out and get another one until you get your gun back from the authorities. You don't want to be walking around defenseless. It could take months to over a year (or years), before you will get your sidearm back. It could take many months before you head to court, but that doesn't mean that you cannot still carry (unless you have been ordered by the courts that you can't).

You don't need to pay big bucks on a firearm for self-defense. Be wise, don't carry around a real expensive sidearm for protection. If it gets lost, stolen, or confiscated, you're out of a real nice piece of machinery and a good chunk of money.

YOU DON'T NEED NO STINK'N BADGES

Did you know that there are concealed carry badges that you can purchase online? Do you think you need one? Most people think this is a horrible idea since it looks like you're impersonating law enforcement. Others who open carry or hook one to their holster while carrying concealed may believe that having a piece of tin is going to avoid problems with the general public from calling the cops on them, especially if your carrying concealed and your firearm is accidentally seen with your badge (like bending over or reaching for something). But people may assume your law enforcement and ask no questions, or you might have an actual officer introduce themselves to you and want to swap some stories. Then they discover you're not one of them and that embarrassing conversation could go sideways.

Some people carry a concealed carry badge to avoid people reporting them for brandishing by accident. The problem here, people assume you're law enforcement, but in reality, you're not. I look at it as opening up a can of worms when someone assumes you are an officer of the law. They may actually need the law, it could be a life or death situation and they approach you because you're publicly displaying a shield that looks like an actual badge for law enforcement. Then you have to explain to them that you're not an officer and you end up wasting their valuable time. They may just report you to the police telling them that you are impersonating an officer. If that person dies while they were trying to get help from you, you may end up in court defending yourself. Things could get real dicey and out of control when you're trying to explain to the court the reasons why you carry a badge and you are not an officer of the law.

If you do wear one, you are not impersonating an officer. You can legally wear a uniform that looks like a police officer, but as long as you are not going around acting like law enforcement. But why would you wear one anyways except for a party or Halloween? Do you really want to go down that road?

There are wannabes out there who actually trick people into thinking they are the law and use that power for or against people. They will eventually get caught and convicted if they start acting and performing duties like law enforcement. If you're such a person, pull your head out, grow up, talk to a therapist, get laid or all of the above. Do something for your community except pretending to be the police. You'll end up in a bad place, like in a cell, playing hand puppets with your new roommate and that's putting it delicately.

I look at it this way, you should be concealing your sidearm and there is no need for a badge since no one will know you are armed. That's the point behind concealed carry. I personally think concealed carry badges are a real bad idea since it becomes a conversation piece that you don't want to talk about and it confuses people as to who you are.

It might get you into trouble, depending if law enforcement is involved; where someone is complaining about you and your badge. If I were you, I would stay away from concealed carry badges altogether. Honestly, you really don't need it. All you need is your permit (if needed for your state) and nothing else. Why create more attention and problems for yourself? Why make yourself known while you can be the gray ghost (blending in with your environment, unnoticeable to others)?

I have been seeing ads on the Internet that advertise concealed carry classes and actually has someone showing a concealed carry badge in their hand. If you look at these advertisements, does it convince you to take these classes because you can carry this shiny little badge when you receive your permit? AVOID THESE CLASSES!!!! A big red flag should be going off in your head. It's just eye-candy to get you to sign up for a class. Getting a concealed badge is not your goal here, it is to meet state standards and to carry legally. These types of ads give the wrong message to those who want to carry a sidearm. This is my opinion, but when I look at ads like these, to me it says, "Get your badge and your gun after you take a concealed carry class without being in law enforcement".

I am not disputing that what they say is untrue in the advertisement - You can get your certification, carry legally and if you wish, you can get a shield. But remember, you don't need no stink'n badges to carry a firearm.

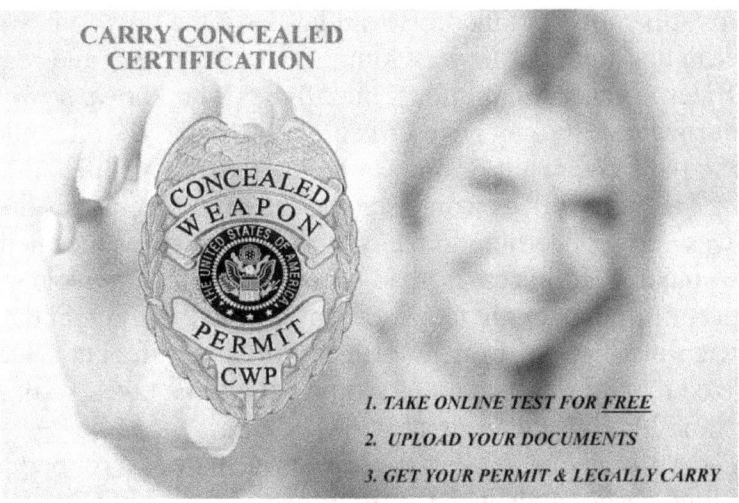

You don't need a badge to carry a firearm!

If you want an honest to goodness badge, then get training in law enforcement and become an officer of the law. If you feel a concealed carry permit badge is what you need to make you complete, then feel free to do so. <u>DO NOT</u> impersonate the law and please don't take the law into you own hands. If you do, you'll tarnish the reputation for those who are responsible armed citizens in the concealed carry community. Having a concealed carry badge does not make you someone who can enforce the law. If you carry one of those badges, then you may not be as serious or responsible than you think you are when you carry.

GETTING PULLED OVER BY THE POLICE

You're driving down the road, jamming to your tunes and you notice a squad car behind you. The sirens come on, you are about to be pulled over and you're armed. What should you do? Depending on the law in your state, if you are carrying, you may or may not have to inform the officer that you have a firearm.

While working on this book (2016), there was a shooting in Minnesota, where a concealed carrier was shot by the officer while he was going for his ID. He DID follow the instructions from the officer, but was still shot and killed. He did not have the duty to inform the officer in his state, but he was doing it out of courtesy and respect for the officer. If he did not inform the officer, who knows how it could have turned out. It may have turned out differently, or it could have come to the same result of this young man losing his life.

In 2017, the officer won his court case and all charges dropped. This was very concerning to me because I too carry concealed. Because of the outcome of this case, I had to rethink in how to avoid such a situation from happening to me and my readers. I thought that just following instructions from an officer would be safe, but since that day, I realized that extra precautions would have to be taken so that something like this never repeats itself again.

The officer believed that the driver was part of a robbery that was committed earlier and since the driver was a law abiding citizen with a permit to carry a firearm, he did not know that he was also a suspect of a crime. This can happen to any one of if we're matching a description of a suspect. They police may have a limited description of the suspect and officers are going by what they have, even though it could possibly be inaccurate. This was a difficult situation for this young man to be in. I am not going to talk about the case, but I do know is that he was one of us, a concealed carrier and what happened was unfortunate.

I will go through some things that you should do when you do get pulled over and actions that you should take to hopefully prevent a similar situation. This is not going to cover every situation since this is impossible to predict, but should be helpful for some of the basics.

With our fallen concealed carrier in Minnesota, presenting your permit and informing the officer is still a good idea, no matter what state you're in (the right to inform or not). Why? The laws in your state may have changed and you may have not been aware of that change. It may have changed that very day where you have to inform the officer and if you don't, this could be a problem. Especially if the officer ends up patting you down and you're armed.

Your body language is also important so that the officer is not perceiving you as a threat. BEFORE the officer gets to the window, have your permit (if required) and license in your hand and your hands on the top of the steering wheel. ALWAYS smile, don't be a smart ass and be as courteous as possible. I have my permit in a small card holder and this is separate from my wallet. I have it in the pocket of my shirt so I don't have to dig for it in my pants pocket while the officer is approaching the car. If you have a purse, have it reachable and available in a few seconds time before the officer gets to your window. Don't be digging in your purse looking for it while the officer is waiting. You may have a firearm in your purse and if the officer sees it, there may be trouble. Have your ID ready before they see you.

    The officer will think that something suspicious is happening if you are digging in your back pocket, your purse, opening up the glove compartment or some other console. Your body language may be misunderstood. I remember I was trying to find my drivers permit as a kid, it was in my glove compartment and when I opened it, all my music tapes fell to the floor (they would be equivalent to a CD for those who don't know what cassette tapes are). The officer freaked out, had me exit the vehicle immediately and searched my car. I was young and had no idea what I was doing. I felt I was innocent and trustworthy because that's my reputation with friends and family, but this officer did not know me. So from their side, I could have been reaching for something to use against this officer. So be careful of your movements, be prepared and ready with your ID for the officer.

    You do not want to seem threatening to the officer. You can say to the officer "Hello officer, my name is <*first name*> and as a courtesy for both of our safety, I am a registered concealed carrier, here is my permit. I am armed, I am going to keep my hands on top of the steering wheel and I will follow your instructions to avoid any misunderstanding." This statement is for the safety of the officer and yours.

    Effective communication with the officer is very important. Don't just say "I have a gun...." this may be taken out of context. After giving the statement from above, wait for instructions from the officer. If the officer says no problem or acts like it's no big deal, continue to keep your hands on top of the steering wheel until it is time for you to leave and the officer is back in their vehicle.

    If you have children in the vehicle, ask them to keep quiet. Don't make any sudden moves towards your children to calm them down, keep your hands on the steering wheel. If you have a crying baby, you'll have to remain calm and keep your hands on the steering wheel. Reaching for the child could be misinterpreted. This is going to suck, but the officer does not know your true intentions, so remain calm and in control.

Have your hands in plain view for the officer at all times and never let them drop below your chest. If they want you to remove your weapon, ask them how they want you to do it and always keep your hands in full view and do it very slowly. DO NOT REMOVE YOUR FIREARM FROM YOUR HOLSTER WHILE IN YOUR VEHICLE. Inform the officer that you want to exit the vehicle first. This will remove some of the suspicion of you hiding your sidearm in the vehicle. But remember, you are not giving them the right to search your vehicle. It they want to, they will need a search warrant and let them know this. Don't waive your rights.

If you have to remove your seatbelt, inform the officer and ask them how you want to do this. Don't look down at your seatbelt, but keep your eyes engaged with the officer and do it real slow when releasing the buckle. Let them read your face. Use only one hand while doing this and keep the other hand up high in plain view. Then slowly raise that hand to match your other after you unbuckle the seatbelt. Then exit the vehicle with both hands raised. I do not carry my firearm on my hip in the vehicle, I have a holster attached to the inside of the car. So if the officer wants to have my firearm, I can leave the vehicle and leave it there. If they ask me where it is, I tell them.

Always listen carefully to the directions being given by the officer. If you don't understand something, tell them to repeat it or tell them you're not understanding their request. If they are yelling at you, remain calm and do not make any sudden moves. Repeat again that you are not understanding their directions. Again, they do not know you and since you have a loaded weapon and you are not law enforcement, they are doing this for everyone's safety. They want to make it home safely that day to see their family, the same as you do.

I would not feel comfortable in removing my sidearm from my holster but would ask that the officer or their partner remove it from me, but with my hands over my head. They may handcuff me and they may call for another officer to assist if one is not present. I don't want anything interpreted as aggression if I remove my sidearm from my holster. Again, remain polite and courteous.

If the officer is not listening to you when they pull you over, make sure that they hear you loud and clear that you have a permit and you are carrying. If the officer seems distracted or interrupts, try to get his/her attention. It's imperative that you need to inform the officer, especially if your state requires it.

There was an instance in Canton, Ohio where the officer continuously interrupted and did not allow the driver to speak. Even though the young man was trying to tell him that he was carrying, the officer kept cutting him off and decided to call his dispatcher. The dispatcher pulled up the driver's record and informed the officer that this young man had a permit to carry.

The officer arrested this poor man for not informing him that he was armed. It went completely sideways and this was no fault of the driver. The officer even threatened to shoot the driver multiple times when he had him in the back of the squad car. The officer was freaked out, again not the fault of the young man, but the officer refused to listen, which was his fault. Luckily it was all recorded on video and you can find this on the Internet. A great training video to put yourself into this young man's position and ask yourself what you would have done differently to change the situation. It's unfortunate that there are officers like this, but try your best to communicate with the officer.

You may also end up in the back of the squad car while they're running a check on you. Hopefully you won't go through all of this, but if you do, remain calm. If you have injuries where you cannot raise your hands, inform the officer in a clear and understandable voice. "Sir/Ma'am, I have an injured arm and cannot raise it. Do you have any other suggestions on where you want my hands?"

So how do you avoid from being pulled over? Make sure that all your lights work (headlights and taillights), tabs are up to date, no strange markings on your car to attract yourself, don't have darkened windows that are considered illegal, make sure there is nothing on your rear view mirror to attract yourself (like an air freshener - some consider this drug paraphernalia), or something that would gain attention.

Also don't speed or be aggressive on the road. I have known people that for over two decades, they have never been pulled over. They follow the rules of the road, they make sure their vehicle is safe and don't gain any attraction. Make sure your vehicle is in great mechanical condition so you don't have to worry if your car dies on the highway and an officer comes to assist. If they do and you have a pistol strapped on you, I would suggest you inform the officer so that they're not alarmed if they see the sidearm and you now have a gun pointing at you. Don't make yourself a target so that you need to get pulled over. Stay off of the radar and you should be fine.

So what do you do if you are not carrying or you do not have a weapon in the vehicle and you get pulled over? Don't volunteer anything. Keep your hands on top of the steering wheel at all times until they are back in their car and ready to leave. If they run a check and it shows that you do have a permit, they will ask questions. Inform them that you do not have your firearm with you today and follow any further instructions that the officer presents to you. Again keep your hands on the steering wheel so they are in plain view at all times. Otherwise, there is no need to let them know unless you ARE carrying.

If you are an armed passenger in the car, I would recommend that you have your license and permit ready. Keep your hands on the dashboard at all times, or if in the back, keep it on top of the headrest of the seat in front of you at all times. Traffic stops by police are the most dangerous things they do, so keep your hands in plain view at all times. Don't mess around with this. If you have passengers that carry, they too should have their hands in plain view and inform the officer.

Pulled Over in the Dark

If you get pulled over in the dark, find a well-lit area, like a gas station, mall, restaurant, anything with people and the ability to be seen. If you are on the highway, take the next exit and find a place that has lights. Don't speed up and have the officer chase you. If you have no choice, pull over, turn your dome light on and any other lights on in the vehicle. Have your license and permit (if needed) all ready to go. Follow the procedures as mentioned above (hands on steering wheel, effectively communicating with the officer, etc.). The officer will have their search light on your vehicle, so remain calm and don't make any sudden moves. Pulling people over at night for officers is very dangerous and again, they do not know who you are and your intent.

So if you are alone and you feel that a safe location is best with a lot of lighting, just call 911 and tell the dispatcher that there is a squad car behind you, it's too dark and you want to be in a lighted area, so you will be going to the next exit. You don't need to mention that you are armed to the dispatcher.

YOU ARE NOT THE LAW

There was an incident that just happened in Winston-Salem, North Carolina as I was writing this book. Daniel Ray Brown who was new to the concept of concealed carry, saw an incident in the parking lot of a mall. There was three people surrounding a single person and it looked very suspicious to him. He took it as a position of authority and went up to the people and pulled his gun on them. Then he demanded that they show their ID. You can see where this is already going to go sideways. Can you point out where he went wrong?

The three people were in the medical profession trying to control a situation with their mentally challenged person who was having an episode. They were not harming this person but trying to help him. The concealed carrier asked for their identification and they told him to put the gun away, but the concealed carrier decided to give them a warning shot by shooting at the ground near them. Again, can you see where the mistakes are clearly being made here?

The judge revoked his concealed carry permit and will be facing charges. This person should have called 911 and then became a good witness, but instead he decided to take the law into his own hands, drawing his firearm and asking for their ID. If you are not law enforcement, then you are not the law. Do not take it upon yourself to get involved in situations that you have no idea what's going on. It will bite you in the rear. Call 911 or have someone do it for you. If you have a cell phone, record the situation and be a good witness.

In this case, the guy told the judge that he thought it was a drug deal gone badly or loan sharks collecting. That was his defense in court. These are all assumptions. He also thought that "stand your ground" was in effect so he could produce his sidearm since in his mind lethal force was necessary.

Again, know the laws in your state. If it says castle doctrine or stand your ground, do your research so you know exactly what it means in your state. Don't take hearsay from a friend. Each state has its own concealed carry laws posted on their websites. States may have their own interpretation on what their own castle doctrine or stand your ground means to them. Understand these and don't assume. A bad drug deal or loan sharks collecting, how ridiculous is that? He had that itchy trigger finger. He lacked the training, education and it landed him in jail.

IT'S A PAIN IN THE ASS, BUT IT'S THE LAW

Once you start carrying, you're going to find that at times, it's a pain in the ass. Each state have their own laws on where you can carry a firearm and you're going to find out quickly about areas where you're not permitted to carry (like hospitals, churches, federal buildings, post offices, courts, etc.). You're also going to need to know the laws around federal properties. Before you enter these places, you'll have to lock up your sidearm. When you return to your vehicle, you unlock your gun safe and start carrying again. If you travel by train, taxi, bus, foot, bicycle, or other mode of transportation, you may not have a place to lock up your firearm before you can enter these restricted locations. Yes, it's a pain in the ass.

Here's an example. Say a relative is in the hospital. You're at work (where firearms are not legally allowed, even in the parking lot) and you receive a call about a loved one who was injured and hospitalized. The hospital they were admitted to is in a very rough neighborhood. Your sidearm is at home locked in a safe (remember, you can't have a firearm on work property) and going home will probably add 30 minutes or more to your time. When you get home, you strap on your sidearm and have to drive another 30-40 minutes to the hospital. The hospital and their parking lot does not allow firearms, so you have to find a place in the street to park and lock it up in your vehicle. See the monotony in this? Yes, this has happened to me.

You're options are very limited. I shared this story with a friend of mine and he told me that he has caches of arms around town. He rents small storage lockers. He's the kind of guy who is prepared for the apocalypse and some sort of zombie attacks (bless his heart). So if he needs to drop off or grab his firearm before or after he leaves his federal job, it's nearby and available to him. You don't have to go to this extreme, but consider the ramifications if you decide to have a firearm on federal grounds or at a hospital. This could be the biggest mistake of your life.

Let's add some more to this scenario. You're at the hospital visiting and family members decide that they want to go out for lunch and take your car. It's legal to have your firearm locked up in your vehicle (off hospital grounds), but you have friends, family and a guest that have no idea you carry and you want to keep it that way. But your firearm is locked away in your vehicle. What do you do?

What if there is no room in your vehicle and they want to pile into someone else's? Do you leave your firearm in your vehicle and go to lunch? Do you take the risk that no one will rob the place where you'll be eating? Does your magic eight ball tell you the future so you know what places to avoid? Will you have to bite the bullet on this one? What I have done in the past are a couple of things that have helped, depending on what vehicle is being taken.

If we are all leaving in my car to go eat, I would excuse myself from the hospital room and ask people to give me a five minutes head start to clean out the front/back seat of my car so I can put my stuff in the trunk. This gives me time to sit in my car, look around several times so no one sees me and re-holster my sidearm from my gun safe. Or if I will be riding in another vehicle, I excuse myself and tell my party that I have to grab my wallet from my car. Then I will get in my car and grab my sidearm from out of the safe.

I can walk back to their vehicle or have them come by and pick me up. When I get back to the hospital, I can lock it up again in my car on the street. I just tell them that I have to put something back into my car and walk back to it and lock up my firearm. If people are inside my vehicle because we had lunch together, I just tell them that I will meet them in the hospital room while I make a private call (this is when they leave and I can lock up my firearm in the safe again). I think you get the idea here.

You're going to run into gun-free zones where you cannot legally carry and that's going to drive you crazy. And you're going to have to be prepared and think quickly on your feet. You're going to need to know the laws also. Can you have a locked firearm on hospital property or parking lot? What if it's a church? Are you visiting an area owned by the Army Corp of Engineers? They don't allow firearms on their property either. Know the laws in those states you'll be carrying. A friend of mine told me in his state that when concealed carry became available, local newspapers went wild and cried that it would be like the old west in the streets. Many years later, it still hasn't happened. But many small businesses were educated along the way that a gun free zone made them a target for violent crimes. So many smart business owners removed those "gun-free zone" signs.

Please respect those establishments who still have those signs posted. It is their prerogative to post those signs. In some states these signs are not enforceable by law. It depends on the local laws. You can't avoid all gun-free zones. Things are slowly changing where people are realizing that the bad people (predators) are the problem and not the people who carry to defend themselves. They're slowly understanding that removing the gun-free zone sign invites those who carry concealed into their establishment and it helps reduce violent crime in their business.

Store owners with these "No Guns" signs (enforceable by law in some states) are losing money to those who carry concealed since they refuse to shop in these places. These are dangerous places because they are inviting criminals and we don't want to put ourselves or family members in danger. Most concealed carriers have boycotted those stores, even if the law states they can carry in those "Gun-Free" zones. The ones that have removed their signs do get business by those who carry concealed. If you're a store owner and want to attract our business and eliminate or reduce robberies, put a pro concealed carry sign in the window. Like "Lawful Concealed Carry Welcomed", "Guns are Welcomed on Premises" and you'll find many more like these on the Internet that you can order.

It's a pain in the ass, but the law is the law and you have to respect gun-free zones. You don't have to like it, but you do have to follow it if it's the law in your state. Just come up with alternate plans if you have no choice and you have to visit. If a situation presents itself where you cannot be armed with a firearm, then there are other carry options like a knife, flashlight (some are called DNA collectors), tactical pen, pepper spray, etc. But you'll need training on these also. Having another type of object around you that can be used as a weapon may be your only option at times, but at least you have something to defend yourself.

Make these tools part of you every day carry (EDC). I carry a sidearm(s), spare ammo, a flashlight, a knife, a multi-tool in its pouch on my belt and a first-aid kit for gunshot wounds. At the end of this book, you'll be able to see my entire EDC.

CONCEALED CARRY CARD HOLDER FOR PERMIT

I have a wallet that has a small removable slide out for my credit cards. I use the wallet for money, credit cards and other items. This is kept in my pants pocket and I keep the slide out card holder separate from my wallet and in a different location. The slide out card holder enables me to hold a photo on one side (family photo) and on the other it holds credit cards. I use this small little pull out to put my driver's license, my conceal carry permits, along with my attorney's contact info. I also have a card that has a script on it that I can use to read to the police when I have to remove my weapon to defend myself. It basically says that I was attacked, I had to defend myself, I am willing to cooperate at 100%, you do not have permission to search my vehicle and that I would like to talk to my attorney.

My mini card-wallet holding my concealed carry permits and state ID.

What's really nice about it is that I can carry it separately from my wallet and I keep it in my shirt pocket or somewhere where it's easily accessible when I get pulled over by the police. I can quickly have it ready and present it to the peace officer in about a second, so I can inform them that I have a permit, that I am armed and that I will keep my hands on the steering wheel. It's a lot better than telling them that you are armed and then reaching for your wallet in your back pocket.

For the ladies, I would also suggest that you have a similar type of card holder. Keep it small, one that can carry your ID and permit(s) along with anything else you will need to show law enforcement, plus have your attorney's business card inside. Have this quickly accessible from your purse, or if you're carrying light that day, in another location that is away from your sidearm and at chest level (if possible due to having a pocket on your blouse) so there are no misunderstandings between you and the officer when you're reaching for it.

I also have photocopies of my ID and my permits. I keep these in my vehicles in case I forget my originals or if my originals were stolen off my person. The IDs are blown up by the photocopier so they are large and easy to read for law enforcement. Just in case your ID or wallet gets stolen by one of the criminals, you have something you can present if needed. I also carry a set inside my magazine holder. It has an ID pocket stitched into it and I can use this also if I am away from my vehicle.

CHAPTER EIGHT

Have Gun Will Travel

*"Thou canst not travel on the path
before thou has become the path itself"*

Helena Petrovna Blavatsky

TENTS, NATURE, & FIREARMS

So you're going on a camping trip to experience the great outdoors, being one with nature, having fun with friends, family, or maybe you've decided to do it alone. When heading out into the wild, you're going to need your firearm, hence the word "wild". When I go camping, I continue to conceal my firearm. I never know who or what I'll bump into while in the woods (human or animal) and having secrecy on my side is paramount in case someone wants to harm me.

I live in the city, there's a stretch of land that has been preserved and it's around 1000 acres. It's used as a public nature park. It has wild animals, forests, lakes, hiking trails, etc. Just two years ago, a hiker accidentally found a body of a missing man who disappeared just 6 months earlier and it was hidden in the woods. Police say that he was murdered. Like I said, this is a public park, it's very beautiful and you never know who you'll bump into. Nothing like this has ever happened before in this city.

My every day carrying routine can also be adopted for camping. I will have my holster, an extra magazine on the belt, multi-tool, knife, medical kit and flashlight. Only difference is that I bring along a floppy pocket holster that I keep in the tent when I sleep. I carry IWB (Inside the Waistband) since with the many activities I do (hiking, canoeing, carrying my canoe through portages and some lite climbing), there are less objects that get in the way of my sidearm. Especially walking through thick woods, the branches aren't hitting it or possibly lifting it out of my holster since half of it is in my pants and under my shirt. The disadvantage is with backpacks. Having an IWB makes it a little harder to get to your weapon. Depending on the type of pack you're carrying, mine gets in the way of my sidearm and it's difficult to get to.

Depending on the type of OWB (Outside the Waistband) you're using, the pack may still get in the way. There are all different types of OWB and backpacks. The type you have may give you easy access or create a challenge. If you have the type of holster that straps to your leg, then you have easier access to your firearm. But you risk the chance of others seeing it, unless you're in an area that you have a very slim chance of bumping into anyone.

My holster is configurable so it can be an IWB or OWB. This flexibility will enable me to adapt for that day on what activities I will do. The only problem with this is that I have to have tools to make the change (screwdrivers) and I can't predict what activity I will do that day unless I plan for it and think ahead. But you never know what's going to happen. There are many holsters that are out there and you might find one that can quickly be modified without tools and can be switched between IWB and OWB on the fly. But you may end up carrying extra pieces for that holster. If you can't find one like this right now, I am sure one of these days someone will invent one.

There are several options to choose from depending on what type of adventure you're going on. If you will be climbing up a face of a cliff or rafting down rapids, you obviously want a higher retention level for your holster. You don't want to lose your firearm while you're climbing or if your water craft flips over.

There are also possibilities of meeting a dangerous wild animal, like a bear, cougar, bobcat, bison, alligator, deer, wolverine, boars, etc., while walking about. Some people have a firearm strapped across their chest for easy access while hiking with a pack, others may carry appendix style, but that depends on your frame, body size and how high your leg will be rising on the path when you are hiking. Or you can put a holster in your pocket and carry your firearm there.

Before you head out to the woods, wear your backpack at home, make any changes necessary so you can quickly and easily access your firearm. Don't find out while camping that the position you chose for your firearm doesn't work for you and your gear. Take care of this at home first or you might end up suffering from this mistake later on during your trip.

Depending if you're in a state park, you'll probably be bumping into people on the path and sometimes you'll see the state park rangers. While walking, I just want to blend in, I don't want to gain any attention to myself, plus I don't know who these people are that I bump into, their intention, especially if they see me toting a firearm. They could be wanted for all I know or disagree about me carrying a firearm and decide they want to do something about it. I continue to wear a shirt that hangs down and over my sidearm to keep it concealed.

Bathroom and the great outdoors.

When I am about to go to bed in a sleeping bag, I will remove my firearm from my holster since I don't want any accidental discharges happening if my sidearm slides out and the trigger gets pulled while I am sleeping. Plus rolling over on your firearm is very uncomfortable. My holster is comfortable enough to sleep in, so this stays on. Why? Just in case I have to go to the bathroom in the middle of the night. I don't want to fumble with putting on the IWB/OWB on again in the dark. Yes, I sleep in my clothes. You never know when there could be an emergency and you have to get out right away. I don't want to be running around the woods naked and defenseless.

On my Glock, I have Trijicon sights (Tritium gas lamps that glow on their own for up to a decade or more). Since they produce their own light, I can see my firearm while I am sleeping and I don't have to rummage through things near my sleeping bag in trying to find it. It glows in the darkness, all night long and very visible in case I have to grab it. When it's in the floppy holster, I can see the rear sights glowing. And I always keep a round in the chamber in case something happens.

I'll pull out my firearm from my floppy holster and put it back into my waist holster before I exit the tent. If your holster is not comfortable enough to sleep in and you need to leave the tent, then take the firearm that's inside the floppy holster and put it in your pants pocket before you go outside in the dark. And of course have your flashlight ready to be taken with you. When I am outside walking in the dark, I keep my ears open and I sweep the area with my flashlight looking for animals. When I am squatting, doing my business, the same thing.

Now, it's going to be tricky with a sidearm while going to the bathroom while sitting or squatting. A flashlight in one hand, a firearm down to your ankles. If I am carrying the firearm in my IWB/OWB, I will remove it and place it inside my floppy holster, but keep it real close to me while sitting/squatting. I might even have it laying on the crotch inside of my pants. It all depends on the situation. I will do occasional sweeps with my flashlight, especially if I hear sounds near me. Remember, animals can see in the dark, we can't. So keeping that light on is real important. My flashlight has three colors. Red, white and purple for tracking blood in the dark (great for hunters tracking animals that are bleeding).

I did a test while camping. I slept with my firearm in the sleeping bag (without it being loaded) and I noticed that it does get jostled around if you're not a light sleeper. It's also really uncomfortable if you switch from your back or stomach to your hip side with the firearm on it. Plus if I needed to draw, I have to fish for it in the bag (if it gets loose), plus my motor skills are diminished from limited arm movement in the bag. Getting on target within seconds would be next to impossible.

I have asked others where they put their weapon and some say they just put it under their pillow and sleep on it. For me, I am a restless sleeper, so I would be tossing and turning and always adjusting my pillow. This would not work for me and I am very cautious and literally scared to put a loaded firearm under my head. I feel better if I keep it above my head and able to grab it. I recommend while sleeping in a tent, to keep your sidearm as far away from the tent door as possible. This will prevent people from quietly opening up the tent door, rummaging through your stuff and stealing your weapon within their arms reach while you're sleeping.

I will put my sidearm into my floppy pocket holster (outside the sleeping bag) and it will be close to me. And I don't have to worry about an accidental discharge since the trigger is covered by the holster. I will have it in a place where I can quickly retrieve it. I like to sleep in the center of the tent and my feet facing the door. If there is an attack on any sides of the tent (like a wild animal), I will be in the middle and will be able to aim at any of the sides of the tent.

If something or someone is trying to get into my tent in the dead of night, I'll have a round in the chamber and my hand on the gun in less than a second. Every millisecond counts. If they enter from the zippered doorway, you can always put a small jingle bell on it, which would alert you. You may want to practice at home with your weapon unloaded while inside a sleeping bag to find the best way to access and draw your firearm before you go camping. There are so many types of sleeping bags out there in how they wrap around your body.

I have heard of others who drag their gun safe with them (especially when children are around) when they go camping, but lugging a heavy safe is not my idea of fun. Some good safes can be 15 lbs. or more. If you do decide to bring a safe, make sure it is very lite and with quick access and lockable to keep the youngsters out. Make sure you can open it up in the dead of night with no lights.

If I am with a group of adults, I use a waterproof box with locking hinges on it. It keeps it nice and secure (not secure from children) and if it rains really hard and there's a lot of moisture in the air, it will keep my weapon dry. It's actually a fishing tackle box for lures, but it works really well for my sidearm. I even customized it with foam and it's outlined to hold my firearm. I have also spray painted the inside so no one can see the contents. It just looks like a regular tackle box. So it fits perfectly and won't rattle around.

Have fun and a safe camping trip!

PLANO clear waterproof fishing tackle case.
Spray painted gold inside to hide contents.
Holds one Glock and three magazines.

AIRLINE TRAVELING & DECLARING A FIREARM

There might be a point in your life where you'll need to fly to another state, hopefully one that accepts you carrying a concealed firearm. Before you travel, make sure you know the laws of that state for carrying a firearm; including the type of ammo that is legal, if there is a limit for magazine rounds, if the type of firearm you carry is allowed and if the permit you have is legal there. I will only discuss about the United States and airline travel and not overseas since these are constantly changing and there are too many countries to list. These are just the basics for traveling in the US.

Several days before you head out to the airport, make sure you're prepared for your flight when it comes to your firearm. You don't want to do this at the last minute and forget something important or be unaware of a law that you might be breaking. You're also going to have to visit the TSA and airline(s) website to print the regulations for traveling with a firearm. Each airlines have their own policies. So if you're using different airlines to travel, you'll have to read up on them. Keep copies of the regulations from these websites for that particular airline(s) you will be flying with. This will eliminate any confusion with the TSA agent, since they may be going through your stuff. It's unfortunate, but some of your TSA agents will not be educated around the laws and rules. So you may end up pulling out your copy and showing it to them to help clarify their misunderstanding.

You'll also want to write down the serial number, make, type and model of the firearm(s). This will help you if your firearm is lost, stolen, or misplaced. I keep photos on my phone showing the serial numbers. If there are also accessories, have those included on your list with the serial numbers. I also have the value of each item just in case it gets lost or stolen. They may also ask what kind of ammo you have and how many rounds. There are rules with airlines on how much ammo you can have and how it's packed.

There are also rules on how you will be transporting your firearm. Usually it's going to be in a hard case with a lock on it, but double-check with the airlines and TSA. I put my sidearms inside a pelican case and include plastic zip ties. The plastic zip ties are a little longer than the length of my barrel. It is also a bright neon color. The zip tie is inserted into the barrel and out my ejector port.

Firearm with zip tie through the barrel.

You can do the same thing for a revolver. Just put it through the barrel and out the cylinder. Just in case your stuff gets searched, this visual inspection shows the TSA agent that there is no ammo in the barrel. I also have a lock around the trigger for extra precautions. When the TSA agent sees it, they know that it won't fire. So visually to them, it looks unloaded and can't be fired. The case is going to go inside your checked bags. DO NOT put your firearm in your carry on. You will be arrested at the TSA checkpoint. In the United States, during the first eight months of 2016, TSA had discovered more than 2,150 firearms in passengers' carry-ons during their routine screening at security checkpoints. That's a lot of mistakes, ones that come with a very unforgiving penalty.

Once you arrive at the airport, I would recommend being the first one in line at the ticket counter, since you will be talking to the airline agent and informing them that you are declaring a firearm. DO NOT take your firearm to the TSA checkpoint, you will be arrested. Also do no declare your firearm with the baggage people at the curb outside the airport. These are not the right people to check your firearm.

When you're at the ticketing counter, you are NOT going to tell them that you have a gun. State the following, "I want to declare an <u>unloaded</u> firearm". Use these exact words so the ticket agent doesn't freak out. Say it in a voice that will not carry outside your conversation between you and the agent. You want to avoid the other passengers from freaking out as well because you have a gun. You don't want more attention to yourself at this point. Plus you don't want to put a target on your back and have someone try to take that firearm away from you after you land at your destination.

You will be given a tag to fill out declaring that the firearm is unloaded and you will have to date and sign it. This will be attached to the hard case in which your firearm is locked in. Here is an example of what it may say:

I declare as required by federal air regulation 108.11, that the firearm in my luggage is unloaded and my luggage does not have more than 12 pounds of ammunition per firearm transported. Furthermore, the luggage containing the declared firearm(s) is locked and I alone am in possession of the key or combination.

Statements like the one above will vary per airline.

The ticketing agent is not allowed to touch your firearm. They will ask if it's unloaded, but will not check it. Make sure your firearm is unloaded, packed, the case is locked and follow the rules of the airlines. Stay with your firearm until it is checked in by TSA or until it is taken by the agent and put on the conveyor or through the scanner.

Some airports are changing policies to make sure there is added security to checking in and out your firearm. This is due to the airport shooting in Florida, by the guy who took his declared firearm, went into the bathroom and came out shooting. Make sure you follow the lead of TSA or the airline agent.

Make sure your gun case has a lock on it that ONLY YOU have the key. I have a range bag that will hold a pelican case for my sidearm(s). The pelican case has two holes so that I can put my own locks on it and I have the only keys for it. I will put it in my range bag and put an additional lock on the zipper where the firearm is stowed. This would be a TSA approved lock. These are not going to stop anyone from breaking in, that's why you have a very solid lock on your hard case. I would recommend you have some extra TSA locks since I have heard complaints from others that the locks are cheap Chinese quality and they sometimes break, or after you set the combination you cannot unlock it, so keep some spares in case they are broken.

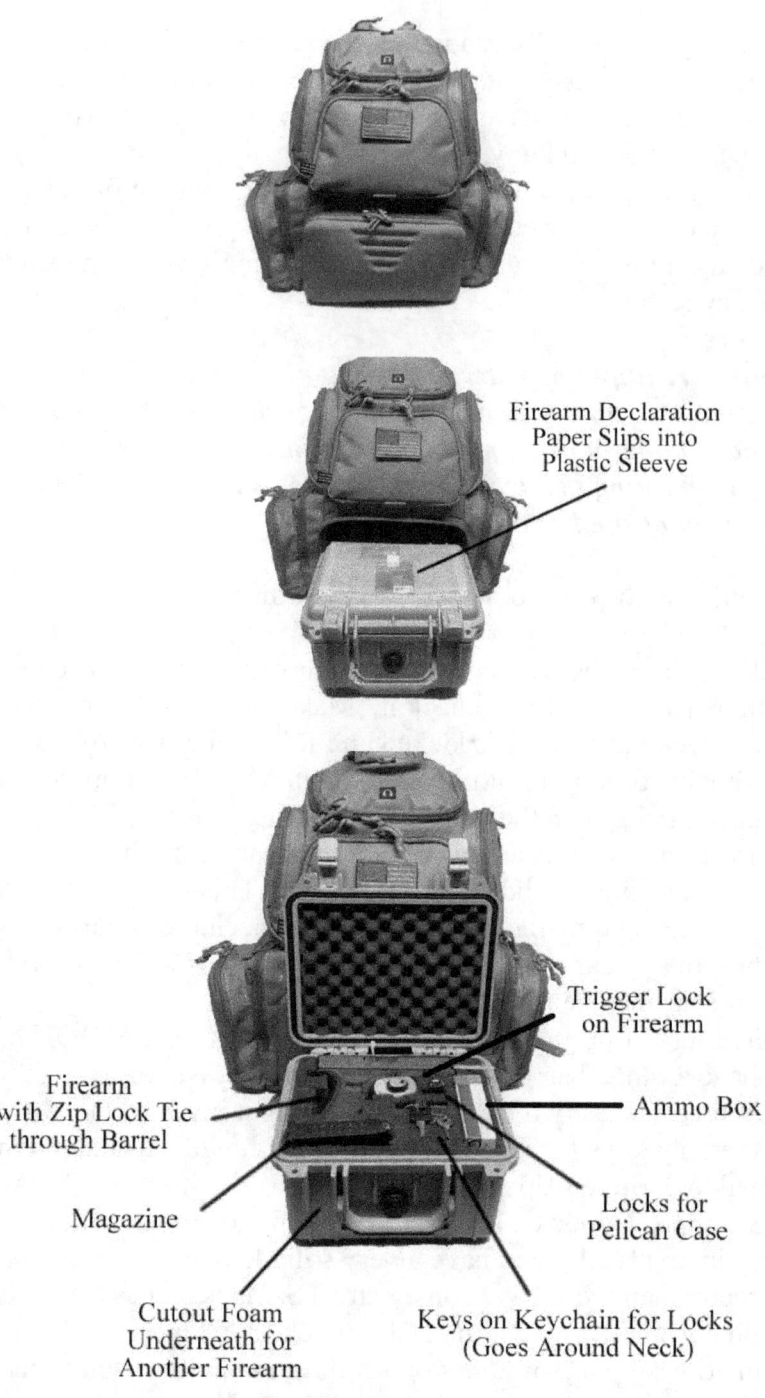

Range bag with Pelican Case ready for airport travel.

Having these TSA approved locks enables the agent to inspect your gear without cutting these locks. They have their own master key to the TSA approved locks. I have two types of locks. The TSA lock for the zipper on the range bag so they can get access inside to see my hard case and a nice solid lock on my case where I am the only one who has a key.

I prefer the TSA locks that have an indicator on them which will inform me if they unlocked it and tried to gain access to the inside of my range bag. I also attach my declaration to my pelican case (which I put a plastic sleeve on it to hold the paperwork). So when they open up my range bag, they will see the case and the paperwork attached to it. So they know right away that it was checked in. TSA may cut the locks on your case (so have some spare for the return trip), but with that declaration tag, this rarely happens.

If your flight is diverted and you land in another state, laws may prohibit you from removing your firearm from the airport. You may get arrested for illegal carrying. If this happens, make sure your firearm is with the airlines (it's in their possession). If you decide to leave the airport and take an alternative way to travel (like a car rental) because you have to be at your destination by a certain time, have the airlines ship your firearm to the original airport of destination and pick it up there. You don't want to end up behind bars on your trip.

If you'll be using connected flights, make sure that the state you will be connecting accepts your concealed carry permit. If for example you connect in New York and your plane was late or cancelled, you will get arrested if you take possession of your baggage with a firearm in it. New York has very strict laws. Avoid those states that you will be landing in (either connecting or just visiting) that do not recognize you carrying a firearm (or does not recognize your permit to carry). Hit the Internet and read stories about people who have been arrested at the airport with a firearm and they have a permit to legally carry, but it's not valid for that state. Reading their stories will prepare you on what not to do.

BOATING & CARRYING

Some states do not allow firearms on boats. You'll have to visit your states website for updated information. There may be county and city laws that may be different from the state law. Research this. If you have any questions, you may have to talk to an attorney.

If you'll be armed and boating in international waters, there are federal laws that you need to educate yourself on. When you arrive in different non-US ports, you will have to research about the laws of that port of call.

If law enforcement pulls you over in your boat and if firearm permits are required in that state, get your IDs out immediately, stop the motor and drop anchor. Don't have your ID and permit near your sidearm. If you're reaching for your wallet in your pockets and your sidearm is seen, it could be mistaken as if you're going for your weapon.

Always have your ID and permit in a location that is accessible within seconds. I keep mine about chest level. If life vests are being worn, very few of these have a pocket to hold an ID. But having a shirt/blouse with a pocket worn behind the vest with your IDs would be one of your best options. The type of life vest that you may be wearing could also get in the way of your firearm if you are carrying concealed (something to think about). Remember, if you're on a small boat, there is no cover and every movement can be seen by the officer. So don't make any moves that can be interpreted as hostile.

Some boat owners have a holster attached somewhere near the steering wheel with their sidearm in it for easy access. Keeping this hidden from the general public is key in not having someone calling the authorities, even if it's completely legal on your part. People are people and if they see something out of the norm, they don't mind calling the police.

Depending on your state and the laws, law enforcement may be able to board your vessel without a search warrant. It doesn't make sense, but if they believe there are probable cause, they will board your craft. No matter if you are boarded or not, if anyone on the watercraft is carrying, inform the officer. As usual, keep your hands in a position of being non-threatening. Just sit down, cross your arms, smile and wait for instructions from the officer. It's not going to be too much different then driving a car and getting pulled over, except the officer would be in another boat next to yours or inside your watercraft.

Depending on the size of your vessel and the number of people you have, you will have to get everyone onboard assembled together in the same area in view of the officer(s). Not much problem here with a small fishing boat. Inform your passengers to keep their hands in view and wait for instructions from the officer. If any of your passengers carry, they will have to have their ID and permit (if required) ready before being boarded.

I understand that some states say that you do not have to show your permit if you get pulled over, but as a courtesy and for safety reasons for both parties, inform them. This includes all parties on the watercraft.

I love to fish and I have had some great opportunities to do so on the ocean, rivers and many lakes throughout the United States. On the river and some of these lakes, it can get crowded and there are those who like to drink and enjoy boating. Some people like to congregate their watercraft in areas where they like to party, like on a sandbar, an island, or a popular shoreline. These parties can be fun, but since I carry, I don't drink. If it gets out of control, I will leave. But with drunks, things can happen and these people are unpredictable. They may even be armed. Make sure you have your cell phone with you just in case you need to call 911 if an incident is about to happen or your forced to use your firearm in self-defense. Be the first one to make the call and if there is a medical emergency, make sure you have them send the paramedics.

Happy Boating!!!

CHAPTER NINE

At Home

"To accept some idea of truth without experiencing it is like a painting of a cake on paper which you cannot eat."

Suzuki Roshi

IN THE BATHROOM

When you're carrying, there will be a time when you will have to use either a public or private bathroom. In public, you don't want your defenses down, especially when your pants are around your ankles. Same thing for home. You can never know these days, people can really surprise you. Let's say that you're at home, in the bathroom and someone entered your home undetected (unless you have your alarm system on 24x7). Your sitting on the throne, text messaging on your phone, some stranger walks in and surprises you. That's frightening. There's not going to be much difference in an ambush when carrying while in a public bathroom, a friend's bathroom, or your own.

If I am in a public bathroom (gas station, highway rest stop, grocery store, shopping mall, etc.), I'll take the furthest stall from the entrance. This gives me distance from the entrance. In doing so, this can add a few seconds to my time if I need to prepare, just in case something is about to happen. If there's suspicious activity outside the door stall, I can have my sidearm ready in my hands and wait.

I wear my firearm on my belt. When I am sitting in a bathroom stall, with my pants down, I keep my sidearm at knee level. I am able draw it and point it at the door within a second if needed. Try to keep your pants/skirt belt-line above the knees. If your holster is at the 3-4:00 or the 8-9:00 position and it's canted, keep your belt near the knees while sitting, you'll notice that your gun is accessible and at a decent angle.

If you carry appendix style and there is no clip on the holster, you can lay it in the crotch of your underpants. If you have a belt clip for your appendix holster, it would stay where it's at. If you carry in the 5-7 o'clock position area (behind your back), you may be at the best angle to reach for it, if not, just lay it in the crotch area of your underpants (with a floppy holster protecting the trigger). Since floppy holsters are so easy to tuck away, plus they are flexible, I usually carry one in my back pocket. Or if you wear pants with many pockets, you'll be able to store it anywhere. If the weather is cooler, a jacket will do.

After I do my business and there is no activity outside my stall, with my sidearm at my hip, I'll pull up my underpants (trying not to snag the grip of my firearm while pulling them up) and then I slowly pull up my pants. Rushing may push the gun out of your holster and it could hit the floor. So you want to be extra careful here in not discharging your firearm (accidentally hitting the trigger with your finger if your sidearm gets lose outside of your holster).

If you have a gun belt, you'll want to double-check your holster clips to make sure they didn't get out of place or slip off before you buckle up. Sometimes it does shift. I've had this happen to me a few times where my sidearm is just hanging and I didn't even notice. It felt funny on my side (a clue) and I noticed that the clips were popped off the belt. So I had to disappear back into the bathroom again to fix the problem. Make sure everything is secure before you leave the bathroom.

I'd rather take the handicap stall since it has more room. It will give me more space to move around and not be boxed in or trapped in a smaller space with limited movement. I know we all don't want to be caught with our pants down, but if someone decides to kick in the door, you'll be ready to defend yourself with equal force.

As mentioned before, while seated and your sidearm is laying in your underpants, please make sure the muzzle is facing away from you and towards the stall door. You can still pull the trigger, just angle up the muzzle in your pants to get hits in the pelvic girdle or higher. Yes, you can fire through your pants. If you're going commando, you will have to put your jacket (depends on the season) inside your pants and place your sidearm inside so it will hold and not fall and hit the ground. But this all depends on what you're wearing for the weather that day. I'll wear a jean jacket sometimes in the summer (depending on the heat index), or a rain jacket if it's raining. If you wear a skirt with no panties, then a light jacket will do. You'll have to be creative in this area.

Do not squeeze your legs together while seated and try to hold your sidearm there, because it may slip and drop out onto the floor. This could also be disastrous if it discharges (when you're fumbling with it), or the person in the next stall may see it or decide to grab it.

If you have your sidearm at the 5-7:00 position, you don't want to drop it in the toilet while you drop your drawers, so keep this in the back of your mind. That's how most cell phones fall in. Move a few inches in front of the toilet, work on what you have to do to drop your pants/skirt (unbuttoning/unbuckling). Then slowly drop your pants/skirt. Then step back a few inches towards the toilet and sit down (or hover). This is a good idea in case your sidearm is loose in your holster so it won't bounce out and drop in the toilet.

Some people may be using an appendix style holster located at their backside. You'll have to remove your firearm, remove the holster, put them back together again and place it in your pants pocket (make sure there are no other objects in your pocket), then drop your drawers. When you sit down, you can keep it in the pocket or move it to the crotch area of your underpants.

I've heard of someone using a lanyard around their neck, but I would be worrisome on where on the firearm it would attach to (hopefully not on the trigger guard) and if you're able to fire it while attached to your neck. They may have a spare pocket holster with them and somehow have a key ring on it to attach to the lanyard. I have not tried this, so I am not sure if this works or not. All I know is that I just try not to go commando and use my undergarments as a shelf for my pistol if necessary. This seems to be the easiest way.

For women who are not wearing a belt, they would most likely have it in their bra, in their bellyband, in a shoulder holster, strapped to their leg or in their purse. These will obviously work while business is getting done without any special tricks. Keep your purse near you and ready to go if your firearm is needed.

When I am in the bathroom at home and the little ones barge through the door, I have my underwear over my sidearm (which is at ankle level) so there's no spark of curiosity from them since they do not see it.

If you're in a stall and you have a gun strapped to your ankle, make sure no one can see it while you're seated on the throne. You don't want someone calling the authorities and you have to explain yourself. Also never hang your gun from the hook of the door stall. I have heard of people doing this. If the stall door gets kicked in, you're screwed. If you put it in your jacket and hang it on the hook, it will take longer to get to it or if the door is kicked in, your luck just ran out. Sometimes crooks will reach over the door stall and grab your jacket off the hook.

If you're in a stall where people can see you through the door slits and if you carry in the 9 or 3 o'clock position, then take your underwear and pull it over your sidearm. This will prevent those who are curious, especially the bad people from seeing it and wanting it.

Never let your sidearm away from your body. Don't put it on the toilet paper holder, behind you on the toilet, on the baby changing station, or the handicap metal bar. I would not recommend this. Some people have left their firearms in these places. When they come back it's gone. Seriously, this does happen. You don't want the next person to be a child who enters that stall and finds your gun. I don't want to imagine what would happen after that. I shudder at the thought. Believe me, this does happen, especially when the mindset starts treating the sidearm like a set of car keys and it accidentally gets set down somewhere and forgotten. Don't get into this habit. It could be detrimental. Keep it on your person at all times, even while in the bathroom stall. Keep it concealed and out of sight while sitting on the porcelain thrown.

I've heard of people using a shopping bag, or some other item to hide their weapon and place it on the floor in the public bathroom. If you have items in a shopping bag, briefcase or purse and place it on the floor, watch it go bye-bye. Thieves will grab it in a heartbeat if they see something of value and it's easily accessible. They will take it and by the time you have your pants/skirt on and out the stall door, they will be gone. Then you'll have to call the police and explain what happened.

When you are done with your business and want to stand up, depending on the weight of your sidearm, it becomes difficult to keep your pants up while you're trying to fasten your belt and zip your fly. What I do is lean my back up against the wall (at home or in a stall), pull up my pants, lean my butt up against the wall and this will hold my pants up. Now I fasten my gun belt and zip my fly. I have found this to be one of the easiest ways to get my belt fastened with all the weight on it.

When you're carrying your EDC (Every Day Carry) equipment, it adds weight. Holster, sidearm, extra magazine and holder, extra firearm, knife, keys, wallet, money, cell phone, extra tools (like a multi-tool) and anything else you may carry. All of this does add weight and trying to pull it up and fasten your pants becomes a challenge. Just lean up against a wall, pull your pants up and fasten your belt. Now you're good to go.

URINALS

For those who need to use the urinal, you're going to run into some problems. If you can just use your fly to use the urinal, that's fine. But for some of us, depending on what we're wearing, we need to unbuckle our belts and make some adjustments. I don't use the urinals anymore when I am carrying. I am armed and if someone discovers I am carrying, they can easily come up behind me and disarm me. If you want to do situational awareness at the urinal, you may get some strange looks from the guys next to you while you're looking at them. This could make them nervous or start a conversation that may make you uncomfortable and I am sure that you just don't want to go there.

When armed, even though I just have to pee, I grab a stall and sit down and urinate. Or hover like most women (some of those bathroom are really disgusting). You have a lot of weight if you're carrying on your belt and gravity will pull your pants down at a urinal if you decide to unzip the fly and unbutton the pants. The advantage of using the stall is that your back is against the wall, the door is in front of you and you can easily draw if someone decides to come through that stall door. Just standing in a stall urinating with the door behind you can easily turn into a situation if someone wants to kick the door in and your backside is facing it. You'll never know what hit you.

IN THE SHOWER

You never know where life and circumstances will take you, especially in places where you never would have imagined you would be. I've learned that what goes on in the mind of planning things out, about 99% of the time, it never happens exactly as the way you plan it. Let's say you're traveling by car and it breaks down in a place you would have never imagined, like bum-chuck Egypt. It will take about a day or so to repair your vehicle.

You found a place to stay, it's the only motel in town and it looks pretty seedy. You check in, your room is on the first floor and the door is on the outside of the building facing the parking lot. You take your key, unlock the door and you notice that it has been repaired due to someone kicking it in. You look in the room and it's very tiny. It's a very hot day (around 100 degrees), you turn on the AC and a funky smell of vomit comes out of it, the bed is right next to the door (only a few feet away) and the AC unit is at the edge of the bed. When you go to use the bathroom, the toilet is so close to the bathtub that you have to put your feet in the tub since there is no room to put them in front of you on the floor. You get a gut feeling that this is not a very safe place to be but your choices are very limited.

Oh, I forgot to mention the very busy bar across the parking lot with drunk people staggering around looking for their vehicles and yelling at each other? The whole place just says "Go Away" all over, but unfortunately you're stuck there. Well, something very similar to this happened to me one year while traveling across America.

In that motel, I never slept under the covers that night. I kept my clothes on, laid on top of those covers, put myself in the bed in a position furthest away from the door with my back up against the wall and kept one eye opened the entire night. I think I also had a tire-iron next to me to keep me company. With the temperatures exceeding 100 degrees outside, I was stuck with the AC being on with that nasty smell. So in this kind of situation you have to come up with a game plan. From getting out of bed to using the bathroom and taking a shower. Also planning scenarios in your head if someone comes through that front door.

So in a place like this, how do you take a shower? The main important thing here is to keep your weapon dry, accessible and hope that with soap in your hands that your firearm doesn't slip out of your hands. Having non-slip grips may help you if your hands are wet, but you'll have to get creative like MacGyver in finding things you have in your environment to remove the disadvantages. For example, in this hotel you could take your pants, tie the belt around the shower curtain rod and adjust it so you can grab your weapon if someone decides to break into the room. Keep a dry towel handy on the pants so that if you have soap in your face or hands, you can quickly dry them and grab your firearm. Or if there is a shower cap, you can try covering it to keep it dry. These may not be the best ideas, since your belt and gun may get wet, but if it's the only option, go for it. You may come up with other ideas depending on what's available around you.

At home I keep my sidearm on the end of my sink, inside a flimsy holster (which covers the trigger) near the shower door, with my flashlight clipped to the holster. Why the flashlight? Just in case the power goes out or someone flips the light switch to the off position. Then I will be able to see in the dark.

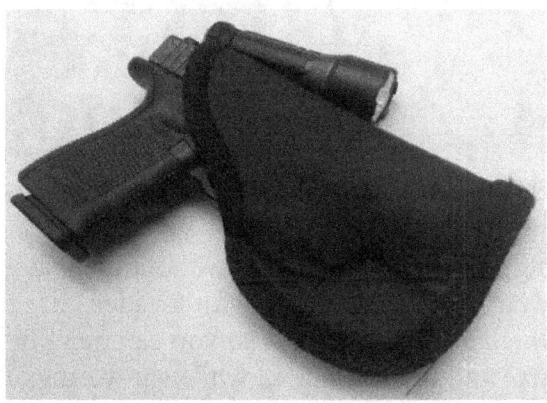

Floppy Holster with Tactical Light Clipped onto it.

If there is a prowler in the house while you're in the shower, don't try to shoot through the shower door if it's glass. You'll end up walking barefoot on the broken glass. You can just wear flip flops in the shower in case you have to shoot through the glass door. I also have my clothes on top of my firearm (but only showing the grip of the gun towards me so I can grab it) just in case a prowler comes into the bathroom.

Because of the clothes on top of the firearm and the position of my pistol relative to the door, they won't see it and use it against me. It just looks like a lump of dirty clothes with dirty underwear on top of it. Thieves won't touch that.

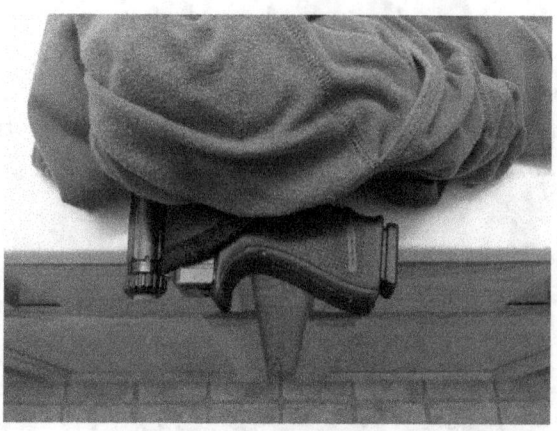
Clothes Hiding Firearm on Countertop in Bathroom Facing Away from Door.

Try practicing in your own shower (without the water and no ammo) and see what you can come up with for ideas of retrieving your sidearm. Like which areas are closest so you can quickly and easily access your firearm and the driest area while showering, etc. You may just want to put spare flip flops in the shower just in case you have to shoot through the glass.

Remember, the shower at the hotel/motel may be completely different than yours at home, so you will have to scope out some options when you get there. For at home, you may end up putting a small shelf above the shower line (opposite of the shower head) that would be easy access for you and dry for your firearm. Put a plant next to it to conceal it. It may even brighten up the place. You can even put up a holster that is plastic and not reachable by water (the driest area in the shower) and have it mounted.

ALARMS AND SECURED DOORS

There are many choices for security systems and different ways to protect your home to alert you of an intruder. If you want to be like Fort Knox, you'll pay the cost for such a system. If you're on a tight budget, I have suggestion that can be affordable and will do the job that it was designed for. Some alarm systems are expensive and others are not. I'll provide you with some simple and effective ways that will signal criminals to go away and make things difficult for them.

What's important is that you have some sort of routine around your house when you do have a security system. Like turning your system back on when you get home. Most people will disable their alarms until they go to bed. Why not be alerted while you're somewhere in the house (bathroom, taking a shower, in the basement, etc.) and give yourself time to arm yourself if an intruder enters your dwelling. Why walk into an ambush? Ambushes happen in split-seconds, not minutes.

If you decide to go with a monitored alarm system, don't plant the brand name of your security system sign out in your yard. This tells the criminals about the type of system you have. This gives them the ability to research and learn how to disable your system. You can get a generic sign or use a competitor's sign so they will have the incorrect information or no information at all. Maybe swap signs with a neighbor from down the street (with their permission of course).

Also, most alarm systems have a default delay time of 15-30 seconds so you can log into your control panel when you get home and disable the system. Thieves will know this important detail. They can plan around that time, so they know how long they have to grab what they want and they can get a lot of high valued merchandise during that 15-30 second window before the alarm sounds. Plus your police could be 6-8 minutes away, or longer, which gives them a better advantage. Why not surprise them by setting it up with a shorter time than the default settings?

I also put up a "beware of dog" sign with a picture of a vicious dog on it. It's not the words that scare burglars, it's that image of a terrifying dog. I also put dog dishes out, one filled with water. I leave the other empty since I don't want to feed the rodents outside. I don't have a dog because the place I stay in does not allow them.

I also have a motion detector flood light. It goes off and on in the driveway when people drive by. There is also one in the back. If you can light the dark areas on the outside of your home (even the sides), this will deter people from entering your yard at night. Criminals will drive buy to find easy marks. Which do you think they would pick? A front lawn with no alarm sign, darken areas around the home, no dog sign and no evidence of a pooch? Or a house that says go away all over with all the previous mentioned seen from the road?

For lower windows of a home, put some real prickly bushes there. Something that will bite if someone tries to go through the bushes to get to the windows. There are also products on the market that will make your windows shatter proof. It's a film that you install on the inside of your windows. It can be used to protect windows during severe storms and those who are trying to break in. You can rev-up your search engine and put in the key words "*window security safety film*" to find products that will stop thieves from breaking into your house via the windows. Read the reviews on these to make sure you find something that will work for you.

If you're not able to afford a fancy alarm system, go out and buy a cheap one. I have gone to a local hardware store, bought alarms that can be attached to the door and they can give a doorbell sound and an alarm sound. They can be attached to sliding glass doors, regular doors and windows. We keep them on all the time when we are in the house and away from home. If we need to exit a door, we just flip the switch to disable the alarm, but the door chime (really loud) is still active. This alerts others in the house if someone walks in or out.

Can be added to doors, windows and sliding glass doors

We also have an adjustable door security bar that props up against the door knob and the other end has a rubber foot on the floor. For the main doors, we have both the security bar and the alarms. You can search online with the keywords of "*adjustable security bar for door*". We also use these for hotel rooms to keep people from kicking down the door. I have tried kicking down the door with one of these things and on the other side of the door, it will hardly budge. So if someone does happen to get through (which will take some time and alert the rest of us), the alarm will go off and either scare those breaking in, or if they choose to come inside, I will have already been alerted, armed and have 911 informed of my situation. For under $100, I have alarms on the doors, windows, sliding glass door and three steel security door bars.

You will have to get into a routine of arming and disarming, along with using the steel bars to protect yourself and your home. You will also have to have family members follow the same routine. I double-check everything before I go to bed each night just to make sure nothing was missed. It just takes that one time to forget and with Murphy's Law randomly visiting people, someone will be attempting to break in at that time.

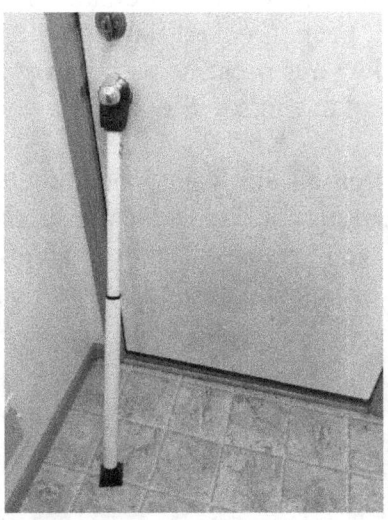

Adjustable security bar for door.

DO YOU KEEP YOUR FIREARM IN YOUR VEHICLE WHILE YOU'RE AT HOME?

I just saw a news article about a man who was sleeping in his bed (Huntsville, TX), someone broke into his home and he went outside to retrieve his firearm from his car.

Why would you leave your firearm in your vehicle while at home? Especially if you're sleeping. You shouldn't. You should have your sidearm with you…. Always! Vehicles can be stolen, they can be broken into and they can be towed. And if it's not within reach and your home is being broken into, you may never make it to your vehicle.

In this case, as soon as the guy woke up, he ran to his car and the two intruders were right behind him. He ended up killing one and wounding the other. Seconds count. If he was delayed by a few extra seconds getting to his car, or if he had his firearm locked up in it and fumbling in the dark trying to unlock the safe, he may not be alive to tell his story. I am sure in this case, he did not have his firearm locked up in his vehicle. That's being an irresponsible firearm owner.

Your sidearm should be with you at all times if you're going to use it for defensive purposes. It shouldn't' remain in your vehicle, especially if you don't keep it locked (lock on the handgun or in a safe). So if you're home, take your firearms with you and don't leave it up to chance. If this guy couldn't make it to his car, who knows what could have happened.

Be smart about firearms and your protection. Have your sidearm with you all the time, if permitted. In the above situation, he should have had it with him while he was sleeping, not outside in his car. This man is very lucky and I hope he has learned something valuable from this experience.

87 MINUTES AWAY

There was a very interesting story of a home invasion in Dallas, Texas. Instead of the average time of eight minutes for the police to reach this person's home, the nearest officer was 87 minutes away. The story starts out with this man lying in his bed and being awoken to a gun in his face after his wife left for the airport. They did not harm this individual, thank goodness, but they did rob his place and after 911 was called, the nearest officer was 87 minutes away. Let's think about this. Help is 87 minutes away, which is 1 hour and 27 minutes. So if a few minutes feels like eternity, how does almost an hour and a half fee like?

A lot can happen during this time when your life is threatened. Most people believe that if they need help by local police that they will be there within seconds. The reason why they were so late is due to shortage in staffing. This can happen anywhere and at any time, especially if a disaster happens where many other people are impacted.

I remember reviewing two 911 calls of a home invasion. The first 911 caller was a women who was scared for her life on the phone. She was telling the 911 operator that the person was coming up the stairs. She yelled at the intruder and told them that she had 911 on the phone and the police were on their way. The intruder didn't care and started breaking down the bedroom door. She kept telling the intruder that 911 was on the phone, thinking that this will scare the intruder and they would run away. Still, the door was still being kicked in. She was telling the 911 operator that they were still breaking into her bedroom and she sounded dumbfounded on the phone that this intruder wasn't listening to her and was continuing to break down her bedroom door.

The door finally gave way and the women started to scream and then the phone went dead. Now keep that in the back of your mind - 1 hour and 27 minutes (87 minutes) and someone breaking into your home and no police on their way. It doesn't matter if its 87 minutes or 1 minute, things happen very quickly. The 911 call was 1 minute and 30 seconds long.

The second 911 call was very similar, but our homeowner was armed. Same thing, an intruder breaking into the house, the homeowner on the phone with 911 describing what is happening, but in this instance, she told the operator that she was armed. The intruder broke into her bedroom and she fired shots. The intruder stopped. There were no screams and the phone did not go dead like the first 911 call, but instead there was a sigh of relief in her voice. I am not sure if he was dead, but the homeowner saved her life by defending herself and not becoming the victim. Who knows what could have happened if she was not armed. So if she had to wait those 87 minutes for help, she would have not had any problems since her attacker was stopped. This 911 call was 1 minute and 39 seconds long. Again, things happen so quickly.

So which person would you rather be in these 911 calls, the unarmed or armed individual?

On average, police arrive around 8 minutes, but that's still too much time. Police rarely prevent crimes, they're usually there after the fact. So a lot can happen in 8 minutes. The 911 recordings I listened to were an average of one and a half minutes. From the initial call to the end results. So that's 6.5 minutes left over before police arrive. That's scary.

With 87 minutes, I can accomplish any of the following in that amount of time:

- Get the kids, drive to the store with a list of 25 items, find them, put them in my cart, and get them bagged, drive back home.
- Go bowling by myself, using non-dominant hand. Complete around 2-3 games.
- Shoot over 2000 rounds at the range (including practice drills)
- Watch a movie on TV.
- Eat a thanksgiving dinner with relatives, turn on the TV, start watching a show, then pass out on the couch.
- Walk over 4.5 miles and not even break a sweat.

Now I hope your understanding that 87 minutes is a lot of time especially with a shortage of police officers. Police cannot be everywhere and your wait time may be longer if you live in a highly populated area. So if your house is broken into (you're armed) and you have successfully defended yourself without any life threatening injuries, then you can do any of the following items listed above or do something else until the police arrive. Hopefully they won't take over an hour, but as you know, seconds count, not minutes. A lot can happen in 1.5 minutes as heard in these 911 calls.

So always be armed and don't end up like one of the many people who call 911 and become victims in their own homes. You cannot rely on police being there within seconds or in a few minutes to protect you. This is your responsibility if its 1 minute or 87.

CHILDREN IN THE HOUSE

There's a time in your life where you won't have any children living with you. Maybe you're young and single, or have a relationship with someone, or possibly married. Your day to day routine includes you being armed, maybe you've been a concealed carrier for many years. Things begin to change as time progresses, then that day comes in your life where you're expecting a child. Either through adoption, your loved one is carrying a baby, or you're taking care of someone else's child until the parent(s) can get back on their feet again. Whatever the situation, you're going to have a child in your home. Congratulations!!!

Now what do you do? You obviously will have to childproof your entire home if you have a very young child. Whatever the age, or whenever you're taking care of these children in your life, things are going to have to change when it comes to firearms. It doesn't matter if you are expecting children to live with you, or you currently have kids and you just decided to conceal carry, you will either have to change your routine or form a new one.

If you're a veteran carrier, you're going to have to reprogram yourself to break some of the habits you've created and form new ones around the children and this can take several months to do. So start preparing. Also keep in the back of your mind that your kid(s) will also have friends coming over. Your child may be up on their firearm safety, but a visiting friend of theirs may not. So it's best to be safe for everyone instead of having a disaster on your hands.

If you're in the habit of putting your sidearm on a table when you get home, on your nightstand, on the kitchen countertop, or anywhere else, you'll have to stop doing this. The safest thing to do is carry that sidearm from the time you get up (taking it out of your gun safe) and holstering it, until you go to bed (putting it back into the safe). Start getting into this habit. The firearm you carry on your person will be safe from children since it's on you and not accessible.

If you have firearms that you don't carry with you, definitely keep those locked up and out of site. Kids are smarter than you think. They may act like they don't see things going on, but they do. They are probably more aware of what's going on around them then you are. They're very intelligent and they see things, so they can pretty much piece the clues together without any problem. If you think that they don't know you have a firearm, guess again, I bet they do and they probably know where you store it.

No matter if you have children or not, you will have to have a gun safe. You want one that is only accessibly by you and if necessary, by another responsible adult. Do your research on gun safes. When I was researching for the best type of safe for my own personal use, I found a YouTube video of a gentleman that tests gun safes. What I saw was that some safes are unsafe and this was very disturbing. This man tested well known portable gun safes to see how difficult it was for someone to get into them, even children. Criminals will also find these types of videos online to educate themselves on how they can access your safe. So before you buy, act like a criminal, go online and see if other people have discovered a way to hack into the gun safe your looking to purchase.

One way this guy tested these safes, he would use real life situations, like give it to his youngest child and ask them to get into it. With some of these safes, the child was able to open it up. Some within a few minutes. Some of these are well-known brand name gun safes that have the electronic push buttons (biometrics or keypad locks). I was shocked to see how these popular gun safes were opened by a toddler without even given them instructions. It makes me really wonder if some of these gun safe companies actually test their own products for the safety of children. But as you can see in these videos, they can easily be opened by a child.

I highly recommend the very thick and heavy safes with the non-electronic push buttons on the lid. Some start at 24 pounds. Find the ones with the push buttons to open the safe and a knob to unlock it. Some of these are extremely difficult to get into. Chances of getting into one of these is slim to none without the combination.

Non-electronic safe with manual keypad.

If a child can get into one of these portable safes, then your criminal element will also. What they do to get into these high tech safes is very low tech. They simply drop it on the floor, the lid pops open and the firearm falls out. Very scary. Search YouTube and you will be shocked as I was, especially with many of those top brand name safes.

Don't end up in a situation where you come home and the burglar already has your firearm because of a cheaply made safe or you just simply left your gun out. Gun owners have been killed by their weapon, in their own homes, when criminals get access to them. So basically, change your routine when you have children in your home.

Make sure firearms are locked up and not easily accessible and get your children trained on what to do if they see a firearm (outside, in your home, or at a friend's house). There are great training videos out there to teach children on what to do when they come across a firearm. It'll save their life someday or those around them. Research gun safes that you're interested in and find them on the Internet. See how easy or difficult to open one of these. This will give you piece of mind in knowing that you purchased a tested and reliable safe to keep children out.

CHAPTER TEN

Essentials

"Only when you can be extremely pliable and soft can you be extremely hard and strong."

Zen Proverb

WHAT IS SITUATIONAL AWARENESS?

You'll hear this all the time in the concealed carry world and it's something you must learn and use all the time, it's called Situational Awareness. It's a simple technique used to become more aware of what's going on in your surroundings. As a responsible armed citizen, this is extremely important since you're carrying a firearm. If you're attacked and you're not paying attention, you're attacker could find your firearm and use it against you. So keeping your head on a swivel is just as important as carrying a firearm. In the military, we were always taught to keep aware of our surroundings, especially when we visited other countries. Carrying a firearm or not, you should be using situational awareness all the time.

The late Colonel Jeff Cooper introduced the Cooper Color Code for situational awareness. I recommend learning more about the history of this man, he was ahead of his time when it came to personal self-defense. His color code system was created around one's state of mind and not around the combat mindset. He believed that a weapon or your martial skill set was not primary when it came to lethal confrontations, but basically your state of mind. He created this technique to help people prepare for confrontational situations and if possible, to avoid them. He came up with a color coded system to make things easier to move from one level of mindset to another and while you're at that level of alert, you'll know how to handle that situation.

There are four colors to remember (in this order). White, Yellow, Orange and Red.

White: This is the mindset of most people who are walking about these days. They are plugged into their electronic devices and completely unaware of their surroundings. These people are completely unprepared and can become a victim and lose their life. This is the level that most of your criminals look for in ambushing. In this level of awareness, the victim would be ill-prepared if something happens to them.

Yellow: You should <u>always</u> be in yellow condition while carrying a firearm or not. This level is a relaxed level where there is no apparent threat, but you remain alert to what's going on around you. Your life may be in danger and you may have to do something about it. This is when you're aware of your surroundings, you have a mindset that something could happen, and you are alert in unfamiliar territory amongst people you don't know.

Orange: Something has your attention, the situation doesn't feel right and you've got the gut feeling that something may escalate. You turn your focus on whatever is going on, trying to determine if there is a real threat. Your mindset has changed from relaxed to "something is about to go down". You're looking around and trying to piece together if something is going to happen where there is a potential threat and you're prepared to unholster your firearm. This level can be a bit stressful, your adrenaline may start pumping through your body and you start playing the "what if" in your mind. You are looking for exits to escape this threat and if there are none, you are prepared since you're in this state of mind. You're ready to take action, but you're not in lethal mode yet. You can stay in this alert level for a while and if nothing proves to be a threat, you can change your mindset back to condition yellow.

Red: This is when things are going to go sideways. You're in fighting mode and this is when you're taking certain actions in defending yourself. At this point, you have already made the decision to use lethal force and you will use it if the situation warrants it.

    As a concealed carrier, you should make yourself aware of these different levels. So when you are out and about, keep it in yellow. In yellow, you can always play the "what if" game in your head and create different scenarios based on the environment that you're currently in.

WHAT IS CASTLE DOCTRINE, STAND YOUR GROUND, & DUTY TO RETREAT?

These are the most talked about laws in the country when it comes to people defending themselves. I am not an attorney, I don't play one on TV and I am not giving you any legal advice. Each state is different in how they write laws for Castle Doctrine, Stand Your Ground and Duty to Retreat, so if you want more information on the laws in your state, consult an attorney. We'll just do a brief overview of what these mean.

Let's start with Castle Doctrine First.

Castle Doctrine:

It will go by several names, but it pretty much means the same thing. You will also hear it referred to as Castle Law or Defense of Habitation Law. Its roots are from English law, where a man's home is his castle and he has a right to defend it. Castle law is limited to real property, like your home or place of business and your vehicle. The purpose of this law allows you to defend yourself in these areas where you can use deadly force without retreating from the attacker(s) without any legal prosecution. If you are fearing for your life and use deadly force, this law should protect you, even from civil lawsuits. But each state is different in Castle Doctrine Laws. You'll have to speak to an attorney from your state to find out exactly how you are protected.

Not all states have Castle Doctrine, which is sort of silly. They expect you to use all means of escape if someone is trying to harm you. If you have a chance to use the back door to escape, but decided to use deadly force instead on that person, you could end up in jail. I have read stories about those who have disabilities use deadly force (crippled and cannot run, or some other medical issue preventing escape) and the courts have accepted these without persecution (as far I know).

Duty to Retreat:

Some states require a Duty to Retreat. This law means you tried every possible way to escape, but you could not and you had to use deadly force. So if you are under threat, you must retreat. Now some of us will not be able to outrun a marathon runner, or someone with better stamina, so retreating may be difficult. How about a 19 year old chasing down a 75 year old? Yes, some laws are silly, but again, you will have to check with an attorney. If you retreated and tried everything you could to get away, but couldn't, then using equal deadly force is warranted. Again, the courts may have to decided, depending on the situation.

Stand Your Ground:

Now with Stand Your Ground, this is somewhat similar to Castle Doctrine, but instead of being in your home or vehicle, you are outside. Again, not all states have Stand Your Ground. You will have to check with an attorney to see if your state has this law. Stand Your Ground replaces Duty to Retreat. Again, if your life is in imminent danger or you think you will experience personal harm, you can defend yourself with equal deadly force. So a claim of self-defense offers protection from prosecution, under certain circumstances. But the courts may have to determine this, depending on the situation.

Each state has its own laws and it is your responsibility to find out what those laws are when it comes to Castle Doctrine, Stand Your Ground and Duty to Retreat. The above is just a brief overview and does not tell you the laws in your state.

PURCHASING YOUR FIRST FIREARM

When I registered for my concealed carry class several months out, this gave me time to save up some money to purchase a firearm since I pretty much live from paycheck to paycheck. So I had to cut back on things to save some extra money for my upcoming future purchase. After I completed the class, I went down to the sheriff's office and put in my paperwork. About three weeks later, I got my concealed carry permit in the mail. Since I had enough money saved by that time, I decided to set a date to go shopping for my first firearm before my big camping trip.

I knew what sidearm that I wanted to carry and I asked a friend of mine to come out with me to the gun store since I never had the experience of purchasing a firearm. Unfortunately, he was unable to make it due to his schedule, so I went alone. Since this was going to be my first time, I asked friends about their experience and also read articles about what to do in the store when I visited one.

The number one thing I took away from peoples experiences is to always follow the four basic firearm rules. If this is your first time, you'll get a little nervous, especially if you're doing it alone. You may think that everyone is looking at you wondering what your experiences are in firearms, so don't worry, put this feeling aside. People can't read your mind. And I have also seen those who have years of experience with firearms not follow the safety rules. This is a rookie move on their part and after reading this, you'll won't be making the same mistakes.

I was just at a gun store recently checking out some sales and the fellow down a few glass cases from me was playing with a pistol. He kept pointing the muzzle at me. So I backed away from the glass case and out of the way. He got the message real quick and he apologized. Loaded or not, he was failing the basic rules. He knew a lot about firearms, since I could hear this in his conversation with the salesperson, but he failed the basics. He was making rookie mistakes. To the trained eye, he acted like an irresponsible gun owner.

So don't be nervous if you go by yourself. Remember, the people behind the counter are only interested in selling you a product. They care about sales and may get a commission off of your purchase. They don't care how proficient you are in firearms. So, I would suggest you do your research on what type of firearm you want before you hit a gun store and talk to a salesperson. I'd hate to have you purchase something and regret it.

By researching (which I would recommend), this will help you narrow down a selection of what matches your needs, plus you'll feel more comfortable around your selection and a little more educated. If you can rent and try some at the range, this will also save you some time and money. Some salespeople will try to sell you something that you don't need and you'll end up with something that is not right for you. Don't let the salesperson intimidate you or make decisions for you. If you feel pressured, then go somewhere else. After you buy a firearm, it's yours. There are no returns after that.

The folks behind the counter should also be following the firearm safety rules. When they check the gun for any ammo (which they should be doing), you will be doing the same after they hand it off to you. Don't rely on the buddy system (talked about later), it's **not** one of the universal safety firearm rules. If you don't check and it's loaded, you can harm or kill someone. Take a look at it for yourself and verify that the chamber is empty. Put your finger in there to make sure you feel an empty chamber and inspect the magazine well to make sure there is no ammo. For revolvers, check the cylinder to make sure there are no rounds and don't flip the cylinder back into the frame like they do in the movies. This will damage the firearm.

Do not point the gun at yourself to check the muzzle. If you decide to dry-fire, make sure you do not point it at anyone. Continue following the safety rules, even if it's unloaded. Keep an eye on that muzzle at all times and at what direction it is pointing. Do not point it at the clerk or the people to the right or left of you.

If you want to learn mistakes from others who should know the basic firearm safety rules, here are two videos of law enforcement who decided not to follow the rules. Do a search for these two videos. "***DEA shoots self in school***" and "***Police officer shoots self at gun store***".

This DEA agent used the buddy system, which is a big no no and not recommended for good reasons. This is when he relied on his buddy to check the chamber for him, which you will see what the results were in the video. These people did not follow the safety rules. In one video, he shot himself in the foot and in the other video, he lost part of his finger.

If the folks behind the counter are not friendly at all and you don't feel comfortable, you can always leave. I've noticed that some gun stores treat women differently, they like to ignore them, or they think that women are not part of the good old boy gun network. Sometimes they are taken advantage of and sold something they don't need or it's not the right fit for them. Like a large size handgun for small hands. If this happens to you, just walk away and find someone else.

I remember a woman who had about $1,200 cash to spend at one of the local gun stores and they completely ignored her. Obviously they did not want her business. She left, purchased from a competitor and posted on one of the search engine websites about her experience with that gun store (where you can give ratings about businesses) and she gave them 1/2 star.

I could tell that she was pissed off. She talked about her experience with these guys in that gun store and now other women who want to purchase from this store will see this posting. This will definitely deter others from having a similar bad experience and take their money somewhere else. I don't shop there either since she wasn't the only one complaining. Everyone should be helped and not ignored.

Remember, this posting will be on the Internet FOREVER. This company will lose business as word spreads. So before you visit a gun store, research the comments from others about that establishment. It can save you headaches.

WOMEN PURCHASING FIREARMS

Sometimes it's a man's world out there, but it shouldn't be, especially when it comes to firearms. Ladies before you decide to purchase a firearm from a dealer, research what other women are using. Look on either the Internet, ask a friend or relative, or just ask other women at the gun range. Find someone who is about the same height and similar build as you. They can give you some pointers.

Take advice from men with a grain of salt when it comes to selecting a sidearm for a woman. They are not you when it comes to making a decision in finding the right firearm. If your 5 foot and 5 inches tall with tiny hands, you don't want to end up with a .50 caliber handgun for your everyday concealed carry. That would be ridiculous.

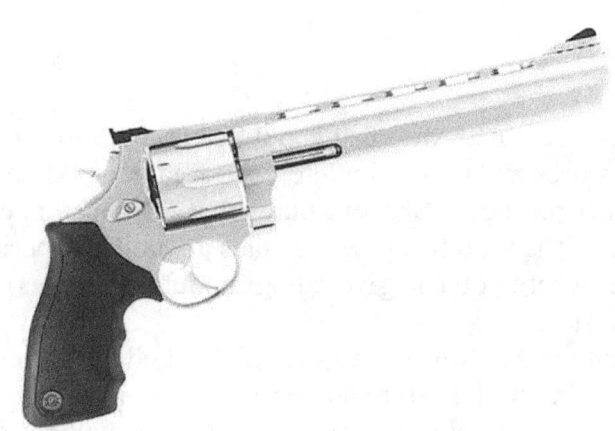

Ridiculous firearm for concealed carry use, but sweet looking.

    I would suggest that you find a gun range that rents sidearms. You can test the ones you researched to make sure it fits in your hands, that it feels comfortable when you shoot (small amount of recoil) and that you're hitting your target. If you know of a friend or family members that have the type of sidearm that you're interested in, ask if you can try it out on the range.

    Once you do decide on your new firearm, visit a gun shop that's friendly with women. I have heard stories of ladies being ignored or treated differently because of their gender. If you get a feeling that you're being treated differently, then don't spend a single penny at these stores. Find another gun store that is informative, has a great reputation, treats people kindly and respects women. I would suggest that you search on people's comments about that particular store before you visit. If you see any negative experiences from other women, move onto another store.

    Also, beware of those behind the counter trying to sell you a firearm. Some will just sell you anything just to make a sale. Do your research first before you decide to purchase and always follow the universal gun safety rules. Accidents do happen and I would hate that your first experience be a horrible one if they pass along a firearm that is loaded. It has happened before, even experienced people forget to check the chamber and the gun fires accidentally and someone ends up damaging property, getting hurt or killed.

    Also, not all manufacturers of handguns are specific for women, but they like to try to get your attention by making them pink or some pretty cool colors. This is a marketing ploy. These sidearms were probably designed by guys, not women. Ignore the gun-candy, move onto a good sidearm that is best for you, and don't go by how pretty it is. This is for concealed carry anyways, not many people will see it and you really don't want to show it off anyways to the general public. It doesn't matter if it's ugly or not, it's the mechanics behind it. It must function to protect a life. I am sure the market will change when firearms are created for women by women.

So remember, talk to people, do your research and take things from the guys with a grain of salt.

YOUR EVERY DAY CARRY (EDC) LOCATION

Once you've decided on what gear you'll be carrying, you'll need to also figure out where you're going to put it. Will you carry your gear on one of your legs (or both), in your pockets, on your belt, inside your shirt, in your boots, under your jacket, etc.?

For every piece of equipment you carry, consider the weight, the location, ease of accessing it, if it's comfortable while sitting (or driving) and does it get in the way of your hands if you need to reach into your pockets?

Location is very important. Once you've found your sweet spot for your holster and your sidearm, where is the rest of the equipment going to go? Will your spare magazine or speed loaders be accessible in case your gun jams or you run out of bullets? What if you carry a knife? Let's say you have it in your left-front pocket of your pants. Is your spare magazine located right above that pocket and it's preventing you from gaining access to your knife, your wallet or keys?

How about your multi-tool to assist you with mechanical problems with your sidearm, like a jammed cartridge? Is it located on your hip in an area where you won't be confused between your ammo and your tool pouch? Is your gear in places where it's creating difficulties while trying to get in and out of your vehicle? Is it grabbing your seatbelt or seat while you're moving? Can you draw your sidearm with your seatbelt off without your equipment getting in the way?

Location, location, location, is all very important. You don't want to have your everyday carry gear in your way. Plus everything still has to remain concealable. What about the pants you're wearing? Do the belt loops get in the way of where you want to put your gear? For the pants that you already have, are all the belt loops located in the same area, or do you have to readjust your gear around those loop holes for every different pairs of pants?

Consider wearing pants with the belt loops in the exact same position, so you don't end up changing your gear around for every pair of pants you wear. This can be frustrating after a while since you have to make adjustments every time. So there is a lot to consider in how you're going to organize your gear. You have to strategically put your gear in locations where it is easily accessible (especially in a fight for your life), the weight is distributed evenly, you gear is concealable and it's comfortable for daily wear and tear. Some of your cargo or tactical pants have pockets that can accommodate your gear.

What most people carry for their everyday carry varies amongst individuals. I for one carry a flashlight, cell phone, sidearm, spare magazine, multi-tool, knife, first aid kit and tourniquet. Others may add mace/pepper spray, an additional firearm, Para cord, tactical pen, body cam, notebook, etc. At the end of this book you will see a list of what I carry for EDC.

CLEANING & MAINTENANCE

Before cleaning, unload your firearm, keep ammo away from you by putting it into another room and ALWAYS follow the universal firearm safety rules. You don't want any ammo around you while you're cleaning. This will eliminate the total chance of an accidental discharge. There's plenty of stories out there where people shoot themselves or others while their cleaning their firearms. I even read a story about one that happened as I was writing this. It's sad, but happens frequently. That's one reason for putting this book together, to educate people to help reduce the chances of people harming themselves or others.

While you're carrying your firearm, it will experience a multitude of changes from the environment it's exposed to. It can be the exposure of the weather (heat, cold, humidity, dampness, etc.), to the perspiration from your skin, dirt, lint and other elements that will have an impact on your sidearm. The first thing you want to do is grab a calendar (I use my cell phone) and set up a preventive maintenance schedule. I have my calendar on my phone set for every 2nd Sunday of each month to clean my sidearm for several years out. This is a great auto-reminder. You just set it and forget it.

Cleaning your firearm(s), even if you don't put rounds through it, is a great way for new gun owners to learn how to clean, build familiarity around their tool and create a great habit. If you're experienced with firearms, it's still a good idea to clean them frequently to keep them up to par. Frequent cleanings also prevent any corrosion and buildup. Your firearms won't be vacuumed sealed, so they are still targeted by the elements in your environment. You want your firearm to be in tip top condition and not fail you when you need it the most. Plus this will keep costs down on repairs. It's also a great idea to clean your firearms right after they've been fired. Don't let excuses get in the way of cleaning. You take care of them, they'll take care of you.

Once you get into this monthly routine, you'll see that it will take less time to clean it, your familiarity will grow on how to disassemble and reassemble. Always follow the firearm owner's manual on how to clean and oil it. If you don't have one, you can always go online and watch videos posted. Just search for the type of sidearm you have and follow the instructions.

After my sidearm is cleaned and oiled, I also clean my holster and remove any fuzz that was put there by my clothes, eliminate any dirt collected and check for cracks or damage. I also check the hardware (like the screws) on the holster, make any adjustments to be sure that nothing is loose and nothing is missing. Then I test the retention of my sidearm to make sure it's not too tight or too loose when holstering or re-holstering. You want to make sure everything is perfect.

If you have a Kydex holster and it's cracked, so far, there is no way to repair it. I have tried almost everything and have read attempts made by others, but so far nothing. If you have a good warranty on it, you'll have to contact the manufacturer to have it replaced. I have a cracked one right now and still trying different things to try and repair it, but for now, nothing so far is repairing and holding the two pieces together. I hope someone comes up with a product to repair it. I don't want to be a day without my holster. It could be the day I need it.

Don't forget to check your sights and if you have a laser/light on yours, also make sure that it's properly aligned and tightened down. Sometimes my front sight moves after a period of time, especially doing a lot of dry-fire practice runs (holstering/reholstering) or running a lot of ammo through it over a period of time. So this is on my monthly calendar as well to check when I clean my sidearm.

I would recommend purchasing a firearm cleaning kit made in the USA. There are a lot of Chinese made cleaning kits and many are just crap and they break after a short period of time. Find a really good American made kit and it will last you a very long time, possibly several lifetimes. If I were you, get a gun matt that is stain and oil resistant. It is totally worth the investment.

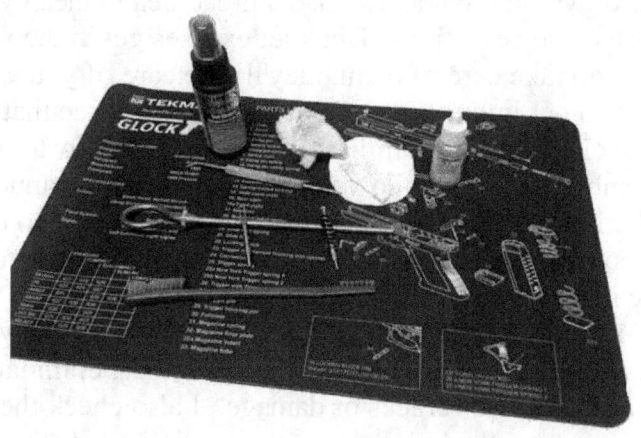

Firearm cleaning kit on top of gun mat.

THE DAILY ROUTINE

I wanted to share my daily routine with you to give you a better idea on how to maintain your edge when it comes to self-defense with a handgun.

6:30 am: Wake up

7:00 am: Take a shower

7:30 am (Tuesdays, Thursdays, Saturdays - Training Days): Strap on the pants, pick a shirt for the day, get my firearm (follow the 4 basic safety rules), set up my training area (bedroom, kitchen, or living room) and practice drawing and moving off the "X" (shooting while moving). I'll do different drills, like quick drawing, time myself in how many times I can pull the trigger in 5 seconds and a few others. Practicing is around 15-20 min.

8:00 am (Monday - Friday): I'll jump online to read a few articles. I'll check out USA Carry (USACarry.com) and jump over to Concealed Nation (ConcealedNation.org). These are great resources and they usually have news articles posted daily from Monday to Friday. This keeps me up to date on real stories about the criminal element and their interactions with gun owners.

8:30 am: Leave for work.

Noon: (Monday - Friday): Then during my breaks/lunch, I'll watch videos from any of these resources on YouTube: United States Concealed Carry Association (USCCA). They have different videos throughout the week: Into the Fray, Tactical Tuesday, USCCA Gun Vault, Ask USCCA, Clear Impact, Cover vs. Concealment, Drill of the Month and other very informative videos.

Other videos I watch are Active Self Protection (ASP), which is basically a video per day with John Correia. He discusses video footages that people submit to him from around the U.S and other countries on how to better protect yourself in real life situations involving knives, guns, etc. There are some really great takeaways in these videos. They can happen to anyone. Then there's First Person Defender (they have several seasons). They take people who already carry concealed and set the stage for real attacks to see how defenders respond and in these real life dangerous situations.

End of the Day: I also carry while at home and if it's after work, I'll decompress by enjoying time with the family, get ready for the next day and start the routine all over again. On the weekends, if there are any new postings and videos, I save them for the weekday so I have something to look forward to. The weekends are a small pause between work lives so I want to enjoy the fruits of my labor. I also make it a habit to insure the home is secure to protect the family and check it again before I go to bed. Then I put my firearm into my floppy holster, keep it near me and start all over again the next day.

Obviously everyone has different schedules, but if you can set one up for yourself and continue with watching and reading from really great resources, it'll keep your mind sharp. When I have additional time, I will read Concealed Carry Magazine on my computer tablet. The USCCA (United States Concealed Carry Association) puts out this magazine and they also do one for women (the first of its kind), which I am grateful they have. There is so much great information presented by these writers, I would highly recommend reading them.

Some of the articles have also helped me learn more about women's views on firearms and their experiences. The information gained in these articles will also help any firearms instructor who will be training women. This information is invaluable in helping to educate and bridge the gap; to bring women closer to learning more about firearms and balance the education across the sexes. I can see it very helpful for instructors learning more about their audience so they can become better teachers.

BUILD YOUR OWN TARGET STAND

When you go to an outside target range, some ranges do not provide targets or stands. So it might be a good idea to make your own. I am going to share with you the plans that I've created to build your own. These are pretty easy to make. I made three of these so I can do drills. If I bring others along to share time at the range, I have plenty to go around.

I went to a retail store, bought a duffle bag to carry them in. It even has wheels on the bottom and a handle bar at the top so I can roll it across the floor. I have even added five small orange rubber safety cones in my collection to be used for drills. I have three target stands, the paper targets and the cones in one bag.

After you're done with building the stands, you can spray paint them to whatever color your like. I have decided to provide a link instead of putting the instructions in this book. It would take up several pages and I would like to keep the price down for this book. These do it yourself plans have color pictures and step by step instructions.

Just visit the website: www.WayOfTheConcealedCarrier.com and download your free copy today.

CHAPTER ELEVEN

Tips and Tricks

"Simplicity is the ultimate sophistication."

Leonardo da Vinci

COVER AND CONCEALMENT

Sometimes people are confused over the differences between cover and concealment. When I first heard these two, I thought that they meant the same. But I was incorrect since this might have been something that I may have picked up from the movies (Hollywood education). So let me explain the differences between them.

Concealment will hide your position. You are concealed (hidden in plain view)........ Maybe under a desk, behind a curtain, in the closet, behind a mailbox, behind a car door, a light post, a filing cabinet, a dresser, behind a door or a sheet rocked wall. These types of locations hide you, but they will not protect you from a bullet. Bullets will go through over 95% of manufactured doors, unless they are designed to be bullet proof or they are really hard and thick that it may completely stop or slow down the projectile.

Cars will not stop a bullet. That's why they have bullet-proof cars. All those rounds that are shot will penetrate and go through your most common (non-bullet proof) vehicles. But in Hollywood movies, they show bullet holes in the car, but no bullet holes in the passengers. I call it Hollywood science, not to be confused with real-life science. Remember, their goal is to sell movies using illusions, not train you in how to protect yourself. This also includes television shows.

Cover will stop bullets. Make yourself a difficult target, find yourself some cover. Like a concrete wall or pillar, a brick wall (not a sheet-rocked wall), a thick tree, a pallet full of sand bags, or behind an engine block of a vehicle. Depending on where you're at, there will probably be more concealment than cover. So keep alert around you, know where cover is, just in case. There are many great videos on the Internet where people test different objects that can provide cover (stopping bullets), or just providing concealment (not stopping bullets but concealing you).

Can cover be used as concealment? Absolutely! Since cover can stop bullets and you're behind cover, no one can see you. Like going behind a brick or concrete wall, a very large concrete planter filled with dirt, behind a wheel on a vehicle and other items that will stop a bullet. As long as your bad person doesn't have X-Ray vision, you'll be fine.

So in a gunfight, cover is your best option over concealment since it will stop rounds from penetrating you. If you have no options, than you're going to have to find concealment and get the hell out of there.

DRAW-CONFIGURATION: INCREASING YOUR DRAW TIME

It's important to be quick on the draw and practicing frequently to decrease your draw time, which is going to be vital in a gunfight. It doesn't mean that if someone has a gun pointed at you that you should draw. You should never draw on a drawn gun. But if someone is going for their sidearm, the first person to be on target is going to have a greater chance in becoming the victor of that gunfight. So it's imperative that you practice, practice, and practice. Your life depends on it.

Below are a list of items that I wanted to share with you in my own experience in reducing draw time.

We'll discuss ways to eliminate some of this bulk to get you up to speed in presenting your firearm as quickly as possible. It's called the Grandpa "G" Draw-Configuration© method. Just one of these methods could eliminate an extra second (or a fraction of a second), but a combination of these can reduce your time when you're reaching for your sidearm and getting on target. Let's take a look at your draw-configuration (sidearm, holster, clothing, your position). Is your configuration set up in a way where it adds time or does it reduce it when you draw?

Practice for several minutes on drawing (with no ammo in your firearm) to see if your draw time is being slowed down or becoming faster because of something you did. Increase and decrease of draw times can be related to where your sidearm is located, what you're wearing, what position your body is in (sitting, standing, laying down, etc.) and the type of holster you have.

I use a laser target and practice in different rooms in the house to mix things up. If you have a shot timer that works well with dry firing, this will also work. I'll try it sitting down, standing up, pretending someone is entering the door, sitting on the bathroom throne doing my business, seated at the dinner table, etc. I am sure you get the idea here.

The laser target has a timer on it and it shows me how many seconds it takes to draw my firearm. The timer will beep, I draw and fire. The laser hits the target and I get a response time of how many seconds between the beeps it hits it. If it takes more than 2 seconds, I try to find out what's causing the problem and then make any adjustments. It could mean a change in my clothing, an adjustment to my holster, changing the position of my body, or something else. But I want to be under the 2 second mark. Under 1.5 seconds is my ideal goal, but less time is better.

These are a list of configurations (below) to consider to decrease your draw time when you try to get your hands on your sidearm, removing it from the holster, presenting it and if necessary, firing it. Does your current draw-configuration enable you to fire in just under two seconds? Your draw-configuration is related to you and your environment.

Here are some things that may steal time away from your draw when your body is at its natural stance……..

- **Sidearm Location:** There are several areas around the waistline where most people carry their sidearm. We use clock positions on the body to reference where something is located. For example, most people carry their pistol around the 9 or 3 o'clock position (right and left hip). Or some will carry around the 11 or 1 o'clock position for their appendix carry (see diagram). Most people avoid carrying in the noon position (the crotch), especially men.

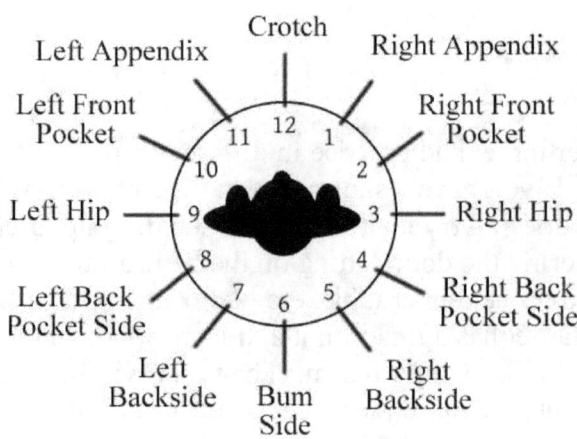

Sidearm Locations around the waistline.

You want your firearm in the most optimal position on the body so that it's quickly accessible. Is your pistol near your hand where it naturally rests, or do you have to reach further away from your hands natural position to reach your weapon? Let's say that your firearm is located somewhere between 3:30 – 8:30 position, the gray area (see figure below). Does it take longer to reach around your back? In this same position in the gray area, is your firearm under your clothing? Could this combination delay your draw time? Your goal here is to get to your sidearm as quickly as possible and you want it as close to your draw hand as possible.

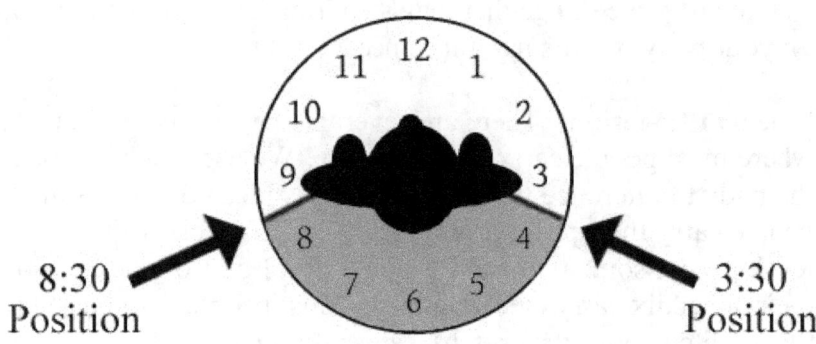

White area - faster draw time. Gray area - delayed draw time.

Now if your hands are resting at another location, like on a table, or your holding something, maybe your arms are crossed, or let's say your hands are up near your face in a defensive position (raised to signal that you're not a threat), obviously your distance will be further from you firearm. But from any natural position, you would like to have your sidearm in its most optimal position. Since your hands can be up, down, or in front of you, your quicker positions for you main sidearm would still be the point on your body where the 8:30 – 3:30 position are (white area). Anything from 3:30 – 8:30 (shaded gray area) will be the furthest points away from your hands, either from a position at your side, your hands up, or in front of you. Reaching around to the 3:30 – 8:30 position can add time to your draw.

Let's say your hands are in a defensive position, you see an opportunity to draw, but your sidearm is at the 5:30 position. How many seconds would it take to put your hands down, reach around your back, unholster your sidearm, move your hands forward again and get on target? Compare this to a 3:00 position instead, would this not be much faster? Or in the appendix position? You're reducing your draw time in the white area and increasing time in the gray area.

This 3:30-8:30 position is the draw-configuration gray zone, an area where your draw time is going to be delayed. The further back you go, the more time it takes to get access to your firearm. You want to close the gap as quickly as possible and stay within the white zone (8:30 – 3:30 position).

- **Safeties:** Do you carry your firearm with the safety on? During an adrenaline dump into your system while you're under threat, will you be able to remember to remove the safety? Having the safety on and remembering to take it off may take seconds, but if you forget and you try to click and there's no trigger movement, this can add to your time and it could be too late since you are trying to diagnose the problem.

- **Clothing:** Does the type of clothes you wear create extra time to draw? Do you have to take extra measures or effort to move your clothing out of the way to access your firearm? Does this add an extra second or more? Is your top too tight and when you pull up your shirt you can't get it over your sidearm? Maybe a wider shirt or a different shirt may be the answer. If your shirt is too long, is it taking longer to pull it up to get access to your sidearm? Dress for success! You want to be successful on the draw and not fumbling around with your clothing trying to gain access to your firearm.

- **Type of Holster:** What retention level is you holster? Level 0, 1, 2, 3, etc.? Do you have to move straps or press a button on your holster to release your firearm? Is the holster retention too tight and you have to make an extra effort in removing your firearm? Make sure that your holster is not too tight for your sidearm so that it causes you problems in trying to get it out. Do your adjustments and make sure that your firearm doesn't fall out, but also not too tight where removing it from the holster becomes difficult. You want the best of both worlds for this one and have this one balanced out (not too tight, not too loose).

- **One in the Chamber:** Do you carry your sidearm loaded and ready to go? Or do you want to take extra steps and time to chamber it after you remove it from the holster? It has been proven that carrying one in the chamber will get the job done faster than fumbling around and trying to get one in the chamber when things have turned upside down. Your gun could even jam in the process. Not having one in the chamber will add seconds to a gunfight when you need it most to save your life.

- **Grip Size:** Is the size of your sidearms grip too big for you hand, or is it too small? You want to have a firearm that will fit into your hands, so that when you present your firearm, you can get on target. It should fit like a glove. There's not going to be a universal grip that will be a one size fits all.

- **Positioning:** This is going to be the position that your body is in. This can be standing, sitting, on one knee (or both), laying down, on your side. These are factors that will have an impact in how quickly you can draw your sidearm. If you're laying down in bed, how quickly can you draw? Do you need to retrieve your firearm from a safe, in your drawer, or a holster on your nightstand? If you're sitting on your couch, love-seat, on the toilet, maybe in a wheelchair, or at the kitchen table, can you quickly get access and draw? Is there anything in your way, like the table or the chair? Are you sunk deep down in your love-seat?

If you're on your side, maybe laying down, can you still draw your firearm? The hip-side where you firearm is located, are you laying on it? If you're standing, is there anything that may be too close to you that will limit your space/distance and you can't get your firearm out all the way? Maybe you're in the corner of an elevator and your gun-side is pushed up against the wall. So how quickly can you get to your firearm from the position you're currently in?

The goal with your draw-configuration is to get your sidearm out of your holster and on target faster than 1.5 seconds, especially under pressure. If you can get it under a second, that's really good. Don't get sloppy with drawing. Once you find the right draw-configuration, keep practicing several times a week for the rest of your life. You don't need anything fancy, just practice in your own home.

There is a saying you'll hear often in the world of firearms: ***Slow is smooth, smooth is fast***. Think about that for a moment. It basically means that you need to start out slow to become faster, but with repetition you'll become smoother at the technique. To do so, just draw slow and smooth for a while to have your muscle memory remember how you're drawing. If you notice any imperfections, try again slowly until you've removed the flaw. You're creating a technique that will program your muscles to do the exact same thing over and over again.

Like the way your dominant hand perfected itself in writing the alphabet. It took a while to learn it. But you drew the letters slowly over a course of time and once you perfected it, you were able to write them, but at a quicker pace than when you first started. Now your hand is automated at writing, it has become second nature. This is your muscle memory at work. This is what you want to do with drawing a firearm.

It's slow at first (slow is smooth), but after many repetitions, your programming your muscle memory to perfect it. Then after a while, you pick up speed. With speed added, you will draw smoothly and your muscle memory will stick to the smoothness of your draw (smooth is fast). Just like writing, you have to do it frequently or your writing starts to get sloppy over time. Can you read your own handwriting?

If your hand gets injured and once it heals, you may have to reprogram your hands again for drawing your weapon. Your muscles will have to relearn how to draw. Just keep practicing.

SILENCE THAT CELL PHONE

Many of us have cell phones with those fancy ringtones when people call or send us text messages. These are great devices for calling 911 when you need help, but they can also give your location away when things go sideways. Let's say there is an active shooter at your workplace and you're trying to conceal your location. You're sitting in a dark room armed, you can hear the gunshots and the ruckus off in the distance. But the sounds from that firearm is getting closer and closer. Then the news crew picks up the story and it is being broadcasted on every channel. A family member sees the news report and knows you're there and they decide to call you to make sure you're okay.

Meanwhile, you are barricaded in a room and you can hear footsteps in the hallway coming towards your location. You know you're in a good position, but there is no cover, just concealment. Then your cellphone rings from a family member and a text message arrives from a friend. The footsteps stop at your door, the active shooter knows your location. What do you do now?

To avoid these type of situations, keep you phone on silence at all times. Things happen so fast, that you may forget to put it in vibrate mode and family members are reaching out to you while you're trying to hide your location from the shooter. If you can, always keep your phone in silent mode so you will not be discovered. You can still text message them while in silent mode. You may want to avoid talking on the phone unless you're positive that the shooter is not near the area you're trying to maintain cover/concealment.

Always have your phone with you, even if you have to leave your desk at work for a short period of time, or you have to use the restroom. I see people leaving their phones on their desks and walk away for several minutes at a time. If you leave your phone behind and something does happen and you're sitting in a bathroom stall, you will not be able to open a line of communications with anyone. Having one will enable law enforcement to give you directions to get you to safety or find you. If a natural disaster hits your area and you're trapped, having your phone with you will enable you to let people know you're alive and get paramedics to you if medical attention is needed. Always, if possible, have it with you.

LOCKING YOUR CAR BEFORE ENTERING

Parking lots are another place where thieves can take you or your car for a ride. It's very important that you're using situational awareness. Keep your head on a swivel, especially when you're approaching your vehicle. You want to enter it as quickly as possible and have it locked right as you close the door (push the lock button on your key fob), then have your key in the ignition and the car started just in case you have to pull away.

I have a remote starter (get one if you don't have one) and I do the following....I remote start the car from a distance to flush out anyone near it. If there is someone hiding by it, it may startle them, or they assume someone is already in the car and might want to check it out. This will give you an idea if someone is there. So when it's clear, unlock your door while the vehicle is running. As you open the door lock it at the same time (key fob), then enter the vehicle and close the door right away. If you need to get away in a moment's notice, you can just insert the key and drive away (unless yours is keyless – push the button).

If you don't have a remote starter, hit the panic alarm on your car to make a lot of noise to flush any people out if they are hiding and trying to ambush you. This will also gain attention by others in the area where they will look in that direction (your witnesses).

Some vehicles are programmable in how it unlocks and locks the doors. Some will unlock the doors if put into park. Or when you put it in drive, the doors automatically lock. Or when the engine is shut off, the doors unlock. Some will only unlock the driver side when put into park. If your vehicle is equipped to configure your door locks, program it to open only the driver side first and not unlock all locks when the ignition is turned off. You don't want someone sneaking in on the passenger side or back seat. This might be a feature to look for in your next vehicle purchase if you don't already have it.

If someone is already in your car when you approach, seek cover/concealment and call 911. While you do this, press the panic button on your key fob to force them out of your vehicle. You can be a good witness to the incident, or even possibly video record it for evidence. You want to avoid getting into a gunfight if at all possible.

Your property can always be replaced.

THROW AWAY PROPS

What I like to do is have some spare money in my pocket which I'll use as a diversion. This is money that I would not spend and something I don't mind losing. I have a bunch of ones wrapped up in a five dollar bill. So if someone wants to take my money in a deadly force situation, I pull out this "throw away" money from my pocket and toss it onto the ground. This hopefully will create a distraction with the gunman/gunwoman and I can either get out quickly (get to cover) or start defending myself right there since they will be on the floor picking up the money.

For carjacking's, I have a spare key from an old vehicle I used to own. If someone wants it, I will pull this out my pocket (if outside the vehicle) and toss it on the ground and look for cover. If I am in the car, I will take the real key out of the ignition (if it's in there) and toss out the fake key onto the ground outside. This creates additional options of either leaving the vehicle for cover (remember, your vehicle is NOT cover), or if the opportunity presents itself, drive away while their back is turned and get the hell out of there and call 911. If there are no other options, I will defend myself with my sidearm.

SMART SHOPPING IN THE FIREARM WORLD

The world of firearms and the products wrapped around the word "self-defense" has an expensive price tag. There's no doubt about it. Anything that's related to a firearm these days, will be a bit high. From tactical pants, knives, flashlights, tools, ammo, etc. Ammo that used to be a few bucks a box not too long ago is now over $10. A bullet that was pennies can be a .20 a shot to well over a dollar. Honestly, it's getting ridiculous. I think everyone should have the ability to defend themselves, but at an affordable price. I hope firearms don't become another product for the wealthy. Remember when Harley's were affordable?

So what do you do?

Since many of your purchases these days are online, you can find some pretty good discounts around the holidays. There will be closeout specials to get rid of old models to bring in the new, brand new products that are trying to be introduced to the public, clearance items and vendor arrangements with a partnered company to give discounts on their product line. A good way to keep up on these specials is to create a throwaway email account just dedicated for the firearm industry. This can be a free online email account and there are plenty of these on the Internet.

I call it a throw away email account because once your email gets out there for a while, it just gets spammed like crazy. After that point, I'll no longer use it and create another and start over again. Once you have an email account set up, go online and sign up for those email newsletters from those companies that you're looking to purchase from. Once in a while, you'll receive discounts in your inbox. You can also compare sales between competitors to see if you're saving money. Be careful though, the price might look like it's the cheapest, but after shipping, you're paying more than the other competitor websites you just visited.

Amazon is a great place to research products. You can see if customers are experiencing problems and what ratings people are giving them. Only read the reviews from people who actually purchased the product, ignore the rest since these can be from anyone who wants to boost the rating of the product or a competitor trying to knock them down a notch. I have seen products with almost 5 stars, but after reading the reviews, the product was crap and most of the high ratings were from people who didn't purchase the item. Just makes you wonder if these sellers are being truthful. Keep your eye on this.

I always start with the 1-2 stars first from purchasers to see if there is a pattern with this item, just to see if it has some type of defect. Having great to excellent customer service is also important, along with having no problems with returns. You don't want to be stuck with something you invested your money in and it doesn't work.

Other websites, if you have your items in the cart and you are about to click on "purchase items", but don't, you may receive a coupon in your email from that company in about 1-3 days asking you to come back and finish your order. Then you can apply the coupon to receive your discount.

Some websites will keep track of your visiting habits and if you have purchased from them before, prices might be higher than someone who is new and visiting the website for the first time. Same product, but different pricing. Unfortunately at this time, it is legal. So if you clear your cookies and use Incognito in your browser, the website cannot determine if you have been there before and may pop up on your screen the discounted price for the item. I have seen on a big brand tactical website where the pricing was different between two different browsers (one browser using incognito and the other not) and this was for the same item. The difference could be a few dollars, but one time I had one which was a $20 difference. So I just went with the cheapest one. Perusing the Internet with software that makes your surfing habits anonymous, can save you money.

Removing your old account on their website and adding a new one later, with a different email address may also save you money. Sometimes return customers will be charged more. New customers (new account) may see a different price. So you'll have to play around with this. Have two email addresses, two accounts (one guest and a current account) on your favorite website and see if there are any differences in pricing. It's not just tactical websites, but you'll notice this with other big commercial websites, especially purchasing plane tickets.

I have also contacted the company of the website that I wanted to purchase from and told them I was looking at an identical item on another website at a cheaper price and asked if they would match it or offer an incentive to purchase from them, like free shipping. Some will be happy to oblige since they want to sell you something. I have asked for a discount on items explaining that I just missed their last sale and was a new visitor to their website. I asked for free shipping (if not offered), or if they can email me a coupon to match that price offered a few weeks ago. You never know until you ask. If I don't get a discount, then I find another website that will be happy to take me on as a customer. It doesn't hurt to try and bargain with these companies since they will have competitors.

For your brick and mortar stores, I have found many of them too expensive and I can go online using my phone in the store and find something cheaper on the same product, with free delivery. So if you need something right away and don't mind paying a higher price, the stores in your area will have to be your go to places. But if you don't mind waiting a few days (and some online stores will ship 2nd day for free), you can save money and apply your savings towards your next purchase. I always compare prices in stores to the ones online. Sometimes local store have a really great deal, but I usually find them cheaper online.

I believe that our retail brick and mortar stores will be downsizing and some will be something of the past in the very near future. They will have to reinvent themselves to compete with online pricing or start matching online prices (which some refuse to do), or they will be going bye-bye. So I guarantee you're going to see some drastic changes in the next few years where companies will feel the pressure from online stores and will have to do something to keep you as a customer or else they'll go bankrupt, start closing stores and go out of business. Unfortunately, some companies have become too big, they don't understand the needs of their customers and have become disconnected. They will be non-existent in the years to come. It's sad, but true.

DON'T FORGET YOUR FIREARM

I decided some time ago to spend the money for a solid holster that was designed to be mounted in a vehicle. I noticed that it was almost impossible to unholster my sidearm while sitting with a seatbelt on. Plus on long trips, it digs into my waist. I also wanted to make sure that it was at arm's length so that I could reach it very quickly if I needed to defend myself. But I ran into the problem of forgetting that it was in that new vehicle holster at times and thought it was on my hip. I knew right away that this could turn into a serious problem.

So I created a technique to help remind me that my firearm is not on my hip, but located in my vehicle mounted holster. I have a small car and I have my vehicle holster near my legs. Before I start to drive, I remove my sidearm from my hip and place it into my secured vehicle holster. I then tie on my bright orange shoestring to my right leg (just above my knee). The right leg is near the mounted holster and the brightly colored shoestring reminds me that my firearm is not on my body. You can't miss it, even while in the dark driving. The neon color of the shoestring still gets my attention. When I stop the vehicle and before getting out, I notice the shoestring (either by color or the feel of it on my leg). Then I'll remove my sidearm attached to the vehicle and reinsert into my on-body holster. Then I remove my bright shoestring and wrap it around my stick shift.

In the past, I have honestly walked out of my car and forgot my sidearm in the vehicle and realized I didn't have it after a few seconds. Why? Because my holster on my hip is so comfortable, I don't feel the sidearm. I can feel the slight pressure from the holster against my hip which in my mind tells me my sidearm is there, but in reality, it's not (I call it a false-positive). So I made this mistake a few times and had to come up with simple method so that I would not form a bad habit of leaving it in the car.

If I walk out of the car and forget to retrieve my firearm, I have that damn funny looking shoestring attached to my leg. This tells me right away that my sidearm is still in the vehicle. This is a great technique that I have used for about a year now and it really has helped me remember to reholster my firearm before I leave my vehicle. Its habit forming, but worth it. It's so easy these days to be distracted and I would hate to walk into an appointment, realized my sidearm is not with me and dash back out to the car to get it.

If people see it in my vehicle, they may report it to the authorities, or if someone wants it, they can just smash the window and grab it (smash and grab). That's why I never leave valuables in plain sight in my vehicle.

Bright shoe string on leg as reminder, firearm in mounted holster under steering column.

Just a reminder, be very careful about reholstering in the vehicle. Depending on what you have on, a piece of your shirt or jacket, or whatever you're wearing can get caught in your trigger.

So when you reinsert it into your holster, do it slowly. If you feel any tug or resistance, then STOP. Remove the sidearm from the holster, put it back in the vehicle mounted holster and double-check yourself to make sure that nothing is in the way. If you force it into the holster and something is caught in the trigger, you're going to have a bad day.

The sidearm should just slide into your holster without any resistance greater than you're usually used to. If it feels different when reinserting, then stop. Put the sidearm back into the vehicle holster and check yourself to make sure parts of your shirt, jacket, sweater, vest, or whatever you're wearing is not getting tucked into your on-body holster. Depending on where you are, you may just get out of your car and insert it into your holster while you're standing.

There are disadvantage of carrying a sidearm on your hip while driving with a seatbelt on. It just adds extra time to draw. But having it near you, attached to your vehicle, gives you a quicker draw time when needed with little to no hassle. While driving with a sidearm on your hip, the seatbelt can get in the way and after driving for a while, you can feel the firearm digging into your hip by the pressure from being strapped in by the seatbelt. If you need to retrieve it quickly, you have to unbuckle the seatbelt, dig for it and this adds seconds to your time.

Keep your secured vehicle holster out of plain sight. There are other vehicles on the highway and if they see your firearm, they may call the authorities and tell them that you were brandishing on the freeway. Maybe they don't like the way you're driving, or they could be an anti-gun person. For whatever reason, they may turn you into the bad person and you weren't doing anything wrong. Plus, being the gray ghost is important here since someone may have seen it in your vehicle and may follow you to try to retrieve it from you later. They may have seen it inside your vehicle while you were both on the road. So keep it hidden to avoid any problems.

I remember a story of a guy who said that they were pulled over by a police officer while they were driving in a designated lane during rush hour and that they needed to have a permit (diamond lane/ride-share lane). In this case, they have never owned one. They were trying to bypass the congested traffic and get to work on time. The ticket is a few hundred dollars. So he told the officer that someone on the highway was brandishing a gun and he wanted to get out of there. So he said he decided to jump into the express lane to get away. He gave a description of a made up car.

Genius idea, but also against the law. So let's say that you're legally carrying a firearm, but the description given by this idiot who is trying to get out of a ticket, matches your car description. So you get pulled over and have no idea what the hell is going on. They may even have you at gunpoint and broadcasting to you to get out of the car with your hands up. Yeah, that sucks!

You'll probably need an attorney at this point.

So I was thinking to myself, if that happened to me, what would I do in this situation? I thought that if I can get the officer to have his witness describe the firearm that was being pointed at them, then this may be helpful in getting out of this bad situation. I would have the officer ask the following question below to the person in the other vehicle:

What color was the firearm that was being brandished at you?
(1). Camouflage
(2). Silver
(3). or a Goldish Color

    Let's say that your sidearm is hot pink. Choose three colors that are not the color of your firearm. Have the officer ask his witness to choose one of the three colors. The reason for this is if the person is lying, they will pick one of the three colors listed. If they are telling the truth, they would say that it was not any of those colors, but it was another color matching your gun (hot pink for example).
    History has shown that when a gun is pointed at someone, they can describe the firearm, even the details of their watch, but not able to describe the person pointing it at them. They get tunnel vision. So if a gun was pointed at this driver, they could possibly describe it in detail, right down to the color. Add that to your defense.
    I would suggest using the multiple choice question about what color your sidearm is. Since the police officer filed a report about someone waving a gun on the highway, he should have a description of the firearm brandished (hopefully) and if not then ask if he can contact that individual and ask those multiple choice questions. Or if this is not possible and you think you need a lawyer, then have your lawyer ask that question.
    People will do the dumbest things to get out of something they did wrong and not take personal responsibility for their own actions and in this case, you get pulled over for absolutely nothing you did. You get in trouble because some jackass wants to get out of a ticket.
    Since there has been an increase in shootings on the highways (road rage, gang related incidents, etc.) and you get pulled over because someone reported shots were coming from your vehicle, you may be in handcuffs for the protection of law enforcement. Ask the officer to check your sidearm to see if it was recently fired. Now if you do cleanings after firing (which is a wise thing to do), you should be okay here. A squeaky clean firearm should be enough evidence to show that you did not fire it and you just happen to be a victim of misidentification. Never go for your sidearm and hand it to the officer, always follow their direction. If you don't clean your sidearm or just left the range, you may need a lawyer at this point. You can ask if the

witness saw your sidearm and have them identify the color of it. But this may not work, but it's worth trying.

Ok, we got off topic a little bit here, but there was a segue in there somewhere. I love to share stories. So try the bright shoestring method to see if this works for you. It's easy, cheap and it will help you remember to take your firearm with you before you leave your vehicle.

CHAPTER TWELVE

Dressing the Part

*"When you don't dress like everyone else,
you don't have to think like everyone else."*

Iris Apfel

DRESSING THE PART

I have found that the best way to get ready for the day is to actually layout my clothes and my gear and start adding it to my outfit while it's laying on the bed. I will feed my gun belt though the pant loops and while I am doing this, I start adding my gear to the belt (spare ammo, multi-tool and medical kit) and to my pockets (flashlight and knife). After this is done, I will clip my holster to my pants (not the belt). Having such a list of items sounds excessive, but if you can keep it small and lite weight, you actually don't notice it at all. It's amazing how many items I use on my belt throughout the week. We are not going to the extreme, like police officers. Since they deal with the criminal elements daily, they need those additional tools (handcuffs, pepper spray, window punch, radio, Taser, flashlight, batteries, gloves, pens or pencils, keys, zip ties, several magazines of ammo and other items as needed).

After I get all my gear in their pockets and on my belt, then I put on my pants. I will then buckle the gun belt and put my unloaded gun in my holster and practice drawing. If I can't feel my sweet spot, then I adjust the holster. Once I have found my comfortable area for drawing, then I remove my sidearm, then attach my clips onto the gun belt (with the pants still on). You may have to unbuckle the belt a little bit to get the clips on. Then I reholster and make sure it feels comfortable. Then I'll draw a few more time, chamber a round and put my gun back into the holster. Now I am ready for the day. If the gun feels like it's sagging a little bit, I re-buckle the belt to the next tighter notch. If you don't have one, then add one. Some people's waists are odd sizes, but most pants and belts are mostly made for even sizes. I have recently noticed that one gun belt company will make belt notches for odd size waists. So you may have to make adjustments with your smoke wagon on your side to make sure it is secure enough, but still comfortable.

I have found this method easier to set up for the day instead of putting the pants on, then the belt, the gear, then sidearm since they are all pulling the pants down and it gets frustrating trying to get everything together. It's not as efficient and becomes a waste of time. So load up your pants before you put them on, make your adjustments and then you're ready for the day.

I like to prepare for the next day, so at the end of the day, I'll find clothes and transfer my stuff over. So when I get up, all my gear is ready to go, all I have to do is holster my sidearm, make a few practice draws with my unloaded sidearm, chamber a round and head out for the day.

WINTERS AND SIDEARMS

I live in the upper-Midwest, so we're part of the multi-coat weather culture in the winter. With multiple changes in temperatures throughout a single day, we may be adding clothing or removing them. What I mean by multi-coat weather is that sometimes you have to change your winter clothing to adapt to the changes in temperatures throughout the day. Maybe it's around 10 degrees in the morning, so you wear something to keep you warm, like long underwear, maybe a sweater, a heavy jacket, etc. These additional articles of clothing can become heavy and restrictive. Then it starts to get a little warmer while getting closer to noon (like around 40 degrees), so we start sweating under our jacket and it can become uncomfortable.

Now I am just sharing some of the extremes that happen in my area, but this may have a small impact in where you live or you may be in a state that has some really decent weather in the winter. Or you live in similar weather conditions like we have in my neck of the woods.

Due to the extreme temperature changes during the day, going from outdoor to indoor, we sometimes have to wear multiple pieces of clothing (a jacket, sweater, a sweatshirt, etc.) to compensate for the change in temperature. The further north you go, the colder it will be, going from a negative temperature outside to an indoor facility that is around 70-80 degrees. It can have a great impact on the body from the clothes that are worn. Then we have to start shedding our winter gear inside the building or the body will start to overheat. Towards the end of the day, when nightfall comes, the temperature starts dropping again and it could hit a negative number. So we're adding on the layers of clothing again to keep warm from the cold temperatures. It can be a pain in the ass, but some people do get acclimated to the weather and end up wearing less clothing.

I remember when I visited Florida in the winter one year, it was in the high 40's, I was wearing shorts and a shirt and people were wearing heavy jackets and gloves. It was a strange cold front that lasted over a week when I was visiting. To me, this was a blessing of warm temperatures since it was around -25 degrees in my state a few days earlier (a cold front that lasted several weeks) when I jumped on a plane for warmer weather. I got some really strange stares and people were muttering silently under their breath when they saw me. I was looked upon as if I escaped an insane asylum. I heard one remark, "Nanook of the North", from a couple that passed me on the sidewalk.

So temperatures nearing 50 degrees to me is nothing since my body was acclimated to the sub-zero climate. To me, I thought they were crazy for wearing winter clothes on such a nice sunny day with no snow on the ground. There were Christmas decorations on people's lawns and green grass growing. That was a very bizarre sight to me since I have never seen this type of scene before in the month of January. It was very alien to me since I am used to several inches (or feet) of snow, seeing my breath and my ears and nose burning from the extreme cold during this time of month.

Yes, if you have visited us in the Midwest during the winter, you may see people in flip flops and shorts when it's around 40 degrees. That's becoming a normal scene now these days. I know, people can be real idiots. Flip flops are the extreme, but strange enough, people are wearing them. I am unsure if they are out of state or the locals. They will dress like its summer, get in their vehicle to go shopping, then when they reach their destination, they will get out of their car and walk into the store. They're clueless about "Murphy's Law". Things that will make your day go bad does happen when you least expect it.

I always wear shoes or boots in all weather conditions. You never know when something could happen and the footwear you have will not adapt to the terrain you're in. Always be prepared. In this case with the flip flops, they could freeze parts of their toes off and possibly their feet if they get stranded, especially during a snow storm or an unforeseen blizzard. Shorts, t-shirt and no winter boots in the dead of winter, I think these people will start winning the Darwin Awards. Weather is always changing and sometimes for the worse. People are not getting any better predicting the weather. How many times has there been no rain in the forecast and boom, it's raining. Or some storm just creeps in and they act surprised when it happens. ALWAYS BE PREPARED!!!

During these times of wearing articles of clothing to keep warm, you're going to have to be creative in getting access to your firearm since it may be a challenge with all the layers you're wearing. When taking off the jacket, you want to make sure that you're not exposing your firearm. I will have to make adjustments to how I wear my winter clothing while moving from one extreme environment to another (-30 degrees outdoors to a 70-80 degrees indoors).

For instance, let's say that I go to a mall or a grocery store. I may just park near the entrance of the building. I'll leave my jacket in the car and keep the winter vest on, walk across the parking lot and into the building. My vest is unzipped at this time. This may not work for most people due to their health. So again, you may have to make some personal adjustments. The establishment may not have shopping carts to put my heavy winter coat inside of it, so I'll just wear the vest. If there are carts, I will put my heavy leather winter jacket in there. I don't want to overheat and I don't want to be carrying a heavy coat. If I don't have a vehicle, but use public transportation instead, I will try to find a locker at the location I arrive at or carry a backpack and stuff it in there.

If I bring my winter jacket with me from the vehicle, I don't zip it up. There is a snap-button at the bottom of my jacket (just below the jackets zipper) that I keep snapped shut to prevent the wind from blowing it open. So when I brush the coat to the side, the bottom of my coat unsnaps and it allows me to quickly access my sidearm. I do not zip up my winter vest if I wear this by itself. If it's a very chilly day, I will wear my heavy winter coat (unzipped) and have my vest on underneath the winter jacket zipped up to keep out the cold. But I make sure that my vest is tucked behind my holster (the gun is not covered by the vest) so I can get access to my firearm.

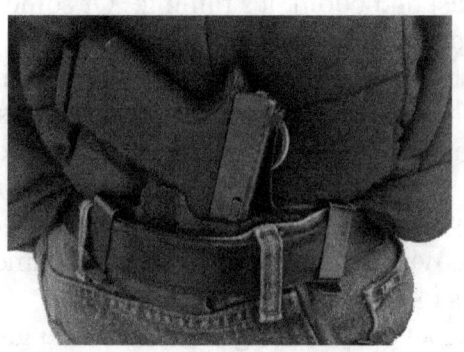

Winter undercoat/vest to keep the body warm and tucked behind holster. Winter coat will be worn over it.

This keeps my body warm, but I can still move my jacket to the side and quickly access my firearm. The reason I keep my front jacket unzipped is that with the many layers of clothing, it can be a struggle (especially with gloves on) to get to my firearm in time when I need it most.

When you go shopping, you can also put your jacket in the shopping cart, have your vest on (which can be moved over your sidearm) and walk around the store unnoticed. At least you will not be overheated, but remain comfortably warm and still have access to your firearm when needed.

The methods discussed above will also work with either OWB (outside the waistband) or IWB (inside the waistband) since the winter vest is covering your gear, but make sure it is long enough to cover in case you have to reach for something or bend over. And what's great about a winter vest, they make them for all genders. What I have also done is wear a sweatshirt and tuck it down my pants behind my firearm/holster. So part of my sweatshirt is still hanging out, but the only part of it is tucked in around the area of my holster to keep it clear so I can get access to my firearm. I will have my winter vest on over my sweatshirt (unzipped) and my sidearm is still hidden, but I can still access it. My sweatshirt will keep me warm along with my thermal underwear underneath (which is breathable and lite). There are also winter gloves designed for your trigger finger. Don't forget to add these types of gloves to your ensemble.

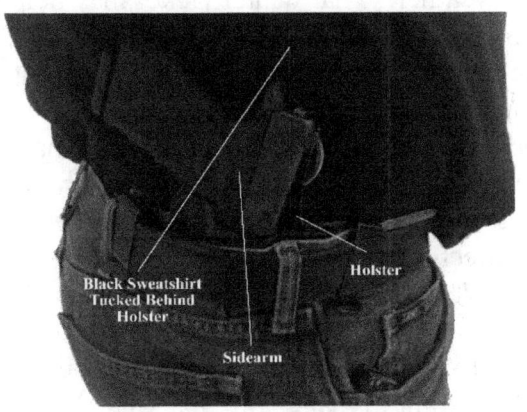

Sweat shirt behind holster before putting on a winter coat or vest.

The best way to beat the severe cold weather is to wear thermal underwear when the conditions ask for it. Here in the Midwest, you will see people in stores without their jackets. Sometimes, these people don't even carry a coat in their car (big mistake for the winter). They really forget where they're at sometimes and how quickly conditions can change.

A few years back, while driving down the interstate, I saw a woman in the ditch. She was struggling outside her car in a mini skirt with high heels, holding her little dog in her hands. She was not wearing a jacket and her car was buried in several feet of snow. It was 15 below zero and snow was coming down hard. She may have been minutes (miles) away from her next destination, but she lost control of her vehicle (probably distracted by the dog while it was on her lap) and she spun out of control and into a ditch. She would be stranded there until a tow truck arrived, but I am sure she was there for several hours since the snow storm had already started.

This is not the proper way to dress in extreme weather. She was ill prepared. If she was in the country and this one turned into a blizzard, she may have gotten frostbite or far worse while waiting for help. Wear a winter jacket and if you like, leave it in the car when you go into a store, but have your sidearm reachable but out of view. When you return to your car, throw on the jacket.

Why put the jacket back on before driving? If you ever end up in a car accident in the winter and possibly unconscious, it's nice to be dressed for the weather. That winter jacket may help you from freezing to death. It's like driving in the summer without any shoes on and your vehicle gets into an accident. If it's a severe accident, there will be glass everywhere, there could be a chance of a concussion to your head and you may wander around the vehicle. And if you have to escape your vehicle, you may find your feet impregnated with glass and car shrapnel because you have no proper foot wear, or lack thereof. Always wear some sort of protection on your feet, its common sense and match it for the weather. Don't wear flip flops/sandals, they can easily be lost in an accident and don't wear them in the winter!

You'll have to go through your winter gear that you'll wear and test it in the fall. You want to make sure that whatever you'll be wearing during the cold seasons, that you're able to access your firearm. Jackets are all different. Winter vests are usually the same (no sleeves, button or zipper). Winter coats can be leather, they can be long or short, and they can be puffy, heavy, or lite weight. So you'll have to play around with these jackets in the fall before it starts getting cold. You will also have to test it out with gloves. There are some great gloves online. You may want to start your search with the words "tactical winter gloves" to see what's out there. Read the reviews and research.

Thermal Underwear and Public Urinals

For men, you will find it difficult using the urinal when you have a sidearm strapped on in the winter. With your belt buckle fastened and your fly open, the thermal underwear will get in the way. You'll find yourself digging around trying to access your Johnson and discover that it may not be as easy as you thought it would be with all that material in the way. Times are wasting since your bladder might be full. My recommendation is to find a bathroom stall. With your winter gear, you'll probably have to put it on the hook of the door. Hopefully there are hooks for your jacket (don't keep your sidearm or valuables in your jacket while on the hook). With all your winter clothes, you'll just have to get creative in your situation depending on what you're wearing and what's available to you in the public stall.

Dressing warm to keep your body at comfortable levels is very important to help maintain the body's temperature at 98.6 degrees. If your internal body temperature changes, you risk the chance of getting sick and if not treated, it could lead to death. If your internal body drops below 98.6 degrees you risk hypothermia, or if it raises above 98.6 degrees, then hyperthermia would set in. So keep a healthy temperature with the clothes you wear in the environment you're living in.

DRESSING UP & GOING OUT

Sometimes in your life you're required to dress up for some social event and you need to think about what you're going to wear. Along with the clothing, you will need your EDC (every day carry) accessories. Will you be wearing your 1911 with the outside the waistband (OWB) and a coat to conceal it? Or will you be strapping on the inside the waistband (IWB) and using your shirt to hide it? Where will you put your spare ammo? Will you also be carrying a spare handgun? Where does your flashlight or knife go? Is there room for your personal medical kit?

Will this event have dancing and you have an ankle holster with a pistol in it? Has this ankle holster ever been tested with dancing, especially long periods of time on the dance floor? How good are the retentions on your other holsters? Will there be a lot of hugging with old friends and relatives? I got snuck up from behind at a wake one year and their arm hit the top of my firearm on my hip, knowing they hurt themselves on the hard metal by the surprise on their face (it's my cell phone I said). Will people discover your sidearm when they hug you? I will focus on hugging in another chapter and share a technique I use.

Take a look at your gun belt. Does it have the right pattern and color for your dress pants? Try putting your gun belt through the loops on the pants. Is the belt too thick to insert in the first belt loop? Make sure that your gun belt can go with your fancy outfit. Or will you have to figure out what plan "B" is so your pants don't fall down due to the weight of all your equipment? You may have to purchase another gun belt just for those special occasions. Or you may have to opt in for a shoulder holster.

If you're wearing a dress, where will you strap all your gear? Will you have a belt? If not, will the bra you're wearing hold up to the firearm bouncing on the dance floor? Will you be strapping on a shoulder holster and your jacket covering it? Since you may be hugging people, will they feel your gear under your arms? If you have a firearm strapped to your inner thigh, will it endure the dance floor and not slide down or pop out?

You also want to make sure that the location where you're going will allow a sidearm. You don't want to go to a party which has "No Gun Zone" signs and they are enforceable by the law. Or the state has designated areas where a firearm is not allowed. That's a felony with time in a prison.

So take the time to research so that you're not handcuffed inside a squad car because you were asked to chaperon at a prom and someone saw you were printing on school grounds and they called 911. So in your state, the law may say that it's illegal to be armed with a sidearm or even a knife in a high school. Don't make a simple mistake that could cost you many years of your life in prison. It's not worth it. Find out the law of the places where you are allowed to carry.

HOW TO DRESS AT THE RANGE

When you visit the range, what should you wear? Always think of safety first. Eye and ear protection is a given, but what about what you're wearing? Are you wearing a low cut blouse? An open top shirt? I have seen people end up with hot casing down their shirt and in their bra. And when you are distracted with this, your firearm may still be loaded. So where is your muzzle pointing as you do the hot potato dance as your trying to remove that burning casing away from your skin? I read a story where this happened to a man and he accidentally shot his 14 year old son. Make sure your shirt is buttoned up or your blouse is closed. Casings will be flying all over the place. I will have my range bag several feet behind me and I will still find casings inside my bag where the top is open.

Also wear a hat with a bill. This stops the hot casings coming down and entering your safety glasses. Some ranges do require a ball cap. Some people think it's idiotic. I would rather be safe than sorry and not have a hot casing hit my eyeball while I have live rounds in my gun and trying to stop my eye from burning. It could end up disastrous.

Try and wear long pants since hot casing may also hit your legs. Having long pants and long sleeve shirts with a ball cap also helps reduce the amount of lead that your body would absorb. Yes, people have died from over exposure to lead from all those rounds they've fired over the years. It will take years of constant exposure, but it does happen. Also remember to wash your hands and face after shooting. There is only one type of soap at this time that removes lead and it's called Lead-Off. Highly recommended. Especially if you have children.

After you go shooting, clean your skin where it is exposed. If possible, change your clothes. Lead will transfer from your clothes to your steering wheel, your seat and anything else you touch. If you have children, you want to also reduce their exposure. When you get home, strip your clothes off and throw them in the wash (but not with your regular laundry). I would recommend that you set aside a pair of clothes just for the range and just use these. And also have a pair of shoes that you hardly use and designate them for the range only. These will pick up lead for sure from the range. You don't want to track this around your car or house.

If possible, have a different set of clothes set aside for the range and a pair to change into when you go home or visiting other locations. When the body is exposed to lead, it does not know what to do with it. So it gets absorbed into the bones. Once it is in your body, it's impossible to remove, so it will build up over time. So start protecting yourself today so you can live a long life and continue enjoying yourself at the range without ending up with lead poisoning down the road.

BELTS, CLIPS, & CONCEALMENT

There are going to be different ways to secure your holster to keep your firearm concealed and this depends on the type you have. Some come with j-clips, c-clips, leather-clips, square clips, paddles and other designs. There are so many types of holsters out there to choose from, they're all going to have different ways to attach onto your gun belt. If you want something solid and going to last you a lifetime, go with metal clips and avoid plastic at all costs. If your concealment is going to be IWB (inside the waistband), my recommendation is to go with the metal clips that are black. The color black doesn't pop out as much as light colors do. Colors like silver, pink, tan, or other bright colors that are noticeable. Plus, black goes with almost everything. Remain stealthy as much as possible and have your clips blend in with your clothing if you're going with IWB (inside the waistband).

I have a gun belt that is made out of saddle leather. Between the leather, there is metal strip that is stitched in, which is used to strengthen the belt to hold heavy objects. I avoid the ones that have plastic inserts between the leather. With extreme weather, along with wear and tear, they break inside and the belt degrades. Friends of mine have switched to metal because the plastic doesn't last as long. The metal insert does provide some flexibility in the belt and it will hold up my gear without drooping or pulling at my pants when my belt buckle is fastened.

With ordinary leather (low quality leather), it stretches and puts your gear out of balance. After a while, the belt starts to deform and droops in those areas where you have added weight. The leather will also deform due to the frequent movements made around the waist and it starts contouring to the shape of your body. After a normal leather belt has been worn awhile (like 6 months or longer without any gear), if you lay it out on a flat surface, you'll notice that it's no longer straight, but bent and twisted.

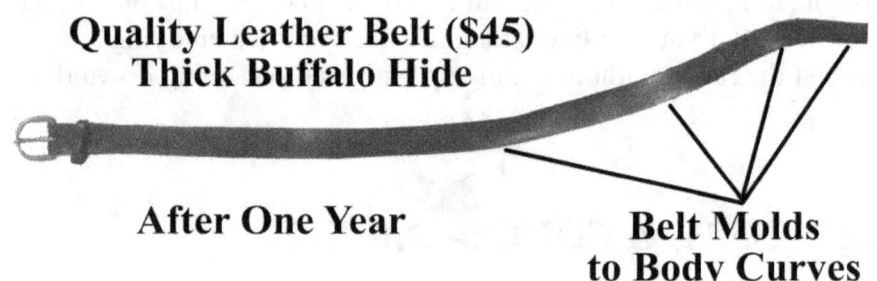

**Quality Leather Belt ($45)
Thick Buffalo Hide**

After One Year   **Belt Molds to Body Curves**

This quality leather belt used to be straight. Not recommended for firearm use. Get a real gun belt.

With plain ordinary leather belts (the non-gun belt types), the sidearm starts to flop up and down while you're walking. When I first started carrying after I got my permit, I used an ordinary thick leather belt that I bought at a mall, thinking that it would be good enough. When I walked, my sidearm would bounce up and down. There was not enough stiffness in the belt to keep it from moving. I kept tightening the belt, but this did not work too well. The buckle started to make a mark on my stomach. So I decided to purchase a real gun belt online. The gun belt came with a metal core. I can coil it up, stand on it and it won't crush under my feet. So I know I have a very durable gun belt. This is an awesome belt and I know that I will get many years out of it. After wearing it with a sidearm for about a year, it has not deformed yet. Don't use a regular type of leather belts. You want a belt that was designed for a sidearm, otherwise you'll run into problems, especially back problems.

Sometimes with my IWB, I may just clip on the front clip of the holster to the belt and leave the rear clip attached to the pants instead of clipping it to my belt. I noticed that with different pants, that moving around from walking, sitting and other activities, the rear clip moves a little to adjust for the movements. Some holster may compensate for the movement, others may not. The front clip is still in place and on the belt, which never moves. So my holster remains in place, even when I draw my firearm. Depending on the pants you're wearing, using both clips on the belt may feel restricted (pinching against your side) and you don't have much movement during your daily activities. This all depends on the type of IWB holster you're using.

If you want to do deep concealment (using IWB), you can just attach the belt clips to your jeans. The gun belt will cover the clips. For some, depending on their waist size and proportion, the clips can move around the pants. Our bodies are all different shapes and sizes, so this method may work great for one person, but not for another. If it was clipped to the belt, then chances are slim that the holster will move. But remember, over time, the metal clips will start cutting into your pants if not clipped to your gun belt.

Since I conceal carry, I always look for others that are carrying. I like to see how concealed they actually are.

Here's an example. One day at a gas station, I saw a gentleman get out of his SUV to pump gas and then I noticed that he was carrying a crossbreed holster since the clips were on the belt. It was an IWB (inside the waistband) with the crossbreed logo (dead giveaway) on the metal clips. The belt was black in color and it was not concealing the brownish/tan clips very well. So it was screaming "I am carrying a sidearm". Otherwise, if the clips matched the color of the belt, it wouldn't have been noticeable.

With different pairs of pants, the loopholes may be in different locations because not all pants are equal. I found myself readjusting my holster between different types of pants and this was wasting my time. So I came up with a method to match up my holster to the correct position every time for each different pair of pants. I took a laundry marker (not a permanent marker) and marked the inside of the pants matching up where my holster goes. Now I can clip on the holster by matching the clips with the pen marks. For any pants I have, I just match the holster clips with the pen marks, put on the pants and belt, then clip the holster onto the belt. With the laundry pen, the clip marks will stay on after many washes.

CLOTHES SHOPPING FOR YOUR FIREARM

When you're looking for clothes to match your concealed carrying lifestyle, the shirt/blouse is one of the most important pieces of clothing in your decision making process. You want to make sure that what you pick out, you can access your rig as quickly as possible. For the ladies, you also have the option to hide a firearm under your skirt, but this would be an area that would take a little longer to get to compared to a blouse since you will be bending and lifting (like going for an ankle holster) to get to your firearm. So this could add an additional second or more depending if you are standing or sitting. If you're Scottish or Irish, then the same would go for your kilt.

If you like to wear your shirts/blouses hanging out, make sure they are hanging at the crotch level (around the zipper line). Having a top that is too long can add to your draw time and having it too short may expose your sidearm when you lift your arms (reaching for something). So you want to test this out first before you go out into the public.

When you pick out your clothes, try to practice your draw in the mirror in the changing room (if you're positive that it's not a two-way mirror). Remember to have no ammo in you firearm when you do this. See if your movements are limited and that your rig remains hidden. Bending over, twisting, reaching upwards are ways to test your new shirt/blouse. How did it feel? Is there plenty of room for movement?

Are you printing (seeing the outline of your firearm in your clothing)? If you don't have your firearm (because gun free zones may be enforceable by law), use your hand motion when sweeping your top up (using your thumb) or raising the garment with your non-dominant hand to access your firearm. Can you get to your firearm? Does your clothing catch on your backside, does it stop you from making a complete draw, or does your gun hand get caught in your clothing?

If you decide to bring your firearm. Pick the last stall in the dressing room. Since you're in the last stall and if there's an active shooter in the area, this will give you time to load your ammo, especially if they do show up in the dressing room. Also make sure you lock the door so no one accidentally walks in on you when you have your gun exposed. You don't want to end up explaining the circumstances to local law enforcement where things could get misinterpreted.

Again, never forget the four universal gun safety rules. While in the dressing room, some mirrors are two-way in clothing department stores. If you draw your weapon (loaded or not) and point it at the mirror, there may be someone on the other end watching you and they may feel threatened, or they may also be carrying and decide to shoot back at you. They won't know your intention. So I would recommend using your finger to sweep up your clothing and drop your hand on your firearm (without drawing) and decide if the shirt will restrict or hinder you. Or turn sideways to the mirror and draw at the wall. But please make sure that your firearm is unloaded before you do this. If it fires, you're in trouble. If you don't have your weapon, then practice as if you had it. Then after you find the right shirts/blouses, purchase your clothes and try them on again at home, in the mirror to make your final decision. It's a little extra work, but you'll get good enough that you may never return things.

Also test your tops to make sure that if you decide to tuck them in your pants that your firearm is not printing. If you wear tight tops, your chances are good that you may be showing others that you carry. You also want to practice pulling up that top while it is tucked in to see how quickly you can get to your firearm.

When you buy things like hoodies or apparel that you will pull over your shirt (for those cool crisp fall days), make sure you don't have any cords that hang out from the bottom of the apparel. Some have a waist cord to tighten up to keep the cold air out. This can get caught by your hand when drawing or it might get caught in you trigger when you holster your sidearm. Or it may cause your firearm to accidentally discharge when you're bending over or sitting and the cord is trapped inside your trigger guard. Just make sure there is nothing getting in the way. Just try and avoid those types of outfits that have a string hanging out. I have cut those strings off of one of my tops to see what happens, but the bottom of the hoodie becomes very flimsy and loose. So cold air blows up my shirt. Having one that has an elastic bottom will work best, but not something too tight to hinder your draw time.

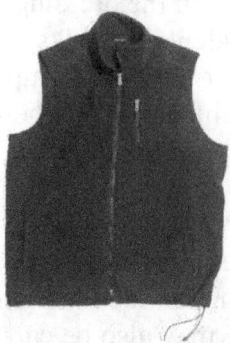

Winter vest with a cord dangling.

If you're buying pants, this can take a little longer since you have to strap on your holster to each pair of pants. Or remove your ankle holster for each pair of pants that you'll put on. To reduce any chances of the firearm from discharging, I remove the ammo and slide my pistol into my flimsy pocket holster and set it on the little chair in the corner of the dressing room and out of the way (but still quickly accessible). I try my everyday carry holster on different pants, make the adjustments, remove my firearm from the flimsy pocket holster (with no ammo and no round in the chamber), then insert it into my holster again.

I will test each pants this way. If you wear an ankle holster, you will need to bend down to get your pistol. You want to make sure that your pants are not too stiff and you're not having problems reaching for it. Or if you're bending your legs to get to the ground to draw, you want to make sure there is flexibility in those pants. When I leave the dressing room to show my clothes and get the nod of approval (yes, I need approval since I am a guy in a relationship, I am not allowed to embarrass others that I walk with), I have my firearm with me and walk around and ask if I am printing.

When you're choosing pants, you want loops in the back that will hold your gear. Make sure there are at least 4 belt-loops spaced out in the back of the pants. I have seen some pants that have only one belt loop in the back and this is not enough stability for you every day carry (EDC). A good pair of pants will have 5 loops which really stabilizes the back of the pants. If there are only one – three, you will notice that you'll find yourself adjusting your pants more frequently since there is not much stability in the back of the pants. Having pants with five belt loops in the back gives better retention to your belt and it doesn't slide up and down as much. You feel like you have more control. Also make sure in the front that you have enough belt loops and they are not spaced out too much.

Preferred Number of Belt Loops.

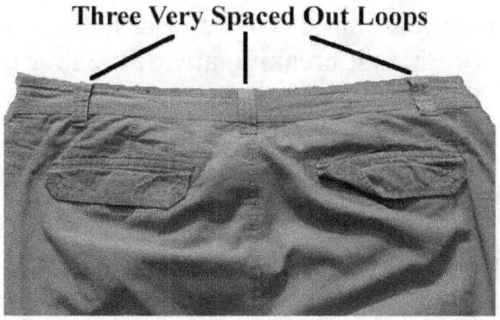

Not preferred due to lack of retention for EDC and lack of ironing.

If you do decide to add a firearm under the skirt, you will have to find the right skirt to easily get access to your pistol. When you try on skirts in the dressing room, make sure you follow the four universal gun safety rules. And make sure your firearm is unloaded. However you have your sidearm strapped onto your thigh, make sure that it's not printing and when you sit down, the skirt is not too short and others can see your firearm. No one wants to have a weapon pointing at them when they accidentally see up your skirt. You want to maintain concealment at all times. You also want to make sure you can reach the hem of the skirt, pull up and draw your firearm. If it's too long, you may have to bend over a little more than you should (while maintaining your balance) to try and grab the skirt to pull up.

You also want to make sure that the material is not slippery where you can't get a grip on the skirt. You'll have to practice drawing in the mirror (pistol unloaded) to see which skirt works best for you. And also test it by sitting in front of a mirror to see if your pistol can be seen pointing back at you. I know that it has to be pretty, but it also has to be practical since you're carrying a loaded weapon.

When you shop for clothes, I like to ask myself these questions:

- Will the garment conceal the firearm?
- Will I be able to access my firearm and draw within a split second?
- If the garment holds my firearm, is the trigger protected from accidental discharge?
- With the type of clothing I will be wearing and how my firearm is being used with it, is it breaking any of the four universal firearm safety rules?

If the garment does not allow you to do any of the important bullet points above, then find another piece of clothing. Don't risk safety for fashion.

Last thing. How can you tell if it's a two-way mirror? Take your finger and place it on the mirror. Is there a gap between your fingernail and the image of the nail on the mirror? If so, it's not a two-way mirror. But if you notice that your fingernail directly touches the image of your nail, then it's a two-way mirror. So you're safe with a gap. No gap, someone may be watching you.

CHAPTER THIRTEEN

What Ifs

"In the sky, there is no distinction of east and west; people create distinctions out of their minds and then believe them to be true."

Buddha

DROP THAT GUN!

We're all in the habit to catch something as it slips out of our hands and try to retrieve it in midair before it hits the ground. What about a firearm? Should you try and catch it?

What do you think would happen if you try to catch a loaded firearm? Here is what you should do when your precious firearm is about to hit the floor… Let it!!!

Yeah, I understand that you have money invested in your sidearm and you don't want to mess up your beautiful finish, or damage that light or laser on it. Ok, so you're afraid that you may damage it, but do you want to take the risk of what the outcome could be? There is a strong possibility that if you try to grab it, your finger may hit the trigger and you may risk injuring or killing someone, or causing damage to someone's property.

Many modern guns have internal safeties that prevent a discharge when dropped. So keep in mind, let it fall, even if it will hit concrete. I would rather repair my weapon instead of it discharging and someone being killed (especially myself) or wounded.

As I was writing this, a very interesting video that came out about the Sig Sauer P320. If the gun hit the floor at a specific angle, it would actually discharge. The internal safety features failed. Unfortunately, it wasn't thoroughly tested. Folks, stuff like this should never happen. After I saw the video and the recall posted by Sig Sauer to upgrade those pistols, I decided to add this note into my book to inform you (a public courtesy). It also made me drop test my own firearms, just to make sure.

With the unloaded pistol, I would drop it at every possible angle to see if the trigger would click. It's not scientific, but I would slam it real hard onto the carpet with a snap cap in it to see if it would fire. Mine did not, so I feel much better about it. It passed with flying colors. So maybe testing out your own firearm (unloaded) to see if the internal safety features are still working may be a good idea after all before you decide to use it.

AFTER THE TRIGGER IS PULLED

Remember, you are responsible for every round that leaves that weapon. So if you're involved in an incident where you're attacked and you end up drawing your weapon, what happens next?

Take note, when that sidearm leaves your holster, be prepared, your world is going to change forever!

Many things are going to happen over the next few days, months and possibly years. First, you're going to have to call 911 to report it no matter what the situation was. As soon as your sidearm leaves your holster in a life-threatening situation, you are going to have to call the authorities. Several things are going to happen in your life once that gun leaves your holster.

Once you present your firearm to someone, you have just bought yourself a ticket on the roller coaster ride of hell. Twists and turns on that ride may play out for a very long time. Hopefully not and the police don't arrest you since there were plenty of witnesses. If they need you to go with them, it's going to be a long day and an emotional ride for you and your family for days to come. If you don't call it in when you sidearm leaves its holster, this can also be used against you in a court of law.

If you draw on someone and they run away, guaranteed, they're going to report you to the authorities. The bad guy/gal will call 911 first to report you. This is something they have learned from others to get out of a bad situation. Why? Because it works and it's very effective. Plus, they just want to ruin your day.

The reason for the bad people calling 911 is to turn the tables on you. They want to look like the victim and make you look like the aggressor in the eyes of the law. So the first one who reaches a 911 operator and reports what happens will be considered the victim (the winner). This has happened in many cases. Yes, I know that it doesn't make sense, but what does lately? They will most definitely use this tactic to stay out of jail.

Rule #1, after that sidearm leaves your holster, be the first to call it in. The clock starts ticking and you're going to have to be the winner. If the bad guy/gal has been shot or you have the situation under control, call it in. If they do run away (even if you present your sidearm and not fire) and you don't report it, someone might have seen you (a bystander) and they may call the police. Or the bad person you drew on will most likely call 911. It may look like you pulled your gun on someone and you're now the bad person. Cover yourself and call it in right away. If not, you may get yourself into some deep kimchi. You'll be a wanted person and it may not be in a good way. Things can be misinterpreted easily.

If you do end up firing your sidearm, leave everything where it's at. This is now an official crime scene. Don't move your ammo casings on the ground, don't move the body, don't do anything. If you had to drop your magazine on the ground, it stays there. The investigators need to examine everything to corroborate your story. If you move things, you are contaminating a crime scene, possibly destroying evidence and this will be used against you.

When the police arrive, make sure you have your weapon away from you if you're not in danger. They don't know who the bad person is here when they arrive at the scene. If they see a gun in your hand when they arrive, it's going to look bad and may not go in your favor. Safety first for those officers that arrive on the scene, they don't want anyone shot, including themselves.

If you have your firearm pointed at the bad person when they arrive, lower your weapon slowly to the ground (don't unload it or make any sudden moves) and follow the directions of the officers. The police are going to assume that you're the assailant and they will take action against you. Giving a description of yourself to 911 will also help them in determining who is who.

If you're safe before the police arrive, your sidearm should have no magazine in it, the chamber should be empty and in the opened position (good for safety reasons also). They may also handcuff you and put you in the squad car. This is normal procedures since they are trying to work a crime scene and identify people.

Do not tamper with the evidence. Yes, you need to understand that this is now a crime scene. If bullets start flying, the casing, magazine(s), the body, anything and everything must remain in its place. If you change things, you will be convicted of tampering with the crime scene and you will be considered the bad person since you are interfering with an investigation. I would suggest taking photos on your phone of the scene after you called the police and your attorney. Just in case someone botches things up and there are questions. Give the photos to your attorney, email yourself a copy.

Do not talk to the police. Keep a tight lid on what happened. You could be in shock. What you say can be used against you. Tell the police that you will cooperate with them 100%, only when your attorney is present. Lawyer up right away to protect yourself. Tell them that you're in shock and need some time to think. You can have a card in your wallet with a typed up message and hand it to the police explaining to them that you will cooperate, you would like to talk to your attorney and that you DO NOT give permission to search your car. I have one that I can use in case that I am unable to speak because I may be in shock. Keep your story to yourself until you see your lawyer. If you have a notepad and you're not in custody, write down what happened. Give yourself at least 24 hours before you do this. Your mind will play tricks with you due to shock. Do not show your notepad to the authorities, save it for your attorney.

The police may confiscate your weapon. If they do, get a receipt for it. It may take some time to get it back (could be months or longer), but this is where your attorney comes in to retrieve it. You are innocent until proven guilty and you should start right away in getting your firearm back. You may also end up in jail until things get sorted out. Someone will have to put up your bail money. While you're in jail, DO NOT talk to anyone about what happened. What you say can be used against you. The District Attorney may interview those who were in the cage with you to see what you said. If you bragged about killing someone, you're screwed!!

The media and your family. The media may also pick up on the shooting and visit your home. The police may also visit your home. I would suggest you let your family know that the police are not allowed in your home, unless they have a search warrant. You have the right to turn them away if they show up at your house. No warrant, NO ENTRY. You may have media camped out at your doorstep, so move yourself and your family to another location. Like a family or friends house. You are going through enough at this point and don't need the additional hassle. Also, DO NOT TALK TO THE MEDIA. What you say on TV can be used against you. Have your attorney speak on your behalf. Have a grab bag to go so you and your family can bug out right away before people start knocking on your door.

Sitting in Jail: If you do get arrested and end up in jail, keep your mouth shut until you have an attorney present. Do not discuss your case with the inmates. If you brag about shooting someone, these people can be a witness against you. They know the game. They will do anything for a reduced sentence and if you're bragging about shooting someone because you think this will make you look tough in jail, think twice. Keep your mouth shut about what happened. If not, you could end up looking like you pulled the trigger on purpose and this does not look good in front of a jury.

It doesn't stop there. You will have to appear in court. This is going to cost you money. You may end up paying up to a million dollars for fees and investigative costs. I suggest you research online for companies that offer you protection (insurance) after you firearm leaves your holster.

You may be sued. Yes, after the court case is done, you're innocent and cleared, but the family members, or the person you shot may come after you in civil court. It's completely crazy, but it's true. The bad person's family (or the bad person) will come up with some excuse that the person you shot supported them, or the family was dependent on that person or some other story (even though that person is a criminal with a long record), but they will go after you. So if the person you shot is dead and they have no family, you shouldn't have any worries. Some people end up bankrupt and divorced when a civil lawsuit is filed against them. If you purchased some sort of insurance to cover your court costs, find out if they also cover civil suits.

STEPS TO TAKE AFTER A SHOOTING

(1) *Call 911*
(2) *Give Your Name*
(3) *Give Your Location*

(4) Say the following: "*I was attacked*". "*I was in fear of my life*" (or fear of a family member, friend, etc.). "*I had to defend myself*"

(5) *I am wearing* _____ (so they can identify you when the police arrive)

(6) "*Please send the police and ambulance*". Even if no one is hurt, get an ambulance so you can get checked out and sent to the hospital. This will give you time to think and have your attorney visit (if possible) and keep you out of jail for the meantime while in the back of the ambulance.

(7). Call your attorney or the company you have insurance with for these situations so they can get the ball rolling.

(8) Call a family member to inform them of the situation (make sure they have your attorney info if you think they need them to call for you - you might be in shock).

(9) If you're not in danger, place your firearm to the side (out of reach) with the gun unloaded and wait for the police.

(10) Shut off your phone when the police arrive.

(11) Do not give permission to search your vehicle.

How to Protect Your Data on Your Mobile Device so it's Not Used Against You: *If you have a mobile device (cell phone, laptop, tablet, any mobile device that holds data) and you get arrested, it will be confiscated. My recommendation is to power off your phone/tablet before the police arrive. In some states, they can legally access your devices using your fingerprint. The good thing with iPhones/iPads is that they are encrypted if they cannot be unlocked. I am not too sure about the android devices since there are so many flavors of that operating system floating around out there. For Microsoft Windows operating systems (for your laptop or desktop), they are easily hackable, so I would recommend a program that encrypts your entire hard drive. With the iPhone/iPad, you need a passcode after a reboot of the mobile device before it lets you in. The fingerprint option will be disabled after a hard reboot (powering off and on). After you successfully enter you passcode, you can access anything with your fingerprint after that (if you have it set up that way).*

So if you want to keep your information private and encrypted with an iPhone/iPad, power it off and don't give up your PIN. Keep your PIN at a minimum of eight characters. Don't use anyone's birthdays, anniversaries, previous home addresses, or PINs that were used on bank accounts or you cell phone. If there is a paper trail or digital fingerprints of any of these numbers (if you have ever used this PIN before), they may find it.

If you use letters and numbers and a special characters in your passcode, this is the best protection, but an eight digit passcode is sufficient with just numbers. Don't use this passcode on any other computers or devices since this could be discovered.

You don't have to legally tell anyone your passcode to unlock your mobile device (this is your 5th amendment right), but if you accidentally give them an incorrect PIN, this just makes it one step closer to wiping your data. Keep your info private so it cannot be used against you in a court of law - so power off that device if law enforcement is involved. Any other biometrics can be cracked, like fingerprint and facial recognition, so always use an 8 digit pin minimum.

Your private life (text messages, notes, surfing habits, emails, photos, music, and social account access) will become public if you don't reboot that iPhone/iPad. I would recommend that you set up your iPhone/iPad to wipe your data after failed log in attempts. The default attempts on an iPhone/iPad is currently set at 10. After the 10th attempt, your mobile device's data will be wiped clean. At this time, there is no setting to change the number of attempts.

If the mobile device is on, you can always send a remote wipe command to instantly wipe its data. You can do this from any device in the world that has an Internet connection and a web browser. Make sure you have "Find my iPhone" / "Find my iPad" turned on in the mobile device. If you don't know how to do this, you will have to search the internet. This also depends on the iOS version installed on your device. To turn this feature on, it's usually under iCloud, in settings.

For example, if your iPhone or iPad is lost or stolen, you can go to www.iCloud.com on your computer, enter your iTunes ID and password, and then try to locate your device. There is an erase feature that enables you to wipe all its contents when it's powered on. If the phone is powered off, you can still send the wipe command. Once the iPhone/iPad is turned on, the signal will reach the mobile device and wipe everything. This is a great way to protect your data from getting into the hands of those who shouldn't have it.

LOST OR STOLEN FIREARM(S)

As a responsible armed citizen, take precautions and lock up your firearm(s) when they're not being used. If your home or vehicle was broken into, immediately report it to the authorities. Make sure you follow the laws in your state when it comes to storing your firearms. You don't want to be in some sort of legal hot water. If you get your gun stolen from your person (a mugging for example), report it. Anytime your firearm is lost or stolen, be a responsible gun owner and report it to the local authorities. Also, depending on your home insurance, you may be covered by your policy to have your firearms replaced. Or if you have some sort of concealed carry insurance, that policy may also cover those lost or stolen weapons.

Keep a record of your firearms and their serial numbers. Taking a picture at different angles showing the serial number is also very helpful to law enforcement when you report it. I like to keep mine on my phone and tablet. My mobile devices are always backed up to the cloud, so if it gets stolen along with my gun(s), I can always get access to those photos on the cloud. Depending on the type of phone or app you have, you can also go online to view your photos. This type of technology helps make it easier to get access to your photos and you can email it to law enforcement.

Just a side note, some states do not require you to report a stolen gun, but it may be in your best interest to do so.

Report your lost or stolen firearm right away to the police. This will help protect you from unforeseen circumstances if your gun is involved in a crime (your fingerprints could be all over it). Since you reported it stolen and if a crime was committed, then you shouldn't be connected to that crime since you filed a report with local law enforcement. Do what you can do to cut any ties to that firearm to prevent any future problems for yourself. You will also need the police report for the insurance company for your coverage. Also keep a copy of the police report and keep it under lock and key, just in case it tries to bite you in the rear later on. The police may not have a copy of it years later since it may have been lost due to a computer upgrade, computer hack, or some fire that destroyed their records.

So if a crime was committed with your gun and it was confiscated; since you reported it stolen, the police will return it back to you.

THE PARANORMAL & FIREARMS

Ok, this is going to be a topic of interest for some and others... Not so much. Well you can just skip to the next topic if you think the paranormal is a bunch of bullcrap, which I don't mind and don't blame you. But with my recent experience, I thought I would give it a shot. So here goes....

My wife and I decided to sleep at a haunted place to see if we would have that paranormal experience like others have talked about. Usually, these places, nothing happens to me and I am a skeptic on some of the stuff I see online or on these reality shows. I haven't seen any concrete proof on these shows, but it's just entertainment to mess with your head and some of it is actually funny. So we found a hotel online that advertised that they had a lot of paranormal activity. This place, over the years has been on several paranormal TV shows and many famous psychics have visited this place too. So I decided to check it out and put it to the test.

This hotel that my wife and I spent a day in is claimed to be the most haunted hotel in our state. We decided to spend one night there on Halloween, the day the veil between both worlds open up for spiritual activity – how spooky. When we checked in, we noticed that there was a couple of binders at the front desk, loaded with stories from hundreds of people who have spent time there in that hotel. They have shared their experiences and one of the most common themes that happens are things moving from one location to another.

I'll give an example of what was read from one of those binders. A gentleman took one of the three ring binders back to his room. He started to read it. Then he went downstairs to get something to eat in the restaurant, but left the binder in his room to read it later. When he left the restaurant, he saw that the binder was back at the front desk, but he was 100% positive that he left it in his room. He asked the hotel clerk if someone was in his room. The reply was "no" and the clerk responded that there was no cleaning being done at that time.

People have also reported their cell phones have moved from one spot to another and objects that seem to follow them. Like a red ball that belonged to a boy who had died 50 years earlier. A couple was in the playroom playing with that ball and left it there when they were done. They left the room and walked down the hallway and saw the exact same ball at the end of the hallway waiting for them. They went back to the play room and the ball was missing from the very spot where they left it.

I heard about this place ahead of time and decided to do some research. Since I read stories online about stuff disappearing and since I carried a firearm, I didn't want to take any chances. I am not an expert at this stuff, but if others claim that items disappear on them, then I am not one who would like to take that chance. I didn't want to have that experience with a deadly weapon getting stolen (ghost or no ghost). I know that it sounds silly, but I don't want something like this to happen on my watch. Can you imagine the conversation with law enforcement…? "Officer, it was in my room and when I woke up, this entity had it in its ghostly hands and poof it was gone." No signs of forced entry, no one cleaning the room while sleeping, hmmm…. This may sound pretty strange in a police report. Or they may get reports like this all the time of things disappearing from this proclaimed haunted establishment.

I am a bit of a skeptic myself, but I am not resistant to the fact that there are some things that cannot be explained, no matter how strange it sounds. During my research of this place, there is a story of a women who was murdered there and she had a reputation of hating men. So I just took that with a grain of salt, never thinking about it, until later.

But one night in this place changed my mind forever. I was actually attacked in my bed while sleeping. Around 3 am, something I could not see was pinning me down in the bed. I was paralyzed, I could not move and I was yelling "Get the hell off me!!" I could hear myself saying it out loud several times, but per my wife, she did not hear anything. She awoke to me struggling in bed trying to move with my eyes wide open and gurgling sounds coming from my mouth (probably me yelling, but nothing coming out). I could see my wife next to me, but I couldn't move. It felt like someone was grabbing my crotch, pushing it down, along with my legs and arms, forcing me down in the bed. Whatever it was, it was very strong and pissing me off. It was getting ever painful in the crotch area while I was being pinned down.

My wife came to my rescue by shaking me and whatever was on top of me, went away. I am a fairly strong person and in good shape, but I have never experienced that before. I had neck pains right after that incident. I wasn't having a stroke either, I am sure of that, I had a physical a month earlier with nothing out of the ordinary. My body immediately went back to normal after that. I could move, talk and walk. So was I attacked by this same woman who had a hatred towards men? Who knows, but I'll be back to see if anything else happens. I really didn't appreciate that kind of hospitality. I know that sounds crazy, but boy it sure got my attention and the pain afterwards lasted for about an hour.

So this is what I did to my sidearm to keep it safe from paranormal activity before I went to bed. Like I said before, this is a deadly weapon and I don't want it in anyone else's possession. So before our one day vacation, I researched what I could do to protect an object (like my firearm) and did the following…

I put circle of sea salt around my firearm. I also sprinkled holy water on my sidearm and put some sage (used in Indian ceremonies) on top of it also. This is supposed to protect it from any poltergeist activities. It creates some sort of firewall to prevent spiritual activities from messing with it. So I can't say that it worked or not, but my firearm was still there and it was right next to me on the floor (there wasn't a night stand on my side) during the time I was attacked.

The experience was strange, but memorable. We had a great time, except for that part of being grabbed and pinned. I would like to go back again and experiment. I would do the same thing with my firearm (creating that firewall) and provide no spiritual protection with a plastic gun, just to see if it disappears and the real firearm remains. That would raise the hairs on my neck for sure if it disappeared or moved to another location. That would just boggle my mind.

I guess with this lesson, do some research on haunted places before you visit and protect that firearm from leaving your side. If you don't believe me, I wouldn't believe it either, but that night chipped a little away from being a skeptic with that experience.

CHAPTER FOURTEEN

Socializing

"When one pays a visit, it is for the purpose of wasting other people's time, not one's own."

Oscar Wilde

CARRYING IN SOMONE ELSE'S HOME

One of these days, you're going to run into a situation where you will be invited into someone's home. So what do you do if you carry every day?

First, you need to check the laws in your state. For example, at the time of writing this, Missouri has a law that homeowners can put up a sign on their premises telling people that they are a gun-free zone.

Here is the verbiage:

"Any private property whose owner has posted the premises as being off-limits to concealed firearms by means of one or more signs displayed in a conspicuous place of a minimum size of eleven inches by fourteen inches with the writing thereon in letters of not less than one inch."

These are enforceable by law. So in this case, you are not allowed to carry in someone's home who displays this sign. So what do you do if you want to carry, but those whom you are visiting are unaware that you have a sidearm?

What are the risks if you do legally carry in someone's home?

- A confrontation with the homeowner?
- A loss of friends?
- You're asked to leave?
- A call to the police?
- An ear full of how you are endangering their family in their own home?

The end result is that you are asked to leave. If they cannot understand your lifestyle, that's okay. You may just never visit that house again, or just not carry. You can just make your apologies and leave. If the police are called, you can just show them your permit and walk away. As long as you did not brandish your firearm or threaten the homeowner, there should be no trouble with the police. So the decision is up to you on what you want to do.

Let me share some examples of events that have already happened in the news when a person visits someone's home.

So what if you are having dinner at a friend's house and someone breaks in, what do you do? Will you be able to defend yourself? Maybe that person was the previous home owner who lost that very house in a foreclosure, he is still pissed off and comes over drunk threatening people with a weapon, blaming the new homeowner for his troubles. Yes, this has happened.

Or you're in a rough neighborhood with a high crime rate. Maybe someone down the street is on drugs and chooses that home you decided to visit that day. While you're there, they come in armed looking for money in a safe. They saw that the homeowner had a new expensive car and they thought this person has money to spare. So they decided to rob the place. Yes, this has happened.

What if you're a home inspector or a female real estate agent and you discover someone broke into the home, or saw you enter and forced themselves in behind you. Yes, this has happened.

The way I look at it, you have the right to carry if you're not breaking the law and you should be able to carry in someone's home, as long as you are a responsible person in their household. I carry in people's homes, but since it is concealed and I have a permit to carry, they will not know that I am armed. Only a select few people know that I carry and those people also carry.

Let's look at it this way. What if I carry a knife in someone's home? I keep one on my belt. A knife can cause just as much damage to a person than a gun. You can be carved up like a thanksgiving turkey or stabbed multiple times. I have seen videos of victims that have been stabbed over 50 times and they did not live and it is a horrible way to die. It happens very fast and once you have been cut, you will be losing blood quickly. If you were shot, your chances are a little bit better, especially if the bullet misses organs and passes through you. So would the homeowner ask you to leave if you carry a knife?

I am not the threat when I carry in someone's home. It is just an instrument to protect myself and others when needed. It is no different than any other object you can use to defend yourself. What if you're a

female real estate agent showing a home for a customer? Should you carry? You are in someone else's home.

What about a home you're visiting where the family has someone who has mental issues. The family just warns you that they act out sometimes, but nothing to worry about, they are harmless. Then you are left alone with them for a few minutes and they see you as a threat and attack you. What would you do? Yes, this has also happened.

Let's say that you are a home inspector and the homeowner is a violent sex offender, or maybe their uncle was recently released from prison on a violent offense and they were asked to let you in, but you did not know any of this before you decided to inspect their home. Would you still carry? Yes, this has happened.

Honestly, I do not inform anyone that I am carrying in their homes. I have a firearm legally, I have gone through the background check, I have had training and I carry concealed. So as long as I am not told up front (verbiage or signage), then I will carry until I am asked not to in that home. The keyword here is concealed. As long as you don't open carry in someone's home, you will be fine. If asked to leave, then just leave. Why take the risk if someone targets that family, or you, when you are visiting someone's home? As you read stories about robberies and violent crimes, you will find similar stuff mentioned above in those news stories.

I don't know people's situations, or the behind the scenes of what's going on in their lives, but let me share some examples. If I was visiting a friend's home, I may not know……

- If they are wanted by the law
- If someone is stalking them and mean to do them harm
- If they owe money and someone is about to collect and do harm if they cannot pay
- They have mental issues
- If they fired an employee and that person is out to get them
- If they are a random target
- If an ex-spouse, who is violent, shows up while you're there and wish to do them harm
- If they have a drug problem or they are a dealer and someone wants their stash

- Or anything else that could lead to violence

You cannot predict situations like these, you have no idea of people's intentions and what their frame of mind is, or what kind of trouble they're in. All you know is 'you' and you should be taking care of you.

HUGGING AND FIREARMS

There will be occasions when someone will want to hug you. At a family event, children, friends, loved ones, etc. And yes, there are those who are not huggers. This is not about them. But if you're one of those people, maybe you should try it. You may like it. Just saying…. This technique works great if you carry on the belt/hip area.

Anyways, when I see someone starting to initiate the hug, I try to take control of the situation. I will use my dominant arm and move it towards them, slide it between their arm and the side of their body, then move my arm upwards towards their armpit and wrap my arm around their back. Their arm will be over mine. They will not get a chance to feel my firearm on my hip since their arm will be above my arm and around my upper back.

Children are a little different because of their height. Sometimes you'll get your legs hugged or your waist. If they are going for your waist, you can just bend your knees and get at their level and have them hug around your chest. You can do the same dominant arm hug so they will not feel your holster. Or you can put your elbow over your sidearm and push your elbow towards your torso and give them a hug. They'll never notice.

If someone hits your sidearm and they give a strange look, just say it's your cell phone, pager, or your multi tool that you always carry with you. They won't give it a second thought, unless they are experienced around firearms. So when hugs are initiated, don't wait for them to make the move, do it before them and take control of the situation. If you're not a hugger, than why are you still reading this?

So hug away everyone!!!

DATING, SEX, FIREARMS, & O-FACES

A topic that you probably never thought you would see in a book. I wonder what things are popping up in your mind at this moment when you saw the title for this topic. Should we worry?

At one point in your life you'll be going out on a date and carrying a sidearm. So what do you do? When do you tell this individual you're carrying?

They could be a person that you've never met before. It could be someone you recently met in person or online. As a concealed carrier, you have a different lifestyle than others and you want to find someone who will not have a problem with you carrying a concealed firearm. There sure will be problems if you date someone who is against them.

I am not here to spread paranoia, but if you're meeting with someone whom you know nothing about, don't let your guard down. There are people on dating sites that will take advantage of you. Some will roll you for your money, steal something of value, or harm you. So please be careful if you either meet them in person, was introduced by someone, or met online. There have been people who have been robbed by gunpoint by these people. There is one story I read about one attempt by someone they met online and they decided to meet at a motel. He was meeting a girl at a hotel, but it ended up being a guy. But they picked the wrong person, he was a concealed carrier and it did not end well for the bad guy. So don't put yourself in these situations. Just meet with them in a public place until you have vetted this person.

We all have a vetting process when we're trying to find that right person who will meet our expectations. That's the point of dating. To find out if they're a match and if you want to share your life with them. With any people you meet, don't let your situational awareness drop.

Remember to follow the law when you're out on a date. If your date wants to meet at a place where you cannot legally carry (like a bar or restaurant for example), then see if you can meet at another location where you are not restricted. Also remember that drinking and firearms don't mix. So order something else, like an ice tea or soda while on your date. You want to have some sort of control over any situation that may arise and not be tipsy or drunk.

Concealed carry is your lifestyle that you will not change and those that love you should accept your lifestyle. If this new person in your life doesn't agree with you in carrying a firearm, then this person will not be a fit for the way you live your life. You'll get those rolling eyes, unnecessary comments, questioned about your lifestyle and then conversations about how you need to stop carrying. Is this the type of person you want to be with for the rest of your life who thinks that you're paranoid and they just don't see the world as you do?

On your first date, you obviously would like to get to know this person and you definitely don't want to reveal that you're carrying at that time. You want to vet this person and see where they stand with firearms. Since you're there, you might as well drop a few things in conversations to see what their thoughts are around guns. Then you can determine at the end of the date if you want to proceed or not.

You should not reveal on the first date that you're carrying since you won't know what kind of reaction you'll get from this person. The date can become very uncomfortable with a lot of silence in between conversations. So start out with baby steps first.

Maybe inject the topic of TV shows. Mention one of those crime drama shows. Tell them that you really like one of those shows. See if they like that type of show and maybe the conversation of guns come into play. You can say that you wanted to be a cop as a young kid. Or you had a relative that was one. Then you can ask if they ever shot a firearm before and see what they say. Just slowly ease into it.

Ask them if they like westerns, pick a movie that you both have seen. Then lead up to asking if there are any hunters in the family. What type of game do they hunt for? Ask them if they ever went hunting with them or even shot some game. They may open up and say they like them, hate them, or are just neutral.

Come up with talking points that could lead to firearms. Then see if they feel comfortable or not. You never know, the person sitting across from you may also be carrying a sidearm. You want to ease into things instead of just dropping the bomb on the first date and say "I am carrying a gun".

You can also throw the following into your conversation to see if they've read this book. Think of it as a covert conversation to see if that the person across from you is someone like you. Ask them what their favorite cocktail is. Whatever their answer is, just respond "I was at this bar in Florida and the bartender made me a drink called the bullet train. Best drink ever". If they ask what's in it, then say "I don't know, but it came in a pineapple and wrapped in a magazine". If the response is "Was the magazine guns & ammo?" you can just smile and the both of you know that you are concealed carriers and have read this book. Now the both of you would have common ground in your conversation. You can take it to the next level and go to the range after dinner. If the conversation doesn't match the one above, then you know they did not read this book and you'll have to use other tactics. I thought I would set something up for my readers so they can quickly get on the same page with their dates and skip all the questioning if they too have read this section on dating.

If you did not get to second base with firearms and you like this person, try a second date and continue with other topics that could lead up to firearms. By the end of the night, if you got nowhere, then towards the end of the date, you might want to lob that grenade. Why? You want to find out if there will be a third date or not and you're probably into this person. You don't want to waste your time and energy on the third date if you have not figured out by this time if they are pro-gun or not. Just ask them towards the end of the date, "I know this is a strange question, but what's your opinion on firearms? The reason I ask is that it's one of my interests and I don't want to alarm or surprise you since some folks are fearful of guns." I wouldn't mention at this point if you carry. If they give the right response, you'll know where you stand for the third date.

Also keep in the back of your mind that you can't change someone and it's not your responsibility to do so. If you really like this person, but they're against firearms, you're not going to change their mind and it's not your duty to change their opinion. You'll just make the situation worse. The relationship will not last long, you'll have differences and the relationship may end up badly. Leave it alone, there are plenty of fish in the sea, find someone else.

I think that you should have a trust relationship with someone before letting them know you carry concealed. I would hate for that person whom you had a failed date with tell everyone that you carry. Then this could lead to other problems if they start spreading the word that you carry. You could end up as a target of someone who wants to challenge you, wish to cause you problems, or just wants your sidearm.

The person you wish to have a relationship with may be against firearms or they may feel completely uncomfortable around them. Since carrying concealed is your lifestyle, you don't have to give it up because someone else disagrees. You can just give them up. Why? It's going to be a headache down the road and why create such an environment for yourself anyways? It could end up toxic. You want someone who has similar interests as you do and who doesn't care one way or the other if you do carry or not.

Opposites do not attract, but it's only true if you're a magnet (not a chick or guy magnet). People who have similar interests will have attractions for each other. If you meet someone who's against firearms, this should be a flag that the relationship won't last long. It will come to a point in the relationship of "Which one are you going to choose, me or that firearm"? Relationships do not last if interests are different. So there's no reason to put so much energy and time into a relationship if there are constant battles due to differences.

Remember, your firearm is now a part of you. It is a tool that is carried daily to help protect your life so you can enjoy a longer time on this planet. You have only one body, a vehicle you travel in to enjoy the things around you and the people you meet in your life. This vehicle that your soul lives in is delicate and must be taken care of (exercise, eat healthy foods to fuel your vehicle, frequent washes, getting tune ups by the doctor, etc.) by doing regular maintenance to keep it running and to protect it so you can continue your travels through life.

It's your responsibility to take care of it and defend it. This is your home until it can no longer support you. So having a partner that understands this is going to be a relationship made in heaven. If your partner is also armed, then you can relax around this topic of interest, build the relationship and grow it to many levels.

Lifestyles of the Bunk Buddies.

Let's say that you're not interested in a relationship at this time, but just want to play the field for a while. So you're going to have to ask yourself if sex and firearms are safe.

If you follow the 4 universal safety rules you should be okay, but with one additional rule for your safety - Keep it hidden. Like many of us, we love sex and on life's journeys, we meet people that we would like to have an intimate relationship with. But as concealed carriers, we live a different lifestyle that most would disagree with. Understandable since our world of realism is different from others.

There are going to be times where life introduces you to people who feel the same urges as you, but aren't interested in a commitment, but just want to have fun. These can end up as very short and hot relationships or just a one night stand exchanging o-faces. Depending on your new friend, they may be curious by nature and having a firearm on you before you're about to go full monty, may raise an eyebrow when they see it....And it could end up going sideways. No sex for you!

I would recommend not sharing with the other person that you have a sidearm. You may not know this person, they may have a fear of guns, their curiosity may get the best of them and with lacking firearm training, and they could get themselves hurt or killed. Or they could simply be a psychopath and in the middle of the night, you could end up getting one in the brain pan. Keep it concealed and have your fun. When you have full trust in that individual and you know they are okay with firearms, then share with them that you carry.

Before you share uglies and start doing the wild thing, maybe you can duck into the bathroom, grab a towel and put your firearm inside of it. You can use the towel as an excuse to clean up after having fun. Or you can just keep it hidden in your pants (your firearm and floppy holster), but near your side. Or hide it somewhere so you can easily access it, but not in the plain sight. If you're into paid performances (prostitution - legal in Nevada), I would highly recommend that you really keep it hidden. You never know what will happen. You could end up with a bullet, or when you wake up, your entertainer is gone along with your money and firearm. Now you will have to report it to the police and that could become very embarrassing, especially if you're married.

If you're married or have been in a long-term relationship, obviously these rules don't apply. If you're cheating on someone, definitely no one should be armed whatsoever. When you're trying to get attention of someone you like, don't use a firearm as a means of flirtation to impress the other person, or try to look macho.

BLACK FRIDAY & BEING ARMED AMONGST THE CRAZIES

Great topic huh? Just as I was writing this section (on Black Friday), there were shootings at a couple of malls today (Reno, Nevada and Atlantic City, NJ). Not inside the establishments, but outside. These people were fighting over something stupid. In one of these cases, a couple of idiots were fighting over a parking spot. In the end, one of them ended up <u>DEAD.</u> Over a stupid parking spot!! I wonder how important that space was to these people and their families. They didn't own it. They couldn't take it with them. After they leave, that spot would have been used by some other random person. Why couldn't they just find another parking spot? What's the point in arguing over a public space that is used by thousands of people every year? Parking spots....THEY HAVE NO VALUE WHATSOEVER!!!!! They are not worth battling over.

Don't be a tool like these people. If idiot people want to fight over a parking spot, let them. Stay armed, remain cool, and don't get involved. If it involves you, give it up and drive away. Let them have it. Don't lose your temper or your life over it. If it involves someone else, be a good witness. It's not worth it my friend. Let those idiots fight amongst themselves. Don't get involved with people who want to fight over stupid stuff. Getting hurt or losing your life over it is not worth it. If you accidentally get involved, deescalate the situation and get the hell out of there. Let them take that parking spot, let them have that big screen TV, let them have that goofy looking red fluffy character that talks, whatever it is, it will be there tomorrow, or at another store, or online. Put your ego aside and <u>LET IT GO!!!</u>

When tempers get out of control, don't end up in prison by drawing down on someone over a space, an object, or something else that upsets you. If someone is not using lethal force against you, then keep it in your holster. THEY are not worth your time or energy. During the holiday seasons, the alternative these days is to shop online. It's quick and easy.

I recently saw a video of a barbershop full of people and children getting their haircut. A woman was losing her temper because the haircut for her child was taking too long. So she pulled a firearm out of her purse and started waving it. She said she could because she had a permit. She was trying to force the woman to speed up the haircut. One of the barbers deescalated the situation by talking to her (and another barber had his gun out in the background, keeping it hidden). No one was hurt, but the police are looking for her. The video was aired on the local news, so she will definitely be caught. She will be facing felony charges. See how people can be stupid?

With these big sales around the holidays, driving to stores is a waste of gas and time. You'll end up fighting for a parking spot, then waiting in line to get into the store, then dealing with angry people, working your way through crowds of people, running from one end of the store to the other trying to find all your items, then waiting in line again. When you're done running around, did you have a great time or do you feel frustrated and drained? Do you feel like you're wasting your time and energy?

So instead of spending 5-8 hours out of your day running between sales, how about ordering your stuff online which would take a few hours of your time or less. This means you don't add miles to your car, waste gas, fight crowds, but instead, you can redirect the time you would have spent shopping doing something else. You won't even have the side of the car dinged or scratched by these people. And the best thing of all, you don't have to deal with people and their attitudes. Instead, you were able to spend quality time with yourself or your loved ones. You were able to watch a movie or do something gratifying for those 5-8 hours and you're not running around like a crazy person.

During these stressful seasons, I find myself making comments about other people's driving because they cut me off, I see people running through red lights to race to a store to get in line and I find myself shaking my head because people are extremely rude these days. If you take a look around, have you noticed the increase in the lack of respect these people have for others and themselves over the years?

I reflect back and notice that I too was contributing to this madness by running around on black Friday or Thanksgiving Day looking for deals. I should've been home on Thanksgiving Day, being thankful for my family and my life. To really get to know those around me, appreciating the time given to me to spend with them since I don't know anyone's expiration date from this world, including my own. I could be spending quality time with those I love since they too may not be making the upcoming holidays. I may not be making the next holiday!

But instead, I am out at the malls, being a mad person like the rest of those people. So I've stopped doing this.

I understand that it's somewhat fun doing this with friends and family, but it not worth the risks. Let the crazies do their frenzy. Be the wise person and do it online or shop some other time and focus your energy somewhere else.

There are crazy people out there and being in a swarm with them at a mall seems like a pretty good target for wacky people who want to vent their frustrations out on others. The world is ever changing and somewhere down the line our society as a whole went sideways and upside down and we went off the tracks somewhere. It's a complete wreck.

Remember, don't put yourself in a situation where you may have to defend yourself or others. If the alley is dark, would you walk through it? If you see a group of people across the street approaching you, would you not go in a different direction or walk into a store and let them pass by? Or would you walk through an area that you knew to be very dangerous? Be a smart and avoid crowds, especially during the silly seasons at all costs.

CHAPTER FIFTEEN

Things You Should Know

*"Knowledge is learning something every day.
Wisdom is letting go of something every day."*

Zen Proverb

FIREARM OWNERS PROTECTION ACT (FOPA)

As a concealed carrier, you are going to be traveling through states that will not recognize your permit through reciprocity. But there is a Federal law called **FOPA** that will allow you to transport your firearm through those states, but as long as you're traveling through and not stopping to visit people or staying for a while. If you do, you'll be breaking the law. If you stop for a while, you are considered no longer traveling and you will lose your legal protection. So if you have a carry permit and a firearm in a state that does not recognize your permit, as long as you are passing through, you're allowed to transport your firearm(s).

Dustin S. Reininger, a former police officer, who in March of 2009, stopped off in New Jersey, took a nap in a parking lot on his way to Texas and was arrested. At around 3:25 am, Officer Gregory Wester knocked on his window, asked a few questions, shined his light in the back seat, saw two cases, asked a few more questions and decided to search the back seat of the SUV (without consent). Firearms were discovered in the cases and he was arrested.

Since he was in a SUV and didn't have a trunk, he had his firearms in two nylon cases behind him in the back seat and he also had a loaded Glock in there. He had hollow points, a shotgun, a rifle and magazines that were considered "High Capacity" - over the 10 bullet limit (a term that makes no sense at all).

Mr. Reininger was a former police officer who can legally own firearms and was sentenced to five years in prison. All because he stopped to take a nap on his trip from Maine to Texas. He stopped in New Jersey for a short nap because he was tired. Some of the stuff he possessed is illegal in New Jersey.

Let's talk about FOPA.

Firearms Owners' Protection Act (FOPA) - Amends the Gun Control Act of 1968 to redefine "gun dealer," excluding those making occasional sales or repairs. Exempts certain activities involving ammunition from current prohibitions. That's just the description, but there is additional things inside that act which you as a concealed carrier should know.

I am only going to focus on one provision called the "Safe Passage" provision, or 18 U.S.C. § 926A -"Permits the interstate transportation of unloaded firearms by any person not prohibited by Federal law from such transportation regardless of any State law or regulation." If you want more information on the bill, you can find it at **https://www.congress.gov/bill/99th-congress/senate-bill/49**

So what is it?

Interstate Transportation of Firearms (§ 926A)*:* "Notwithstanding any other provision of any law or any rule or regulation of a State or any political subdivision thereof, any person who is not otherwise prohibited by this chapter from transporting, shipping, or receiving a firearm shall be entitled to transport a firearm for any lawful purpose from any place where he may lawfully possess and carry such firearm to any other place where he may lawfully possess and carry such firearm if, during such transportation the firearm is unloaded and neither the firearm nor any ammunition being transported is readily accessible or is directly accessible from the passenger compartment of such transporting vehicle: *Provided*, That in the case of a vehicle without a compartment separate from the driver's compartment the firearm or ammunition shall be contained in a locked container other than the glove compartment or console."

Here is the link to the statute:
http://uscode.house.gov/statviewer.htm?volume=100&page=766
just in case you have to present it in court.

So the nitty gritty here is that there are three stipulations that you must follow. But a heads up, there are a few states that will harass you, or arrest you, even though you are following the Federal law. You may end up in court defending yourself telling them about the "Safe Passage" law and hopefully get released after that (key word "hopefully"). Some of the states that are very anti-gun (like New York and New Jersey for example) have a reputation of not wanting to follow the rules like the rest of the states and people end up getting harassed. So be prepared.

This law is vague in some areas, but I'll try to clear it up. For legal purposes, I am not an attorney, or pretend to be one, or play one on TV. I am just trying to interpret what "Safe Passage" is from what I have read and my opinions on what it means. I would recommend talking to an attorney to be safe before you travel to other states with a firearm and also to be sure that you're up to date with the current laws.

Feel free to look up the law yourself to get more familiar with it.

Here are my interpretation of the "Safe Passage":

1. Before you start transporting your firearm through those states where you cannot carry, you must have them locked up, away from everyone in the vehicle and unloaded. I would recommend keeping the firearm(s) in the trunk with the chamber empty, with no loaded magazine in the firearm. All ammo must also be locked and away from everyone's reach. If you have compartments in the vehicle, like any consoles or glove compartment, this does not count. It is still in the reach of people and not locked up.

2. When you do start traveling, the state you **start in** and the state you **end up in** must be places where you can legally carry.

3. Keep "traveling" with short stops in those states that do not recognize your permit. You can stop for gas and food, but not visit people or stay over. Don't take naps at rest areas or any other places. Unfortunately this provision is vague on what the time limit is, so keep moving to avoid spending time in jail.

So just to be clear, make sure you know the laws in those states you visit, if they don't recognize your concealed carry permit, don't stop for anything except to refuel and get the hell out of that state. If you can go around those states, that would be great. Anytime law enforcement is involved with you in a state that does not recognize your permit, it can go sideways, even getting pulled over with out of state plates (which is why Dustin thinks he was targeted because of his Texas plates). So keep moving on. If you're hungry, pack a lunch or get some fast food. With Dustin's situation, I would even think that if he stopped for food and someone saw his cases in the back of his vehicle, he would have still been arrested if law enforcement were involved.

WARNING SHOTS

You see it in the movies all the time or you may have heard it from one of our politicians in an interview about how it's okay to give warning shots in the air. Well, where do you think that bullet will go? Does it magically disappear into the air once it leaves the barrel? Don't take advice from Hollywood on guns or politicians who know nothing about firearm safety (shame on you!). Again, you're responsible for every round that leaves that firearm. **_NEVER EVER_** give a warning shot!!

If you shoot one in the ground, it could ricochet off of a rock in the earth and hit someone, or if you shoot it in the woods, someone may be back there hiking. Or shooting in the air, it will come back down and it may hit someone. People have been killed in their own kitchens when a bullet fell from the sky and went through the roof and hit them in their own homes. Or a bullet comes through a window or wall of a house and kills a child while at their own birthday party. This has happened. Don't make this tragic error and then end up going to prison.

You see it in the movies, but those folks know nothing about gun safety and they just get people in trouble all the time.

Let's say you're at a great distance from your attacker. They present a knife and start walking towards you, you then present your firearm for self-defense (your still at a safe distance), if the sight of a firearm does not stop them, you have every right to pull the trigger. Remember, you can pull the trigger until you can stop the threat. In this situation, you decide to use warning shots.

There are no guarantees that it will stop them. They may not be in the right state of mind or drugged up and a warning shot is nothing to them. They may feel invincible, possibly immortal. They may even think that you're not serious because you're purposely shooting away from them. This does not scare or deter them. Don't take any risks around warning shots, this could cost you dearly. Warning shots are irresponsible and dangerous. It may even bounce back and hit you.

I have seen this on a range where a piece of the bullet ricocheted off of a metal target and embedded itself into the chest of someone on the range. It wasn't a warning shot, but it shows that bullets can bounce back and hit someone. If you're just going to carry a firearm just to scare people, then you shouldn't be carrying. It's not a toy, it's used for defensive purposes. That's why you verbally communicate outloud to people to stay away from you. This is what I call a "Warning Shout", not warning shot. If my "Warning Shout" is not deescalating the situation and my life is still in danger, then I will defend myself, but not with a warning shot. This will not end the threat and could get me or someone else killed instead.

Be responsible, don't do warning shots. If you do, you will go to jail for endangering others.

YOUR DEFENSIVE AMMO

I mentioned before that I am not going to talk about the type of gun or ammo to purchase since there is already a lot of information out there. I just wanted to mention the type of ammo that you should be purchasing. When it comes to your life and the life of others, you're going to have to pick the best type of defensive ammo that is out there which matches the rating for your sidearm. Your life may depend on it.

Do not use hand-loaded or reloaded ammo as your main defensive ammo. You want American made ammo that was designed for self-defense. It is going to be more expensive than the ammo you will plink with at the range, but you are investing in the success of saving your own life. Using low quality ammo for self-defense will have a greater chance of failure. During a gunfight, you don't want your firearm jamming, or your ammo not firing, or it explodes when you pull the trigger. You want ammo made by a quality manufacturer that has been tested for critical defense.

You want to make sure the ammo you use is created to stop the threat. FMJ (Full Metal Jacket) ammo is not considered critical defense ammo. It will over penetrate the body (go right through) if used in a defensive situation. Innocent bystanders may get hit by your bullet after it leaves the body of the person you are using equal deadly force upon. And you are responsible for that bullet. Some states may not allow you to use FMJ rounds for defensive purposes. Statistics have shown that more innocent people are injured or killed when using FMJ in a gun fight.

Defensive ammo (hallow-points or frangible rounds) are designed to go into the body, create a cavity wound and produce additional damage inside the body and not over penetrate. You're trying to stop the threat by using hallow-points and frangible rounds, they are designed to expand on contact to make holes in the body and do as much damage as possible. Frangible rounds are designed to expand and release pedals (pieces of metal from the bullet) that will create more internal damage to the body to stop the threat.

Always test the ammo with your sidearm to make doubly sure that it works. It can be expensive to go through a box of hallow-points or frangible bullets, but your investing in your life to make sure you come out alive after a gunfight.

FIREARMS AND OFF BODY CARRY

Off body carry is when you store your firearm in a different location other than your body. But it should always be near you. You will find purses, briefcases, day planners, man purses, backpacks, hand bags, portfolios, laptop bags and many others used as off body carry devices.

I am kind of the straight to the point person and really don't like to beat around the bush, but I really wouldn't recommend using these. Too many things can go wrong with this type of setup.

Many of the ladies love their purses and there are plenty on the market that incorporate a pocket for firearms. I am going to be totally honest with you all in that I would highly recommend on-body carry. I know that some of you will disagree with me on this but let me bullet point some reasons why off-body is not a great idea.

Grandpa "G" and Grandma "D's" reasons not use off-body as a carry solution for concealed carry.

- Off-body devices are easy to access and steal.

- If you sit down (restaurant, bar, coffee shop, etc.), it will take you longer to access your off-body holder if someone starts assaulting people or you, especially if it's in a location that you have to dig for it (like you have it slung around your chair). Time is of the essence and if you can't get your sidearm out and on target in less than a second, it could cost you your life or a loved one.

- It is not really considered concealed, meaning it is a target for thieves. They may not know what's inside, but they see your off-body carry bag as value and they will do anything to you to get it. Especially if they are coming up behind you with an instrument to make you unconscious for a quick grab.

- You can easily forget your off-body carrying device. How many times have you asked yourself "Where is my purse? Have you seen my keys? Did I shut off the lights? Where is my cell phone?" This is a strong indicator that you will forget your off-body carry in the future. People have forgotten them at restaurants, shopping malls, parks, vehicles, bathrooms, etc.

- It takes away valuable seconds to defend yourself to unzip, dive your hand into the off-body carry bag and present your firearm. By that time it could be too late.

- If the off-body bag/purse is not a cross body style, but like a handbag type, you always have to remember where the zipper is to access your firearm. It may have the zipper on the side and if its facing in the opposite direction where you cannot unzip it, you will have to flip it around to access your handgun while you're under attack.

- If you're under attack, the off body carry may not be in the same place as it was before. It could have been pushed behind you, to an area that is not reachable, or it could be in the hands of the person assaulting you.

- If you use the cross body style bags/purses, it can be used against you by a thief. You can be dragged by the strap until it is broken, you could get entangled when it is grabbed and you cannot access your sidearm, or you could be strangled by the straps. It could happen so quickly like most attacks, you wouldn't know what hit you.

- Some off these off-body carry bags may not have a trigger guard to protect against accidental discharges.

- If you shoot from inside the bag, hopefully there are no objects in the way, plus it is a guessing game if you are able to hit your target.

- You may accidentally put objects in that pocket of the bag/purse and if it lodges itself inside the trigger guard, you could have an accidental discharge.

- Unattended, it can be accessed by children. There are many stories of children getting access to guns in a carry bag/purse and it makes me squeamish just to think about the loss of life of a child, especially when it could have been easily prevented. I do not wish this upon anyone.

After reading the bullet points above and you are still set on using off-body carry, then that's your prerogative, but remember, safety starts between your ears and you are responsible for your own actions or lack thereof.

PURCHASING A FIREARM AS A GIFT FOR SOMEONE

Say that a birthday is coming up for your spouse and you want to purchase a firearm for them. What do you do?

First, you'll have to check out the local laws in your state. And also visit the ATF.gov website and do a search on purchasing firearms to make sure that you're within the law. During the time of this book, federal law allows you to purchase for someone who can legally possess a firearm. If they are going to carry concealed, they will have to follow their state laws, so they may have to have a permit to carry.

According to ATF's website (2017), the following are not allowed to possess a firearm.

1. Has been convicted in any court of a crime punishable by imprisonment for a term exceeding 1 year;
2. Is a fugitive from justice;
3. Is an unlawful user of or addicted to any controlled substance;
4. Has been adjudicated as a mental defective or has been committed to a mental institution;
5. Is an alien illegally or unlawfully in the United States or an alien admitted to the United States under a nonimmigrant visa;
6. Has been discharged from the Armed Forces under dishonorable conditions;
7. Having been a citizen of the United States, has renounced his or her citizenship;
8. Is subject to a court order that restrains the person from harassing, stalking, or threatening an intimate partner or child of such intimate partner; or has been convicted of a misdemeanor crime of domestic violence
9. Cannot lawfully receive, possess, ship, or transport a firearm.
10. A person who is under indictment or information for a crime punishable by imprisonment for a term exceeding 1 year cannot lawfully receive a firearm.

Such person may continue to lawfully possess firearms obtained prior to the indictment or information.
[18 U.S.C. 922(g) and (n), 27 CFR 478.32]

If your spouse (or anyone else) matches any of the items listed above and you purchase them a firearm, then you are involved with what is called "straw purchasing", which is against the law. And since

you gave it or sold it to them, you are now breaking federal laws and of course, it is a felony with 10 years minimum jail time and a $250,000 fine. Basically, you're screwed, so don't even think about doing this.

If your spouse (or anyone else) does not match any of the 10 listed above, then yes, you can purchase a firearm for them. If your spouse (or anyone else) does not carry, but has it at home with them, then they do not need a permit. Again, if they want to carry it outside, off the property, then depending on state laws, they may need a permit to carry.

Remember, after you purchase a firearm, it is nonreturnable, so make sure the gift you give is what the other party is asking for.

WHAT KIND OF CONCEALED FIREARM SHOULD YOU CARRY?

Yes, this question gets asked often and everyone is different in what they want to carry. If you're going to conceal carry, then here are some suggestions on what to look for. These are just the basics to get you thinking and start researching for the firearm that fits your needs. In this section, this is all about concealed carry handguns, not rifles or shotguns. Here are some basic things to consider when purchasing.

(1). *Price:* If you are involved in an incident where your firearm leaves the holster and there are police involved, your firearm may be confiscated. So if you purchase a sidearm worth $1000 or more, then you're going to be out of your investment for a while, unless you have a really good attorney. Always remember to get a receipt if your sidearm is confiscated by police. My recommendation is to keep the price as low as possible when you purchase a defensive sidearm. There are some really good firearms in the $500 range or less. If you have $1000 to spend, why not get two firearms in case one is damaged or in police custody. Then you will not be disarmed until your gun is released from law enforcement. Don't forget to have an extra holster, just in case the one you were carrying also gets confiscated.

(2). ***Grip Size***: Our hands come in many different shapes and sizes, so there are no "one size fits all" firearms. So do some research on quality defense handguns that are out there and find a range that you can rent from and try them out. You might find the one that fits perfectly in your hands, with very little recoil when you shoot. You will really feel it when you put several hundreds of rounds through that handgun. When you sign up for defensive handgun classes, you may end up shooting over 1000 rounds. Will your hands hold up with that type of trigger and grip? I have had friends that have complained that their hands hurt after several hundred rounds. If it fits like a glove and you can get your rounds on target, than you have found the handgun that will work for you.

(3). ***Portability/Concealment:*** There are so many handguns to choose from and what you should focus on is if you can conceal that firearm. Is the butt of the gun too big and printing? Then look at some midsize sidearm. I know that your 1911's are real popular, but some are too large to carry and are difficult to conceal at times. If you carry a large sidearm, how will you hide it during daily activities? Also think about where you will conceal it. Will your full size firearm dig into your body when you carry? Will it be comfortable? Will a compact or subcompact work best?

(4). ***Ammo:*** How much ammo will your sidearm hold? 5, 6, 9, 15 rounds or more? Also remember, you should also be carrying spare ammo in case you need it. If you can find a firearm that has a double-stack magazine, this will hold more ammo. If you ever read interviews of police officers in a gunfight, the topic that always comes up is ammo. "Sometimes, you just don't have enough ammo" is the top response from most of these officers. So you will need to make the decision of how much ammo your gun should have and how many spare magazines you can carry. You will also need to check on the laws in your state around how much you can carry.

Your magazine could be a failure point and if your gun jams, you will have to clear it, but you may have to drop in another magazine in case the one you're firing from fails. I personally like handguns that carry 15 minimum in the magazine, so with a spare magazines I can have 30 rounds and if I happen to have another, that's 45. Two spare magazines and one inside the firearm should be plenty. You will not remember how many rounds you will fire when you have to defend yourself. You could easily empty your firearm in seconds and may have to reload immediately - if you have spare ammo.

It may take up to 9 rounds or more to stop someone from harming you. If they're on a narcotic and they get shot, their body will not respond to it right away, even after hitting them 5 or more times. That adrenaline will be pumping and with the drugs in their system, they are not even feeling the pain yet. The more blood that exits their body will slow them down since this is basically what's keeping them alive and they will eventually experience a system failure. You may end up emptying your magazine and then inserting the second one because usually bad people work in teams and you may have to defend against the second or third person that is coming after you. They usually travel in packs, so be prepared. The more ammo the better for self-defense.

(5) *Reliability:* Do your research to find out if the firearm you're interested in has any recent recalls, if people are complaining about it, or if people are raving about it. There are people who love to torture firearms. Jump online and search for videos on people who really test the hell out of these things. I found one video of a man who took shots at some sort of manikin with a firearm in its hand, pretending it was the bad guy. One of his bullets hit the ejector of the bad guys (manikin) firearm. He took that pistol and tried to fire it and it was still working after that. A nice big dent in the side, but it still fired. It still jammed after each shot, but he was able to get it back into battery and fire it again. You want something that will not let you down when you need it the most.

(6) *Warranty:* What type of manufacturer's warranty comes with your firearm? Does it have a one year warranty? Five Year? A lifetime? How about the place you purchased it from? Do they offer a warranty? Some gun stores offer a lifetime warranty of the firearms they sell. New and used. What's covered by the warranty? You can go online, check out their warranty to see what is covered and what's not. When you send in your firearm to be repaired, you will have to remove any accessories that have been installed on it. If they replace your firearm, you won't get your stuff back. Make sure you keep anything that you

replaced on the firearm and return it as if you just bought it off the shelf with all the original equipment.

(7) **_Weight:_** How much you firearm weighs is also important since you will be carrying it daily, several hours throughout the day. The lighter the better, but having something too light may produce too much recoil when you pull the trigger. This of course is the reason why you should try out firearms first before you purchase so you get something that fits your needs. With all the gear that you might be carrying, every ounce does add up. When you shop for a firearm, think about backpacking in the woods. Every ounce you add to that backpack makes it heavier and heavier. So you want to make sure that your everyday carry (EDC) gear doesn't weigh you down. Too much weight will also contribute to back problems.

(8) **_Ease of Use:_** Is the firearm easy to use? Do you have to fumble around with it to get it to shoot? You basically want something that you can point and shoot since we are talking self-defense here and you need to get on target within seconds.

(9) **_Maintenance:_** Is it too complicated to clean the firearm? Do you need tools to take it apart? Is it easy to put back together? How many pieces are there when disassembled for basic cleaning? Four, Five, More? You are going to need a handgun that is toolless and as few parts as possible when you take it apart. Carrying around extra tools can be a pain in the ass, especially if you lose it or misplace it. If you're out on the firing range and you have a jam, taking it apart may have to be an option to fix the problem. My sidearm when taken apart has the frame, slide, barrel and recoil spring. Just 4 pieces that need to be removed for cleaning. No tools are necessary and it takes about 5 seconds to disassemble.

(10). **_Safety:_** What sort of safety features does the sidearm have? Are they external, internal, or both? What mechanisms are built into the firearm to prevent accidental discharges? Which one works best for you? Is having too many safeties slow you down when you have to draw your firearm? How many manual manipulations do you need before you get the safety off and fire when needed the most? Will you end up pulling the trigger and nothing happens because the safety is still engaged?

There are several types of safeties on firearms. Manual safety, drop safeties, grip safety, decocker, etc. You obviously want a sidearm for your daily carry to be safe, but you want one that you don't have to putts around with to disengage the safety to make it fire. I personally like the internal safety features, which means that the only way the firearm will discharge is when the trigger is pulled. If it gets dropped, the internal safety features prevents it from firing. This is all I need. Just point and shoot. It will not fire on its own, as long as the trigger is protected. You may have a different preference, but find out what type of safety features you need.

CONCEALED CARRY INSURANCE

Now these days, there are companies that will insure you if you have to defend yourself using your firearm. So should you get insurance if you're carrying a firearm for self-defense? I would highly recommend it if you can't afford an attorney or pay for court costs and fees, since these can soar to over a million dollars. There are many reasons to purchase insurance and the number one reason that people do is that attorney fees are expensive. If you do end up killing someone, would you rather have a law firm that has years of experience defending people who have been involved in a shooting, or a public defender that has little to no experience in this area when murder charges are filed against you?

What if your public defender is against civilians having firearms? Would you not want someone who is a 2nd amendment defender and also someone who also carries a firearm? I carry insurance just for that reason. I have read way too many horror stories of innocent people getting locked up by the justice system and ending up in prison because of lack of money or their attorney had limited experience in this area. I have already locked down an attorney that I want to work with and I have already interviewed them and also made sure that they also carry concealed. This shows that they have experience in this area and they are someone like myself who understands the importance of carrying a firearm.

The way things are now, if you don't have the money to defend yourself, your changes are very high that you'll serve time. I would rather have someone experienced in this area that can bail me out of jail and defend me. And the costs per month for this peace of mind are pretty reasonable. This is your life we're talking about.

Some of my friends always say to me that they should also get insurance because if that day comes where they would have to defend themselves, they would be covered. But unfortunately they keep putting it off. They're smart people, but procrastinators. When that day comes, I hope they have won the lottery by that time because they're going to need the money.

I mentioned "peace of mind" and what I mean by that is that if something does happen to me, I won't spend too much time in jail (if any) and I won't have to put my house up as collateral. My bail will be paid for right away and I can go home to see my family, possibly that same day. In my mind, I am covered if anything happens and I know I will be taken care of. And I won't be stuck with a large fee from the bail bondsman.

Yes, if you do have to go to one of those services for your bail, even if you are proven innocent, you will still be paying a hefty fee for that loan and it could be over thousand dollars. For what I currently pay for in conceal carry insurance, that's about a 2.7 years' worth in payments and my current plan already covers for bail and over 1 million dollars for court costs. And I am not giving my money away towards a bail bondsman who is only bailing me out and charging me for it. My investment is wise in selecting an insurance company that covers folks like me. So if something happens to my friends, who are professional procrastinators, they will be jailed and have no money for bail or their court case. They may have to put their home up, give up any assets and anything out of pocket. They may have to drain their 401k retirement to survive. I for one sure don't have that kind of money sitting around, I am not giving up my retirement for anyone else and you probably don't want to either.

Let's say you don't have coverage, you do end up in court to defend yourself and you won. Congratulations. Let's say the bill arrived and it's around $800,000. Your house had to be sold to cover much of the costs since a second mortgage would only cover a fraction of the bill and your paycheck may also have to be garnished to make the payments. And then after you think things are real crappy, well guess what, you've been informed that the person you shot, their family is going to sue you for damages. Poor little Johnny, with a rap sheet of felonies can no longer work to support his family because he is now disabled because of you. They will file a civil lawsuit because Johnny who supported the family financially can no longer do so. And yes, most of the time they win these court cases.

Now things have gone sideways. So now you've lost your home, your family has moved into your folks' home or your friends. You're probably going through a divorce at this time due to the insurmountable bills and the emotional stress this has caused in your marriage. And now you have this pending lawsuit that's going to put you further into debit. All because you had to defend yourself to save your life from some scumbag and since you procrastinated on the insurance coverage, you're in a predicament that could have been resolved by just having "peace of mind". It's pretty messed up, but that's the reality of things these days. I don't sell insurance, I am just trying to give you a heads up.

Again, I would recommend getting some sort of insurance if you're going to carry a firearm to defend yourself. Just a tip, your home insurance will not cover court cases or civil lawsuits. They may cover damages to your home if there was a gunfight in it and they may cover lost or stolen firearms - maybe. So you'll have to check with your homeowners insurance for what is covered.

I've prepared a questionnaire for you to get you started so you can intelligently ask questions to help you become more knowledgeable about the services being offered by these companies and what's covered. It's a lot of questions, but that's fine. It's an important decision to make. You want to compare your notes with other companies that will insure you and then do your pros and cons to see what company is best for you.

Concealed Carry Insurance Interview Questions. I say "interview" because I am hiring them to work for me and I want the best candidate.

- Do the attorneys in your network actually have any experience in defending someone in a deadly-force encounter? What are your standards in selecting these people?

- Do you have a 24x7 phone number to call if something does happen?

- Are there deductibles or co-pays?

- Do I need to pay the money back if I lose my case?

- Are there limits to how many cases a year (for example, let's say I've had a bad year and two times I've been arrested for self-defense)

- Am I covered out of state? If so, do I need to contact an attorney on your list before I go there (example: travel between Texas and Florida and the states in between)

- Am I covered for other areas of self-defense (use of deadly force), for example: Knife, pepper spray, baseball bat, machete, a pencil, etc. or just the firearm only?

- Is accidental discharges covered?

- Is the bail paid for? What is the limit? Does the attorney get paid right away to bail me out? Do I owe this or is it covered?

- How much does your policy cover up to? 1 million dollars or more? Note: Depending on the self-defense case, it could cost you over a million dollars.

- If my One Million Dollar Policy is reached, is that the cap, or will I continue to be covered if it's more?

- Will my emergency contact at your organization connect me to a lawyer when an incident happens, or am I on my own and have to try and reach out to them myself? What if I cannot reach them on my own?

- How long have you been in business offering this type of protection (insurance)?

- What is your insurance rating?

- Are you a member of the BBB (Better Business Bureau)? (Research any complaints against the company on the BBB website)

- Who is your insurer? Have they experience in this area of self-defense and concealed carriers (some do not)?

- Will the attorney come to the scene and interact with the officers?

- How many hours before my attorney connects with me after I make the call for help?

- Do I select the attorney, or do you?

- Do I get a counselor the help me psychologically after the event? I have heard PTSD can happen months or years later. If I am still a paying member months or years after the event, can I still get help from a counselor? How many session can I receive? How much is covered? Do I pay anything out of pocket?

- Are all attorney fees, investigative costs and expert witnesses covered?

- Do I have to pay any funds or fees after the crisis?

- Are mistrials covered? How about retrials?

- Are civil or criminal judgments covered?

- Are civil suit damages covered?

- Do you pay up front or after the verdict? What happens if I am found guilty? Are my costs still covered?

- Are my family members or relatives also covered by your insurance?

- Are my firearms also insured? Is there a full replacement cost?

- Are lost wages covered?

- If there is a gunfight in my home, what's covered? Physical damages to the property? The blood stains on the floor (biohazard)? What if the bullet travels outside my home? Is damage covered for my neighbor's property or any other damages caused by the bullet(s)?

- I already have conceal carry insurance. So how does it work out if I sign up for your service already having coverage? Can I use both, or are there conflicts? Does one have to be the primary and the other secondary? How does this work out?

- What other benefits do I get for becoming a concealed carry insurance member? Do you provide any discounts for products, training, or other paths to help educate me so I am better informed in the ever changing concealed carry world? Or do you just sell insurance?

After you do your own research, you may come up with some additional questions. I am not going to recommend an insurance carrier to you because they do change, like their rates and their policies. It's your responsibility to find out which one is best for you and if there are any other benefits that are added besides just insurance. Companies are becoming more competitive in this area and it's amazing on what you'll find out there. Some are not just selling you insurance, but education and training along with their benefits.

CONCEALED CARRY & GUN SHOWS

If you have a lifestyle of collecting firearms or hunting, gun shows are great for you. They will have a large selection of handguns, knives, scopes, cross bows, rifles, etc. Going to gun shows, you may get an opportunity to fire fully automatic weapons or military guns that are not legal for citizens to own unless they have a special permit. It's a big event for those who want to learn about military history, shoot some antiques (like a Gatling gun or a musket), do some skeet shooting, throw some tomahawks at a log, shoot arrows at a target, use their pistol range, or fire some big guns. You might even find some deals on firearms.

But if you're looking just at the carry concealed side of things, gun shows will not be for you. Gun shows are not really intended for those who live the concealed carry lifestyle. You will have to go to an event that is specialized only for concealed carriers. These are slowly popping up around our nation. Otherwise, you'll have to go online to find products just for your everyday carry.

At these CCW shows, you'll find those who have products just geared for concealed carry. You'll obviously find firearms at these events, but you'll also find classes and training around the topic of carrying. I have been to gun shows, but my interest is only in conceal carry and self-defense. I personally have never found anything that is related to CCW at these events. Their focus is on a different audience. Many of those people do not carry a firearm on them for self-defense.

So if you want to meet others who carry, learn more about this industry, find out about the CCW laws, get some self-defense training and try out some really neat products for your day to day lifestyle, then search online for concealed carry events. This will be your best resource for finding what you need for your CCW lifestyle. They may be slim pickings out there and you may have to travel out of state. But over the next few years, you'll see more and more of them since CCW is turning into a multi-billion dollar industry.

CHAPTER SIXTEEN

Firearm Mentality

"If you correct your mind, the rest of your life will fall into place."

Lao Tzu

IT WON'T HAPPEN TO ME

Some people have some sense of immortality and believe that they'll never be a victim. I have heard so often "I have lived this long without any problems in my life, so nothing bad will ever happen to me now."

The truth is, violent acts can happen to anyone at any time. Read that statement above one more time. Let it sink in. How about those people that are attacked in their 80's or 90's. Maybe nothing bad like this ever happened to them before and here it is almost a hundred years later, they have become a victim of a violent crime. Is that kind of statement said above mean that if you were a victim once, for the rest of your life you will continue to be a victim? It's one of the most ignorant statements I have ever heard. I want to share a hard reality with you, you're not immortal. You will die one of these days, sad but true. You may have a peaceful death or a violent one. So why not prolong your chances of living a longer life to relish in the joy and beauty of those around you? To do so, be prepared by protecting yourself. You only have one body to live in and you must do everything to take care of it and defend it.

It also comes down to survival of the smartest, not the fittest. With a sidearm, you can be the weakest person on this planet, but if you can point and shoot, you are much better off than those who are in excellent shape and think nothing will ever happen to them. Having a firearm is one of the greatest equalizers out there no matter what condition your health or body are in. But if you're attitude is that nothing bad will ever happen to you, then you're head is up your keister. You do not have any say in what will happen to you and you also don't have super powers that will keep you from harm from those who wish to hurt you.

Ask yourself this, have you had a bad day before? Car broke down, a death in the family, your boss hates you, slipped and fell, or even said to yourself "Why is this happening to me? I am a good person". These are the signs that you're not indestructible and anything can happen. The reality of it all, anything can happen to anyone at any time - without warning!

I too have watched the news, seeing people harmed or killed, but never thought that something like that would ever happen to me, but it has. I have been mugged and beaten multiple times in my lifetime. I have also had someone brandish their firearm during a mugging. A sibling of mine was robbed at gunpoint where the firearm was pointed at their temple. This is too close to home. I have had grandparents who were sitting at home watching television and their door was kicked in. They were beaten and robbed. My attitude back in the day was that no harm would ever come my way and that's normal thinking for all of us. But things do happen and I have wised up since then. So I learned to be prepared and expect the unexpected. But I learned it the hard way. I am lucky to be alive today.

If you truly believe that nothing harmful could happen to you, then you may become a victim one of these days and it may cost you your life. Pull you head out and get your head into the game of life where anything can happen. Since you're carrying a firearm, this tells me that you're level headed, responsible for your wellbeing and that you have made the decision to prolong your life in a world of violence. Carrying a firearm is a strong statement that you will not be a victim. I am giving you a virtual "Tip of the Hat" for being a realist and not living in a fantasy world. You have made the right choice.

DON'T GET COMPLACENT

After you start getting used to carrying your firearm, you're going to forget that it's there. It's going to be up there in the category of your cell phone, your car keys, or remote control of your TV. What does that mean? Once you get used to something, it's easy to forget it and you can become complacent. How many times have you lost your cell phone? How many times have you set down the TV remote and you can't find it? How many times have you set your firearm down somewhere and can't remember where you put it?

This is dangerous. You should not be forgetting where you left your firearm. It should be on your person at all times. There may be situations where you may lay it down just for a second, you get distracted by something or someone and put it somewhere for safe keeping. Then you attend to that matter and forget about your firearm.

Let's say you are out doing errands. You get distracted and leave your firearm in your glove compartment while getting money from the ATM, or you drive to a grocery store and forget it on the front seat of the car. Then you come back, find your window broken and your sidearm missing.

Here's another scenario. You have a holster installed in your car for easy access while you are seated. You go to the gas pump to fill up the vehicle and then approached by a homeless person looking for money. They will not leave you alone and now you're getting worried. Is there an accomplice nearby? Will you be ambushed? You finally get that person to leave using verbal judo and when you get back to your car, you discover that you don't have your firearm on you. It's still in the car. This has happened to people, where they forget their firearm in the car.

Don't get into the mindset of having your firearm out of your reach. If you have to attend to something, grab it and keep it on you. I understand that if you sit for long periods of time, the butt of the gun or the holster rubs against you and you need a break from the pain. So you decide to set it on the table. Is there any children around? How about other visitors? You don't want someone accidentally picking it up and it gets discharged. Just don't get into the mindset of losing your weapon. Don't get complacent with your firearm. It is not a remote control, it is not a cell phone, it is not car keys and it's not your wallet. It can be a dangerous weapon in the wrong hands if it's forgotten.

If you stash weapons throughout your house, always keep them in the same location so you're not looking for it in a place where you thought it should be. Then when you need it, you can't find it. Always keep your firearm on you or near you. If it's uncomfortable while carrying, examine the reason why and take care of it. Get a different holster, maybe a different firearm. Maybe move it to a different location on your body. This is a serious matter and the point is not to get complacent with your firearm. It could turn into something very dangerous.

CARRYING IS A 9-5 JOB

Do you carry from 9-5? Just 8 hours of the day? Why? Do you think criminals punch in and out of a time clock during the day and you're safe for those other 16 hours? Think again.

You should have your sidearm with you at all times. Even while you're at home you should be carrying. Why? Predators like to ambush you and when it happens, it's fast and without warning. When you're taking out the trash, working on your car, gardening outside, just opening the door to go outside, shoveling snow, answering the door, watering the grass, cutting the grass, doing dishes, taking a shower, sleeping, walking the dog (or walking the cat if you are one of those type of people), watching TV, going to the bathroom, making out (showing your "O- faces"), eating at the table, or whatever you are doing at home….. You could be attacked in your own house and without warning.

Be prepared since criminals do not care what time of day it is. Criminals do not work a 9-5 job, they will try to get to you 24x7, 365 days a year, on holidays, weekends and leap year. Always carry no matter where you can legally carry. I always carry at home and if I can't have it on me, it is at arm's reach. In the shower, near my bed, wherever, it's always there.

While in bed, I would recommend having your sidearm near you and able to retrieve it within a few seconds.

Let's say you hear a sound (clock is ticking) at night and your waking up from a dead sleep. You scan your bedroom for any sounds or movement (clock is still ticking), then you lean over and place your hand on the safe in the dark, feeling for the combination or using your finger print, pushing buttons, or an electronic wristband. Then the lid opens on the safe (clock is still ticking), you feel for your sidearm, then release it from its case and get out of bed. Then you search for your flashlight, then activate it and start scanning your room for intruders. You firearm is loaded, a bullet chambered and your safeties are off.

Then the clock stops ticking at this point since you're ready and able to defend yourself.

With that scenario, how long do you think it would take you from a dead sleep to arm yourself, then get on your feet, find your flashlight and be ready to defend yourself if necessary?

I guaranteed that it's not going to be a few seconds. From an almost dead sleep, about 10 - 15 seconds to get your hand on your sidearm and another 10-15 seconds to be completely get ready for anything to happen. You are looking at 20 - 30 seconds, or possibly more depending on how alert you are and how quickly you can get out of bed. Being over 50 some years of age, for me about 45 - 55 seconds. If you're older and a little slower, it could turn into minutes.

I was alone in the bedroom one day, I woke up from a dead sleep and I must have been awakened by something outside the bedroom door. I was surprised to see the crack of my bedroom door open for a brief second and it stop. I thought I was imagining it. I turned to look at the clock on the wall to my right to check the time, then turned to my left and my wife was standing there. She walked through that door and it took her 2 seconds or less to get to my side. I didn't notice her walk into the room. I was shocked. What if that was someone else that had no business being in my house? This made me reexamine things when it comes to personal defense while asleep.

So is having a safe a good option? Is it best for you to have your firearm locked up while asleep? Or should it be in your drawer, or in a holster on the night stand next to the bed? Depending on what side you sleep on in the bed and which hand is your dominant hand, seconds could be increased. There is a lot to think about here.

Let's say it will take you an average of 45 seconds to get armed and ready. What should you do? You've trained and trained to reduce the time, but you can't get anything less than 30 seconds. Maybe you should look at it from another angle. Instead of focusing on decreasing the time to get armed, maybe you should re-evaluate the security in your home. Maybe put a deadbolt lock on the bedroom door, or use one of those metal security posts designed to prop up against the doorknob. I take one with me on trips and they do work on carpet. Works great on hotel room doors. This will definitely delay someone. You could also use one of those door jams that are used to prop open doors. It will add additional time to get to your sidearm. You should probably have something in place to give you more time before someone enters your house, your bedroom, etc.

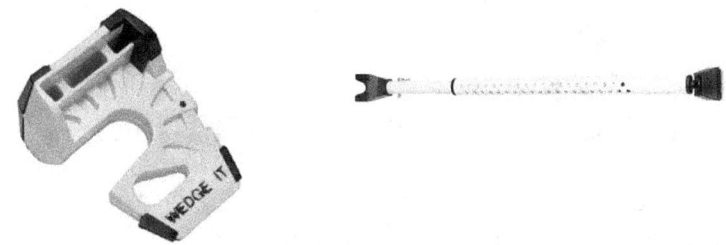

Two items I use to delay or stop entry into my home and rooms.

If you can delay someone's entry or be forewarned, one of those quick unlock safes, the ones that are not dependent on an electrical source, will be okay to use. As long as your adrenaline is not pumping too much, or your hands are not shaking….you should be able to unlock it quickly. I am not a fan of electrical safes, or safes that have a possibility to fail. Anything can happen and when Murphy's Law is come a knocking, it better not be in this position when you need your sidearm the most. If you lose power to your safe and have to find the key for it, or some other method to unlock it, you're going to increase your time into the minutes.

So find the quickest, safest and most efficient way to be in the ready position. Every second counts and you don't want anything to delay or stop you.

Next to my bed, I have a tactical flashlight, firearm and earplugs, just in case I have to fire indoors in the middle of the night. With the flashlight, I need to see what's going on and if I have to pull the trigger, I want some kind of ear protection. If you have a suppressor, then this would also be helpful in protecting your ears. Shooting indoors can be very, very loud and it can damage your hearing. So try to protect your ears so you can stay in the fight longer without the distraction of the gun noise. So having a set of earplugs ready to go on the nightstand may be a great option if you know there is an intruder in your home.

So before you go to bed tonight, practice with an unloaded firearm at how long it takes for you to get access to your firearm, to get out of bed and be ready for the intruder. This could be a drill you try several times a week to work out the kinks and then try it weekly once you've perfected it. Set an alarm for the middle of the night (alarm clock or cell) and see how long it takes you from a dead of sleep to being armed and ready. Look back at your clock and see if it's less than a minute or longer.

BEING IGNORANT ISN'T AN EXCUSE

It's your duty to be informed. What I mean by this is that just don't carry a firearm and call it a day and just stop there. But "G", I have my permit and firearm, isn't that all I need? Being ignorant when it comes to firearms will get you in trouble. Expand your horizons by being up to date on what's happening around you. Find a favorite website that posts concealed carry information on what's going on around the nation. Find those who frequently post videos that keep you up to date on the concealed carry community. Don't be ignorant by purchasing a sidearm and then doing nothing else about educating or training yourself on this great responsibility you have.

It is your responsibility to inform yourself. With great responsibility comes great challenges. There are ongoing changes in the concealed carry community, especially when it comes to the law. You don't want to end up in a place where you're not allowed to carry and didn't know it because you chose not to be informed and now you're being handcuffed. Your life is going to change forever.

As responsible armed-citizens (the key word here is responsible), don't make the common mistakes made by those who concealed carry and have given us a bad rap because they didn't follow the laws. Their mistakes add laws to the books that make it even more difficult to defend ourselves.

Some people just carry because they think it makes them look cool and they think its badass. These are the ones that give us a bad name in the eyes of the general public. They strap on a sidearm and decide they are above the law and make stupid mistakes, which could have been avoided by paying attention. Their ignorance turns into irresponsibility and this impacts the rest of us. There are idiots out there who just carry and know nothing about the laws, or the four universal safety rules. Because of their ignorance, something bad happens and the ripple effect surges through the media and screws it up for the rest of us. They have become that irresponsible armed-citizens, in which their actions floods the news channels and informs the nation that this one incident reflects on the rest of us, but in a negative way.

Don't be like those people. Keep up to date on what's happening in your area and around the nation. It will pay off, trust me. If not, it could land you in jail. Be intelligent on the topics of concealed carry, the basics of firearms and firearm safety. It's not that hard. You will be doing a big favor for the rest of us.

Since you picked up this book and reading this, it tells me that you will do very well in the concealed carry community. You will not stop your frequent training and you'll continue to learn more about this great opportunity that we have. You will feel grateful and realize that other countries will never be able to experience something like this for themselves. By educating ourselves, we stand a greater chance of continuing to defend ourselves in such a violent world we live in and in years to come, the negativity from the media will hopefully decline with more positive lifesaving stories. We must all work together on this through continued education and training.

So if we help each other by educating and training ourselves, we will be able to have a much more enjoyable life with less violence in our nation and gain more trust from neighboring Americans when it comes to carrying a firearm.

THE SELF-PROMISE

First of all, I just want to say that getting old just sucks. Over time there's more maintenance to be done to keep the body and mind going. And as age progresses, you start slowing down. There will be a day where you will not be able to carry a firearm due to a serious illness or disability. Unfortunately for some, that day will come. So what will you do about it?

Let's say you have Alzheimer's disease or maybe suffered a stroke. Because of this mental condition, you can't remember where you left your sidearm and you leave it in places where it is unsafe for others, like children. You can't even remember the four basic firearm safety rules. Due to this mental state, you can end up being a danger to yourself or others. Maybe you've already done some accidental discharges with your firearm. If stuff like this is happening, it may be time to hang up the gloves and retire.

If you have family members, they too will be concerned about your welfare and your firearm(s). So what do you do about this? You will have to make a promise to yourself and your family members and put it in writing. You will have to step aside and have someone else take up the responsibility (if possible). If you don't want harm to come to you or others, then you will have to make this big decision. I wouldn't wait until you get any older, start working on it today – don't procrastinate. Anything can happen to you between the time you read this book and tomorrow. You can be as young as 20 when things happens, because life can throw you under the bus sometimes. I know of people who were in car accidents that are in their twenties and the end results was a disability that impaired them so they can no longer function normally as they once did. When you no longer can carry a firearm, you must put it up for the safety of you and others.

If you have memory issues, I would hate to have you land yourself in prison and not remembering what you did and feel trapped behind bars. Waking up every morning in a strange cold place, with people you don't recognize, a bunk bed and a toilet, with roommates who may want to harm you. You're sitting in a cell, not remembering that you shot and possibly killed a loved one by mistake because you woke up one morning and didn't remember the faces of those around you. They became strangers and you thought they were a threat to you. So you shot at them.

This would be horrible to wake up day after day not knowing where you're at and wondering why you're behind bars. It's a complete nightmare. Can you now see how important it is if you can no longer carry a firearm, that you need to protect the ones you love from yourself? It has happened before. So please seriously think about it.

There was a recent story about a husband in Pennsylvania who shot his 78 year old wife in the bathroom. He was having mental problems at the time and was confused and thought she was the intruder. So imagine yourself having some type of mental issues like dementia, you confuse someone in your house, like a child and you accidentally harm them with your firearm. I don't think you want to go down that road.

I have put together a form where you will have to sign and add a witness to it. I would also have someone video record you reading the form so that if you do have memory issues later on in life, it can be replayed for you so that you understand the reasons why you made such a decision to no longer carry or be around firearms. You may only trust yourself and no one else at that time. Hearing and seeing yourself filling out this form and giving yourself a personal message will convince yourself in the future the reasons why you retired your firearms.

It's a hard thing to do since it has been a part of you and your life for so many years, but someday, if something does happen to you, you have made a promise to yourself to protect you and those around you.

I have created a promise form for this type of situation. One that you can obviously tweak for yourself. If you want to make it legal, then approach an attorney and work with them to draft something up to your liking. I am not an attorney and the form below is not a legal from. It is something created for peace of mind when it may come to the day that I can no longer carry a firearm.

That's why I think that it's really important as a responsible gun owner, to prepare yourself for when that day comes. So this is what I put together.

I, <Your Name Here>, am making a promise to myself and to others that when the day comes that I can no longer use a firearm, that I will relinquish them to my family or friends. I understand that there will be a day that I may physically or mentally be incapable of using a firearm. I understand that I could end up being a threat to myself or others if I do not relinquish my firearm(s). I am signing this form to give consent to the person(s) below to take good care of my firearms.

I would like to give my firearms to the following people who can lawfully possess them.

Firearm Name: Glock 19
Firearm Serial Number: B46ZW57
Bequeath to: Jay Smith
Relationship: Brother-in-Law

Firearm Name: _____
Firearm Serial Number: _____
Bequeath to: _____
Relationship: _____

Firearm Name: _____
Firearm Serial Number: _____
Bequeath to: _____
Relationship: _____

If any of the people above are no longer living or unable to have a firearm, the people below will get the following firearms from above.

Name from Above: Jay Smith
New Firearm Owner: Rita Perch
Firearm Name: Glock 19
Firearm Serial Number: B46ZW57
Relationship: Sister-in-Law

Name from Above: _____
New Firearm Owner: _____
Firearm Name: _____
Firearm Serial Number: _____
Relationship: _____

Name from Above: _____
New Firearm Owner: _____
Firearm Name: _____
Firearm Serial Number: _____
Relationship: _____

Name from Above: _____
New Firearm Owner: _____
Firearm Name: _____
Firearm Serial Number: _____
Relationship: _____

Gun Owner's Name: _____

Today's Date: _____ Video Recorded On: _____

Witness Name: _____
Witness Signature: _____

Witness Name: _____
Witness Signature: _____

    I would recommend that you have it notarized. Once you have it notarized, make copies and hand them out to the people who you trust that will help you in this transition. If any of the names change or you have more firearms to add, do a new form and start over again and get the new one notarized again. Some banks will notarize for free. You can download the form at **Promise.WayOfTheConcealedCarrier.com**

CONVINCING OTHERS TO CARRY

    So you got your permit and your sidearm, but you want others, like your friends or family armed also. So what do you do? This all depends on the individual. They may not have grown up around firearms, they may have a fear of them, or some other belief/reason. Or they have been exposed, but have no interest whatsoever. You may get those who will jump onboard and carry right away.

    All you can do is ask, but don't pressure them. If people are not onboard right away, then it's not your job to convince them. I tried this but failed miserably and the other person was getting pissed off.

    I could not convince them about the benefits of carrying a firearm. I showed videos, gave real life scenarios, but it just made them madder and madder. I love this person and didn't want them to get hurt, but they could not find the reasoning behind defending themselves with a firearm. Sometimes you cannot change people's minds. They have to do this on their own and it's not your job to do so. It has to take a certain type of mindset to carry a firearm to defend yourself. I never had the mindset until later on in life when a friend of mine took me to the range for the first time. Then I wanted to learn more about it and started to educate myself and got training.

Some events in people's lives can change their mindset. Maybe they were attacked, or a friend of theirs was. Maybe someone they knew was murdered. Or there has been frequent break-ins, or rapes in the neighborhood and because of these factors, their mindset changed and their innate state to survive returned. If they're not ready, than they're not. Some people just shouldn't carry a firearm, but later on in life they would be a great candidate to do so.

The way I look at it, as long as I am carrying, than I can defend myself. If others want to take a much harder path to be convinced, than let them take that trip on their own. And don't tell them "I told you so" when they do change their minds. It's childish and in the end, you're probably pissing them off more. Encourage them on their new path and teach them valuable things about firearms. It is what it is, so that should be your mindset if others have no interest in carrying a firearm.

Don't push it, just leave it alone if the other party shows no interest. If they transition over, good for them. If not, then it's not for them or the time is not right.

KEEPING YOUR COOL

There are going to be times when people do stupid things and they're going to piss you off. So what do you do? Since you'll probably be armed, your best bet is to leave them alone. There's no need to start a fight with someone. So what if they pulled in front of you, or you're in the fast lane and someone else is tailgating you and they're trying to push you faster. Big deal, keep your cool and keep your sidearm in its holster. There's no need to brandish it. If you do end up in a fight with someone (and you didn't start it), you'll have to deescalate, run away or fight your way out of it if they are not using deadly force. So don't let an idiot turn you into an idiot.

There are plenty of stories where people just lose it in a non-deadly threat situation and they pull out their firearm and start threatening people.

I remember seeing this young guy on a surveillance camera video who was at a convenience store. He was buying something at the counter and another guy walked into the store and started harassing him. From the video, we do not know if the person who is being belligerent had a confrontation with the guy earlier in the day. They may have known each other or one of them cut the other off in traffic. Whatever the problem was, the guy at the counter was minding his own business and the other guy who followed him into the convenient store was very pissed off.

The pissed off guy was a concealed carrier (CC) and he pushed the guy and started fighting with him. Since the CC started the fight, he is now considered the aggressor. During the fight, the CC was losing and was getting his ass handed to him. He was definitely losing the fight he started.

So what does he do? He pulls out his firearm and threatens the guy he attacked in the first place. This was a big mistake on his part and will probably be going to prison. It was all caught on video surveillance cameras. Don't be a dumbass and start a fight with someone and draw your weapon on them. You're asking for it and you will get it. You may end up dead because they too may also be a permit holder, or you go to prison because you let your tempter take control. Be smart, be a responsible armed citizen. Remain calm and keep your cool so you don't end up in a bad situation like this young man did. Just get out of the area and disconnect yourself from the situation.

Just on the way to work today, I had someone who was an out of state driver merge into my lane and cute me off. So I slowed down, changed lanes to get out of their way and accelerated onto the highway ramp. I presumed that they were lost and had no idea where they were going. So this person decided to change a couple of lanes back over to my side, take the extra effort to follow me onto the highway and tailgate me.

I am not sure the reasoning, but they may have mistook my action as aggressive, or they just wanted to mess with someone that night. It just didn't make any sense to me. There were teenagers in the car, which is strange to me since I have never had problems with teenagers getting aggressive with me on the road, plus the state the vehicle was from is a 24 hour non-stop drive from my state (Midwest to the east coast). So a few flags popped up for me. They were around 15-18 years old inside this yellow Cadillac. So it could have been stolen, they could have been in a gang, or on vacation without any supervision. Whatever their situation, they chased me down the highway. Now if they were in a gang, they could have been armed. So instead of trying to out race them, I merged myself between two cars in the slow lane so they would stop tailgating me. It worked. I could see four young men in the vehicle as they passed by. They just gave up and sped away. So whatever their intentions, they didn't follow through and changed their minds.

I stayed there for several minutes between those two cars and watched that out of state driver up ahead until I could no longer see them. I wanted to see if they were waiting for me. Then I went back into the fast lane and went to work. Many things went through my mind when they decided to tailgate me. Are they armed? How far is it to the next exit? Should I get off the highway and take the side roads? What should I do tactically and if they shot first, how quickly can I get out of the danger zone? I don't want to end up in a gunfight on the highway. Too dangerous for everyone. I was wondering if this is going to end badly and if I will make it to work that day. There has been several shootings on the highway lately, so is it the same people or another idiot? A lot of "what ifs" played out in my mind, just in case they may have been gang bangers looking for someone to hurt. I kept my cool, deescalated the situation and lived another day.

WHY CARRY? -
THERE WILL ALWAYS BE PREDATORS

One of the oldest careers in the world is being a criminal. Everyone has stolen at least one thing in their lives. So what was it that compelled you to do so? Did you learn that it was something wrong? For those who graduated from that class and know the difference between what is mine and what is yours, congratulations. You are ahead of the class. But there are those who failed that lesson, over and over again.

Over the many millenniums, humankind has talked and dreamed about a utopia, a heavenly place where everyone gets along and there is peace across the lands. But we as humans are far from it. We do not live in a civilized world and it will continue this way for thousands of years to come. When there is value placed upon an object or people, then there will be those who will stop at nothing to own it. As long as there is selfishness and greed in the world, with the lack of love and respect, crime will follow. Humans have protected themselves since the beginning of civilization, using knives, spears, swords, rocks and just about anything that can be used in a deadly-force situation.

Times have changed. We have electricity, we have housing, and we have sent probes into space. We have advanced technologically, but as a race, we have not changed very much. Do you think that we have gotten worse as humans? As an advanced species, we have gotten to a point of mass genocide; euthanizing our own kind in the millions. We still have people who want to possess us and our valuables and they will end our lives without giving it a second thought. Many of these criminals have no soul and will take your life just for the hell of it, because they just don't care about you or anyone else. They have lost respect for themselves and of others.

So a very good reason to carry a firearm for self-defense is that humankind has just scratched the surface in becoming civilized as a whole. You'll have to worry about the ones that have decided to go down a different path – the life of a criminal. With those that wish to harm others on this earth, as concealed carriers, we decided to make the decision to protect ourselves and not become a victim.

In this new century of ours, society as a whole has been mediocre around crime-control, where criminals have more protection and rights than those civilized tax payers. I remember one criminal who went to the police and complained that she was shot while she was attempting to beat an old man and rob him in his own home. Seriously?!! She was shocked that some innocent bystander defended themselves. She believed that her rights were violated.

And there are some real violent crimes that are still happening to this day. So concealed carry seems to be the most logical option at this time. Why live in some unfair circumstance where criminals are armed and we're not? Society as a whole doesn't believe in using their primitive instinct to survive, or we have been taught not to use them by being dependent on local law enforcement to be available in seconds to protect us. But in reality, it takes several minutes for the Calvary to arrive. But many people choose to live in a world wearing rose-colored glasses and this seems to be the acceptable norm.

Be smart, get back your primordial instincts and protect yourself and the ones you love. Be the survivor and live another day. Use the ability to arm yourself in one way or another. Train on whatever object you will use to defend yourself.

If you think we live in a perfect society then keep those glasses on. If you watch the news and see all the violent crap that's going on out there every day and around the clock, remember those are real people like you and me. They are no different than anyone else. It's not Hollywood or one of those fake reality shows you see on TV. It's very real and the way the direction that society is going in the US, your rose colored glasses are going to get stomped on and it will be way too late by then. You'll end up as one of those people in the news, a real person with a real tragedy. No actors, no directors, no Hollywood and no stunt person in your place taking shots. These are real honest to goodness people like you. They have a pulse like you, breathe the same air and enjoy the same liberties as you do.

There are so many reasons to carry concealed. You, like everyone else around the world, should have the ability to defend themselves from harm, no matter what it takes to live another day and not be a victim of a predator or justice system.

The people I meet (friends, family and strangers), I don't know their situation. I don't know the trouble they could be in. I am unaware if they are being stalked, have a relative released from prison, pissed someone off, or anything else. For example, I will visit a chiropractor and get adjusted on occasions. What I did not know until later that the women who was my physical therapist has a stalker. It is an old patient of hers and he got her phone number and started texting her about hooking up. The not so funny thing about it, he's also a cop and married. She told the man that she does not date married guys. He was furious about the whole thing, even when the women called his wife and told her that her husband needs to stop calling and texting her. Now I as a patient, lying on a table, could be defenseless if this man decides to show up at her work and possibly be violent. I heard from one of her coworkers that they would pool some money to help with the cost of the restraining order. As we all know, restraining orders will not stop anyone from committing a violent crime. Especially if you're next to them.

So keep in mind, those around you may have troubles brewing on the horizon and you would not be any wiser to it until somebody decides to be crazy and wishes to do harm to those people and those around them. You have no control over this, but you can protect yourself. So always carry where legally possible.

15 REASONS WHY YOU SHOULD NOT CARRY A FIREARM

15. You are suicidal.

14. You want to get respect immediately and don't believe that it's earned.

13. You may think that having a firearm makes you cool. Or even popular. In fact, hardly anyone should know you're carrying - Hence the word "Concealed"

12. You think that a CCW permit is a license to kill. If you think this, you should not be armed. You should get your head checked out.

11. You want to intimidate others. Having such a responsibility is not something to fool around with, unless you want to serve some prison time and be Best Friends Forever (BFF) with your new cellmate.

10. You want to be one of those wannabe cops that consider themselves an enforcer of the law. Like those who get involved with others on the highway and they believe the other driver is not obeying the traffic laws. They truly think it is their responsibility to stop them. Sound familiar? Get over it. Don't get involved in a highway shooting, so mind your own bees wax and keep your eyes on the road.

9. You feel it makes you look like a badass or very sexy.

8. You want to impress your friends by telling them you carry concealed to just get attention. Maybe someone is trying to score points with someone they like. "Look everyone, I got a concealed carry permit" (it's a new badge of honor to them). Or they like to show off their new toy. "Hey, check out this gun in my holster". What's the point of concealed carry if you're telling everyone?

7. You're dealing with anger issues, have a short fuse and enjoy getting into fights. I would **not** recommend Concealed Carry, but would recommend you talk to a specialist who can help with managing your anger.

6. You have issues with someone's gender. Like you have anger issues towards women or men. Again, work this out with a professional.

5. You're the type of person who is reckless and push the envelope and like be on display. You like to get a reaction from others, no matter how far you cross the line. To test the waters for a reaction no matter how nervous and frightening it may be to others.

4. You are not mature yet to carry concealed. At times, you just can't stop being reckless. If you still do stupid stuff and get in trouble for it, stop doing it. For example, your 21 or older and you love to party until you black out. Or you're irresponsible or can't take accountability for your own actions and you lack self-discipline. At this stage in your life, it would not be the best time to get your permit to carry. Just party on until you come to your senses. It could be dangerous to you and others if you are armed and inebriated. Once you get some responsibility under your belt and build that maturity, maybe take a look again at concealed carry.

3. You lack common sense. Safety should be your first priority and you should have control over your firearm and not put people in danger. Safety is paramount for you and everyone around you. If you lack common sense, you'll be lacking in being a responsible armed American. A good example is the guy at the gun store who lacks muzzle discipline and is pointing the firearm at everyone.

2. You're paranoid.

1. You suffer from deep depression or you're a danger to yourself or the public.

I am sure you can think of some more, but I am hoping you're getting the picture here. Having and carrying a firearm is a very big responsibility and it shouldn't be taken too lightly. There are a lot of laws to follow and frequent training is a must to continue carrying concealed. If training is not required by your state to carry a firearm, keep that sword sharpened and find a class that will improve your skillset. Keep up with what's happening in the concealed carry community so you are educated and are aware of any changes.

You now have this great opportunity, so don't abuse it. There are a few bad apples out there that decided to take the law into their own hands, ignore it, or have become completely ignorant. Those who make these choices by ignoring common sense of concealed carry tarnishes the Concealed Carry Community and gives us a bad reputation. There are good people out there who carry, the ones you want on your side when things start hitting the fan. So hopefully you can get some pointers and not end up in the hall of shame for concealed carriers.

CHAPTER SEVENTEEN

Additional Info

"The is the real secret of life – to be completely engaged with what you are doing in the here and now. And instead of calling it work, realize it is play."

Alan Watts

IT'S YOUR RIGHT!!!

You may have heard that a gun is a God-given right or an American right. The way I look at it is that it is your human right to defend yourself no matter what part of the world you live in or what your beliefs are. Humans are a very interesting creatures and they can become dangerous at times. No matter where you are in the world, your life can be in danger at any time by your fellow humans. Those who promote violence do not discriminate on how rich or poor a person is, how healthy or sick someone is, race, color, creed, or anything else. Violence can knock on anyone's door and they could be bringing the grim reaper with them that day. For themselves, you, or all parties. The reaper also does not discriminate.

There is violence in the world, there are predators and no matter who you are or where you're from, you should have the absolute right to defend yourself with any type of weapons. If it's hand to hand combat, a knife, a gun, a spear, sword, a pencil, or whatever you can get your hands on, no one should have the right to harm or take your life away from you.

I don't think laws should dictate on how you can or should defend yourself. You are the good person who is trying to live another day. But there are those who want to harm others and because of these people there are laws in place. These laws for men and women are supposed to protect their lawful citizens, not the criminals. If someone who has crossed over the line and deep down they want to do you harm, then they should not have any rights.

Over the years, things have changed in the laws and the waters have become more muddied. The reasons to defend yourself should never change as long as anyone walks this earth. I am not saying to ignore your laws, I am just saying you should have the right to defend yourself, to save your life (or someone else's) no matter what type of weapon you use. Hopefully someday our lawmakers will take another crack at it and give innocent people more rights than the criminals who do violence to us and our families. So please be armed and be safe out there!

MY EDC (EVERY DAY CARRY)

Here is my Every Day Carry (EDC) gear. Remember you want to keep it as light as possible, but prepared for almost any situation.

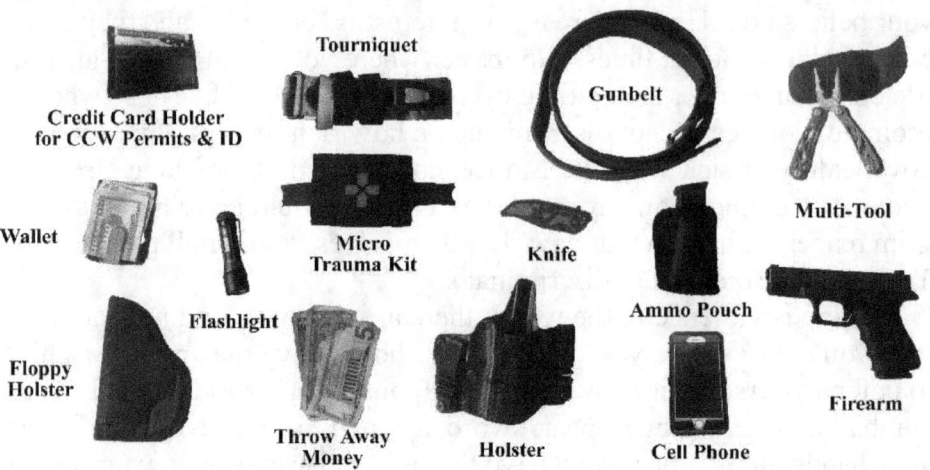

Let's break it down.

- **Knife:** You're looking for a very reliable knife that's portable and easy to pull out for self-defense. I use a locking fold out knife that clips to my pocket, but I am always looking for something better. I don't like the flip knives since you have to do something manually to get the blade out. Now a switch blade with a clip on the side would be great (depending on local laws, it may be illegal). Just pull it out, push a button and the blade comes out. If laws do not permit a switch blade, find something with a sheath that can be clipped to your pocket and easily accessible. You also don't want people seeing it. You want to keep your knife hidden

- **Multi-Tool:** There are some really great products on the market. I personally use Gerber for my multi-tool. They are dependable and affordable. There are some multi-tools out there that are over 100 dollars, but I paid less than half that for mine. Since your weapon is mechanical, having a multi-tool comes in handy. It's not just for your firearm, but for the world you live in. Multi-tools will have screw drivers, a knife, scissors, needle nose pliers, serrated blade and a few other goodies. Avoid the Chinese cheaply made multi-tools. You want something of quality that will last for years with repeated use.

- **Medical Kit:** Since you're now carrying a firearm and if you ever get into a gunfight, you will need to have a medical kit. I have a couple of kits designed specifically for gunshot wounds. I carry one with me in the car and take to the range. It's in my emergency medical backpack which is used for almost any kind of trauma. This goes where I go since I have family and will help multiple people if severely wounded.

    The gunshot wound kit is around $150 dollars (the cheapest I have found that gives you the most bang for the buck). It will handle some serious wounds and was designed by a nurse who has experience in this area. Just do a search on Doom and Bloom.

    I also carry one on my person, a micro-trauma kit for gunshot wounds, along with a ratcheting tourniquet (M2®inc. RMT) strapped to my leg. This is much better than the CAT 7. You can put it on with one hand, no twisting of a bar, just ratchet it. This is around $45, but worth it. Medical kits (like our healthcare industry) are expensive, but invaluable when you need it most.

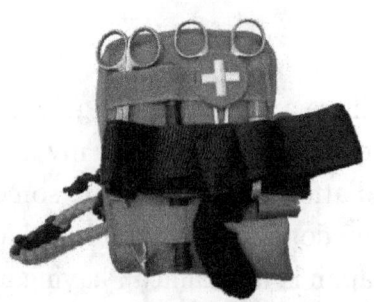

First aid kit for gunshot wounds by Doom and Bloom (kept in medical backpack).

- **Flashlight:** You really need a flashlight, even if you have one mounted on your firearm. You never use the light on your firearm to search for people. You could get into some legal hot water for this. Use a flashlight that has at least 150 lumens and its small enough to clip to the inside of your pocket. You can use this flashlight to blind the attacker and also defend yourself. They call these tactical flashlights DNA collectors (the end of the light has raised metal to collect DNA from your attacker when you hit them on the flesh). I use a Bushnell TRKR T150L. At 150 Lumens (very bright) it has white, red and a purplish color (for tracking blood in the dark) lights. It has a push button on the end of the light. It's under $30, compared to those in the hundreds for a flashlight. I've had mine for over a year. I use it all the time and have had no problems. This little thing comes in real handy, plus mine is beaten up from the abuse, but still works with no problems.

- **Cell Phone:** You will need this to call 911 first before anyone else does. Have it on you all the time and keep it charged. Keep a charger in your car just in case you have a bad battery (like I do). Did you know that you can still use cell phones that are no longer in service? 911 still works on these, but you can't make regular phone calls. Now these days, many of us don't have a landline, but just use our cell phones. I have one dedicated cell phone with no phone service. I keep it in the bedroom just in case I have to call 911 if I left my cell phone somewhere else in the house. We have no land lines since having two phone bills was getting too expensive.

- **Throw Away Money:** I carry a bunch of one dollar and five dollar bills to be used in a robbery. If someone is trying to rob me, I will pull out the wad of bills and throw it on the floor. This is a perfect way to distract them when they pick the money up from the floor while I can exit the situation or start defending myself.

- **Ammo Pouch:** I also carry an extra magazine (15 rounds) so I can get back into the fight if I run out of ammo while shooting, or if my magazine is no longer working. It's my backup for just in case. I also added an adhesive strip on the bottom of the magazine with an arrow on it. I have trained to reload my firearm with the spare magazine with the ammo pointing towards my front. When I get dressed for the day, I will insert my spare magazine into my pouch knowing which direction the bullet is facing. So during a quick reload, I can quickly insert my magazine without checking which way the ammo is pointing. Since the arrow tells me which direction to load it in my pouch, I don't have to mess with it after it is pulled from its little holster. My ammo pouch also has an area to store credit cards. I have a copy of my driver's license, lawyer's contact info and permits instead. So if I do get robbed of my ID, I already have a copy handy for the police officer.

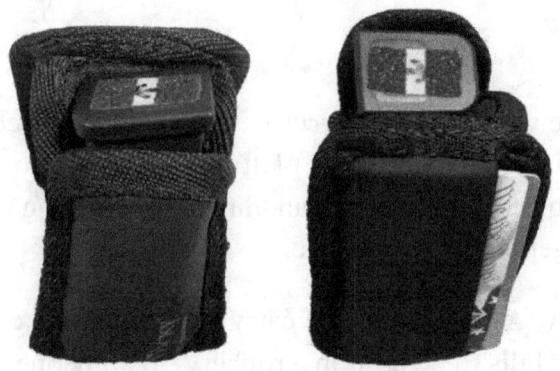

Ammo pouch with adhesive showing direction of ammo with copy of permit and ID in back

- **Floppy Holster:** I carry this with me when I know I need it for later. For example, I am visiting friends at their cabin and staying the weekend. When I am ready for a nap, I will remove my firearm from my regular carry holster and insert it into the floppy holster. Then I will place it in a location where I can retrieve it when needed.

    If I am in a public bathroom and because of what I am wearing, I may need to remove my firearm from its hard shell holster. I can store my firearm in my floppy holster and have it in a convenient location ready to defend myself until my business is done.

- **Gun Belt, Holster and Firearm:** This is pretty much a given.

- **Wallet and Credit Card Holder:** Your wallet is where you'll obviously keep your credit cards, money, etc. Your credit card holder would be used for you permit to carry, contact information of your attorney or concealed carry insurance company, a laminated card to read to the officer after the incident (this person tried to kill me, their weapon is over there, I will cooperate 100% after I talk to my attorney, etc.) and your state ID.

RESOURCES

I wanted to provide you with some resources to help get you started. I do not get paid from any of the resources I mention here, I am only sharing with you what I have found to be as useful and what I use. I believe in safety, but also in quality. What I mention here is top notch and I would like to share them with you.

TRAINING

USCCA (USCCA.com): United States Concealed Carry Association. They provide training videos, a magazine dedicated for concealed carry (also a section for women), books, instructor certification programs, CCW insurance and much more. They are worth checking out. They now have a downloadable app with a lot of excellent information. They offer so much for concealed carriers, I can't list them all here, so check them out, and you won't be disappointed.

Virtual Shooting Range: I personally use ShootOff. It's used for dry practice firing by using laser training. I can make my own home shooting range simulator. I use a white sheet on the wall, a computer with a webcam on it and my laser ammo. I can create my own virtual targets or use my own on the wall. It will detect my laser shots (green or red) on the target using the webcam. There are many drills and features I can practice with this program. It is currently free and works with PC's and MAC's.

The Law of Self Defense - The Indispensable Guide for the Armed Citizen (by Andrew F. Branch, Attorney at Law): I would highly recommend reading this book NOW! It really breaks it down when it comes to using deadly force and it gives real life cases after someone pulls the trigger. The information presented is from an attorney who actually defends concealed carriers. I would suggest this book to anyone who decides to carry a firearm. It will educate you on using deadly force and what could happen afterwards.

I would read this book first, get familiar with what deadly force is, then watch videos. Use the knowledge in this book on whether the situation you saw was a justifiable shooting or not in the eyes of the law. I was scared of carrying since I lacked knowledge of using deadly force. I have read some real horror stories of people who pulled the trigger or used deadly force when it wasn't warranted. But after reading this book, I feel more confident in carrying knowing the law when it comes to deadly force and when to use it.

Active Self Protection (YouTube): John Correia, from ASP, does a wonderful job of narrating videos from around the world on situations involving people caught on video defending their lives against people who are armed with a gun, a knife, or any other weapon. There are many hours of videos from over the years that will open your eyes to the type of world we live in and how things can actually happen to anyone. You'll learn about situation awareness, suggestions on what to do when things go sideways and using the 5 "D's" to defend oneself. John goes through each video and tells us what's going on and how to do it better if we're in those type of situations. Great stuff to cover your ASP!!!

The FireArmGuy (YouTube): The Firearm Guy gives reviews of all sorts of firearms and tactical gear, does range penetration tests and informs us about the gun culture. He also shares his passions about firearms. Some great information for someone new to firearms or experienced. There are some videos that will help those who carry concealed, but if you wanted to expand your horizons on what type of firearms that are out there, this is a great YouTube channel.

Hickok45 (YouTube): Another great resource on different types of firearms. These are some very entertaining videos and Hickok will try out all kinds of firearms, test them and do his review. So if there are any new to the market or old types of firearms, he will test them and post his videos with his results.

BlackScoutSurvival (YouTube): If you have an interest in tactical or survival, this is a great resource to check out. As quoted from their page "To us, 'Survival' is more than just wilderness survival". With a quote like that, this clearly gives you an indication on how serious this YouTuber is about teaching people on different techniques to survive in their environment. You will find all sorts of videos that talk about self-defense, disaster preparation, urban survival, reviews of outdoor/tactical products and much more.

DrBones NurseAmy (YouTube): No matter where you're at, you should have some sort of first aid skills. Dr. Bones and Nurse Amy have a whole archive of videos to teach you these skills, ranging from first aid, prepper medicine, to survival topics and gardening. They are also authors of "The Survival Medicine Handbook", a guide for when medical help is not on the way. Nurse Amy is also a registered Nurse Practitioner with a Master's degree in nursing. Dr. Bones is a medical doctor and surgeon. So you know you're getting information from those who are experienced in this area. You can also purchase medical first aid kits, some designed by them, especially affordable kits for gunshot wounds.

WEBSITES

I am going to share a few websites to get you started. These will keep you busy for a long time and they will also connect you to other websites that are out there.

Concealed Nation (ConcealedNation.org): Their goal is to promote responsible and legal concealed carriers. If you want to know what's going on around the country when it comes to people defending themselves, this is a great place to visit. This websites posts news reports of people who have had to defend themselves with firearms. There are also videos posted too. A great resource of news articles from the concealed carry world.

USA Carry (USACarry.com): A wonderful website that is strictly dedicated for our concealed carry people. They provide resources, maps, forums and articles. You'll find information about changes in government (federal and state) when it comes to concealed carry. You will learn some tips and tricks, stories of survival and anything that deals with concealed carry. They have some great people who write stories for this website. When I first came upon this website, I read everything starting from the very first article posted. If you want to quickly educate yourself on concealed carry, this website is a great resource.

Handgun Laws (HandGunLaws.us): A fabulous resource for concealed carry maps for our great nation. They really put a lot of time and effort into providing our concealed carry community with information about what the laws are in each state when it comes to carrying a firearm. I will download maps of states that I'll be visiting, print them up and highlight information that I think is important. Then I put them into a small binder for traveling. I will educate myself on the laws before entering those states to make sure I can carry legally. Visit the website and check out your state and your neighboring states to determine if your permit(s) is allowed or not.

Beth Alcazar (Facebook): Beth is a great resource, especially for women. She provides excellent information for all concealed carriers. She is a firearms instructor, a writer for Concealed Carry magazine and has worked in the Firearms industry since 2000. She is also a USCCA certified instructor with many online videos helping to share information and training for responsible firearm owners.

Thank You

Thank you for reading my book. I hope it was educational, insightful and entertaining. Please feel free to visit our website at www.WayOfTheConcealedCarrier.com.

© Copyright Notice

Google, Twitter, Facebook, ABC News, NRA, Eddie Eagle Gunsafe, YouTube, Kydex, Nike, Harley Davidson, Laser PET Electronic, The Crow, MacGyver, Office Space, Craigslist, Snap Caps, Mumu, Plano, Pelican, Bushnell (TRKR T150L), Amazon, M2inc, RMT, Ratcheting Medical Tourniquet, USCCA, Sticky Holster, Pilates, Concealed Nation, USA Carry, Handgun Laws, True Lies, Active Self Protection, First Person Defender, Apple iPhone, Android, iCloud, iPad, iTunes, Windows, Springfield 1911, Ruger GP100, Magic Eight Ball, Lead-Off, Hickok45, trademarks or registered trademarks are retained by their owners. All other registered trademarks or trademarks are property of their respective owners. Quotes by Echart Tolle, Jim Butchner, Alan Watts, Helena Petrovna Blavatsky, Suzuki Roshi, Leonardo da Vinci, Iris Apfel, Oscar Wilde, Lao Tzu,